JOURNEY TO THE GODS

Journey to the Gods

John Hillaby

ISIS
LARGE PRINT
Oxford, England

First published in Great Britain 1991
by Constable and Company Limited.

Published in Large Print 1994 by Isɪs Publishing Ltd,
7 Centremead, Osney Mead, Oxford OX2 0ES,
by arrangement with Constable Publishers.

The lines from "The Waste Land" by T. S. Eliot on page 232
are reprinted by permission of Faber and Faber.

British Library Cataloguing in Publication Data
Hillaby, John
Journey to the Gods. – New ed
I. Title
914.540476

ISBN 1-85695-215-0

Printed and bound by Hartnolls Ltd, Bodmin, Cornwall

With gratitude to the pathfinders:
Peter Levi, George Papadopoulos, Palinurus
and a score or more of
invaluable people in the mountains.

CONTENTS

Introduction

The *Flying Tortoise* 1

Down to the start 15

Aspects of Attica 23

Two against Thebes 46

Fruits of the earth 81

Coastal encounters 113

The Sacred Way 148

Prologue to the Pindos 164

High noon at Kaloscopi 190

Whirlwinds and water-nymphs 209

Karpenissi 241

The Place Without a Name 257

Tavropos, tortoises and Trikala 296

The Mountain 317

Among the Gods 342

Index 365

INTRODUCTION

During one blistering hot afternoon on the roof of the High Pindos, the central spine of Greece, we wondered, not for the first time, where on earth we could spend the night. We needed water, urgently, and also a reasonably flat patch of ground devoid of stones and prickly scrub. For hours and hours we had been trudging along narrow mountain ledges with occasional vertical drops on the sinister side. In the heat haze the distant peaks shimmered like a badly focused TV picture. We sweated. Our packs seemed to have redoubled in weight. When the sun began to sink, early, as it does in high places, we noticed that the gorge was spanned by power cables suspended on our side by an immense pylon. It stood on a promontory about sixty feet above us. Could I climb up to it and, if so, could I find a serpentine track well within the competence of Katie who, as the widow of a tea-planter on the slopes of Ceylon can clamber up almost anything?

G. all systems! I found not only something close to grass between the legs of the pylon but a springet of sparkling water. Two short blasts on the whistle we always carry meant I'd located the Arcadian equivalent of the Hilton. With a shove or two I helped her up to where, sheltered that night by the ventilated fly-sheet, we dined on dehydrated chicken soup, noodles and tinned octopus in tomato sauce, commodities I hope never to taste again. Towards dawn — not far from half-past three — the sheet flapped in a warm wind and we heard harmonic howls which were either dogs on the loose, jackals or, possibly, wolves. About an hour later when we were thinking about packing up the sky was zipped open by a streak of lightning. A noise that resembled someone tearing a sheet of calico ended in a double explosion as if both barrels of a shotgun had been fired almost simultaneously. Situated as we were at the foot of one of the highest lightning conductors in the Pindos we had to get out, quick.

More howls before it began to rain with tropical violence. We scrambled down the scree and trudged on and on, until about midday we reached the hospitable hamlet of Marathos where we were looked after by the man who ran the place, "Kaiser" Kapodistrio and his lonely friend Nico who lived in a world of his own making accompanied, occasionally, by a strange woman, a Vlach who "had the sight". An overnight stay there and we were off again. Long days of hard slog but, as used to be said of Africa, *semper aliquid novi.*

Newest of all were the ever-widening sights and insights we gained into the world of classical Greece, that is not merely majestic ruins of temples and monuments preserved in the aspic of tourism; by walking up through narrow passes and gazing down from summits we began to realize how ancient Athens and Delphi maintained their supremacy against the ferocious duplicity of Sparta. Likewise we discovered that the swamps of Boeotia must have been as important to The League north of the Gulf of Corinth as the walls and gates of Thebes.

Before we left we could not have had more erudite or

entertaining instruction than the *Atlas of the Greek World* (1980) by Peter Levi and his translations of Pausanias, one paperback volume of which we carried throughout our whole venture. That gentle scholar Geoffrey Kirk fired our imaginations by much that he has written about Homer and the oral tradition. Apart from the poetic and distinctly theatrical intervention of the Olympian gods, is there any evidence whatever that there had ever been a Trojan War on the scale related in *The Iliad*? We set off with E. V. Rieu's translation and splendid commentaries on both that epic and *The Odyssey*, but were obliged to leave them behind in Delphi because of weight problems.

We read Patrick Leigh Fermor's intriguing accounts of the Vlachs or Wallachians before we struck up an enduring friendship with Nacu (John) Zdru. He still writes to us, regularly. When we returned to London my friend Tom Winnifrith, Chairman of the Joint School of Classics and Comparative Literature at the University of Warwick, an authority on these strange people, gave me abundant help by analysing their language and putting their arrival and departures into historical perspective.

As I shall relate, between the end of the Civil War and the beginning of the military dictatorship in Greece I had some brief employment in Athens and Delphi. On this journey we met the oldsters and the children of that terrible turmoil in the mountains where whole families fought against each other. We heard many stories. Nobody, in my opinion, has expressed them better than the late Kevin Andrews in *The Flight of Ikaros* (1959). I shall paraphrase one of them:

Sphakoanos was described as strong and careless, handsome, modest and generous. He had great style. In his belt he carried two pistols. One of them he called Maria and the other Eleni. One day he came into a village on Sunday at the hour when everyone was at the *Leitourgia*. He walked right into the church and called to the priest, "Stop the Cherubic Hymn, *Dhespoti!*" He stepped up into the sanctuary himself, placed both pistols on the Holy Table and began to pray. "O *Panagia*, accept Maria and Eleni, and inspire all these thy servants to join ELAS this very minute or I'll blow their goddam brains out!"

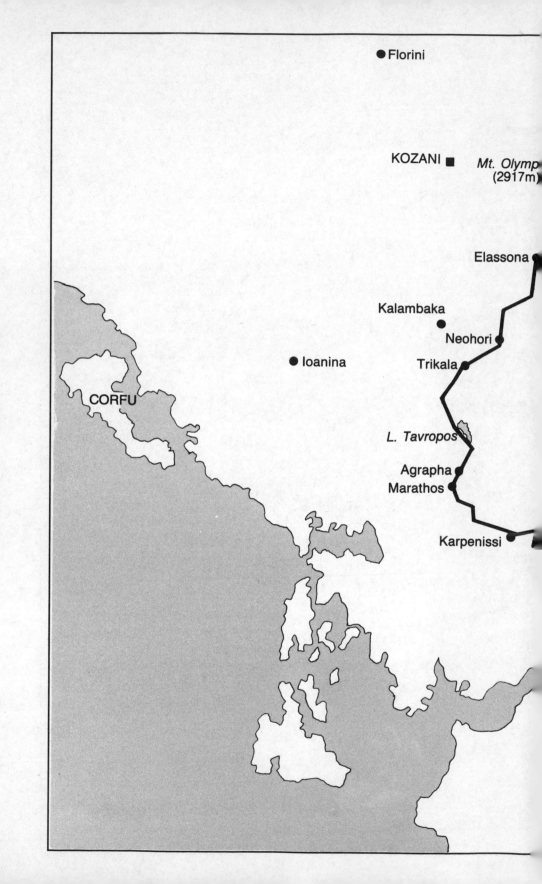

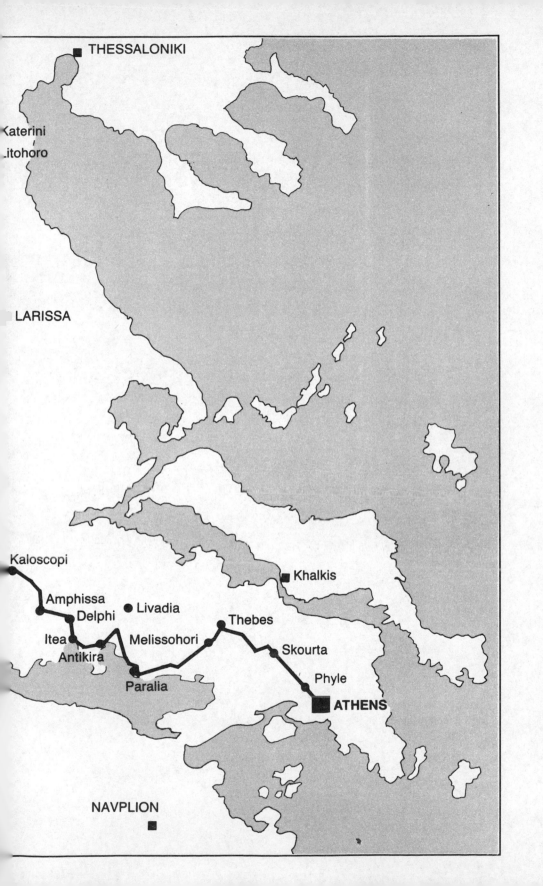

The *Flying Tortoise*

The railway station, the Ferrovia, is the back door, the tradesman's entrance to Venice. International tourists mostly fly to Marco Polo, the airport a dozen or more miles out of town, then they are driven along the narrow causeway across the swamps of the lagoon to the Piazzale Roma opposite the station, a square which, flanked by coaches and cars stacked away in enormous garages, is probably one of the ugliest in Europe. A pity, this. Even after three or four centuries of noble decay Venice is still very much of a piece entire. She has beaten the infernal combustion engine.

At high noon when bell-towers from the Giudecca to the Canale Grande proclaimed the Angelus, we sat at the foot of the Scalzi Bridge, arguing amicably whether to spend one more day in Venice or board the night express to Athens by way of Belgrade and Thessaloniki. Katie had a mind to take another look at the mosaics on the out-lying island of Torcello. I had just one thought, to push on, to start the long haul on foot from Attica to Mount Olympos on the fringe of Macedonia. I had been thinking about it for years.

After a snack we compromised by enquiring about the times of trains at the office in the station. They left each evening a little before six o'clock. "Time to catch it tonight and see Torcello first," I suggested, ever one for the best of all possible worlds.

1

"Not on," said Katie. "Venice isn't for rushing about. We haven't even packed. Let's spin for it. Heads we leave today; tails tomorrow."

I'm a great believer in heads. For decisions on important matters the Roman legionaries spun a coin and called "Heads or ships". Those emblems must be of considerable antiquity. We were carrying a few Greek notes and coins. The current gold-coloured fifty-drach' piece bears the head of Homer on the obverse, and a high-pooped galley of the kind which might have been used by Odysseus on the other side.

I spun it, high. Blind Homer landed face downwards at the foot of a surprised porter. To compound disappointment on this party's part, an immense diesel engine slowly panted in, blowing out oily smoke-rings as if exhausted by her long run from Attica to the northernmost tip of the Adriatic. Whilst the passengers poured out and the cleaners squeezed in I looked at the monster with some curiosity. The logo on her flanks depicted a flying tortoise. Rather heavy symbolism, I thought — a view reinforced when I remembered that Pausanias tells a story about how an eagle, unable to smash the carapace of a tortoise, dropped it on the bald head of the dramatist Aeschylus. What for? Could it be that he had cast doubts on the immortality of mankind? Subsequent events were to lend some substance to that fanciful notion.

In the heat of an unseasonable sirocco we left the station and ambled back along the Lista di Spagna to the Canale di Cannaregio which runs through a nicely dilapidated native quarter free of tourists, including the old ghetto; thence by way of the Terra di S. Leonardo, the haunt of discriminating eaters with shallow pockets, and the Maddalena and the Ca'Rezzonico, where one may still see Browning's deathbed. A five-minute stroll along the Rio dei Gesuiti brings you out to the New Port where the gondoliers park their black swans within sight of the Island of the Dead.

I run over these names with affection since on our way to Greece on several occasions we've stayed in the same little place overlooking the Cannaregio. Venice is a place of coming and going. Those who stay there for any length of time go to escape from the twentieth century. Laurence Scarfe tells an engaging story of an eminent Venetian whose great passion in life used to be the London Underground. Seated in his lovely city he planned imaginary journeys from the Oval to Paddington.

I have little to say about Venetian glass; I don't like it; at least not the modern gimcrackery. But looking into the museum when the boat called at Murano, we marvelled at the nineteenth-century chandeliers, riots of coloured glass, firework displays suspended in mid-air, enormous examples of grandeur and folly. What must they have been like when flicker-lit by a hundred candles?

No stones of the cities of antiquity are quite so trite as those of Venice. They have been worn down, if not out, by centuries of tourism, adulation and literary scepticism. Distinguished visitors with a gift for surprising us object to feeling what they are supposed to feel in the presence of marvels. The "dumpy Doges' Palace" exasperated Herbert Spencer to the point where he felt obliged to explain *how* it should have been built. What about St Mark's? He conceded it was a fine example of barbaric architecture. Towards the end of his life Ruskin, getting progressively grumpier, gave the impression that he would like to pull the place down. Three centuries earlier Montaigne was not so much impressed by the vaunted courtesans — 11,654 of them at that time — as by the police in their cocked hats and sabres, and the high cost of living: *"Les vivres sonts chers comme à Paris."*

The languid island of Torcello is different. Instead of the mouldy, faintly putrescent smell of Venice the atmosphere is mildly marine, marvellously refreshing. Before the mid-season crowds swarm in one might stumble across a quiet garden set in the lagoon. With the need to reverse through acres and acres of reed-beds, the *vaporetto* inches up to a precarious landing-stage. Beyond lies a country lane hedged by hibiscus and tamarisk. On either side spread vineyards, orchards and fields of sweetcorn beset by poppies, long-stalked marguerites and sedge warblers. On that lane there is what looks like a village pub, but without a village since only a few buildings survive alongside the Basilica of Santa Maria Assunta and the double-domed Venetian-Byzantine style church of Santa Fosca.

The breath-taking glories of Maria Assunta, indeed of most if not all places which echo the remains of Venetian thraldom, are the mosaics of the vast barn-like Basilica. Here simplicity does all that the elaboration of St Mark's, St Peter's in Rome and many other less well-known cathedrals can never do. It is, says Scarfe, "a church abandoned and all the better for it". The city which used to be Torcello had gone before the cathedral plans were completed, and most of the marbles and porphyry, the inlays and incrustations, were shipped off to St Mark's.

The great mosaic of the Last Judgement on the west wall is the work of the twelfth and thirteenth centuries and is the only completed portion of what must have been a scheme to cover the whole of the interior. We are left to guess what the rest might have been like. Scarfe describes it as rising "like a glittering cliff of precious stones and gold in an empty cave." As if on ledges the figures are in layers, descending from Christ the Redeemer and the Heavenly Host down, far down, to the naked damned, writhing in an ossuary of shattered bones. In the central apse the lonely figure of the Virgin is curiously attenuated, almost flame-like, making it easier to understand why El Greco, the Cretan, put life into the timeless, the expressionless faces of Byzantine art he had known in his youth. Could it be that the glittering mosaics were inspired by iridescent fish scales, familiar to the restless inhabitants of a sea-kingdom?

Katie and I shouldn't have been there but for Homer, who foresaw that there were better things to do than rush about in trains. Nevertheless in the soft light of the evening I thought of the *Flying Tortoise* thundering towards Greece through the gorges of Slavonia.

The next afternoon we returned to the Ferrovia laden with rucksacks, food, wine and mineral water for two days of quiet window-gazing. We had booked first-class

5

seats and hoped we'd have the compartment to ourselves. To our dismay, about half a minute before doors slammed and whistles shrieked, an elderly Austrian with a shaving brush attached to his deer-stalker clambered in, puffing and hauling up heavy zipped cases, baskets and two pieces of light artillery in canvas bags.

His name, he told us, was Fritzi, and, as if we hadn't guessed, he "voss goin' untink". Only one thing about our fellow-traveller really interested us and that was where he was getting off. Ljubljana he said which I reckoned about two or three hours away. During that time he talked, mostly about himself.

As the train began to ride rapidly over the sea we were absorbed in watching Venice sinking back into the lagoon. In the foreground mooring poles, power pylons and other life supports pierced the mud. Behind them the golden ochre, the pink and white of the campanile of St Mark's and the great green dome of S. Simon Piccolo lost definition in the general haze. Far away and scarcely visible were Murano, Burano and the small dot which I presumed was Torcello. *Clicketty-clank, clicketty-clonk.* We were being carried off, away to deeds of derring-do. The carnival was over, the brightness gone.

The door handle rattled. Passport control? No. An anxious lady from the next compartment broke in thinking we occupied the lavatory. Within half an hour we pulled into Trieste, a handsome city in its upper reaches or so I had read. Fritzi surprised us by saying that thanks largely to Maria Theresa it used to be Austria's most important seaport. He stood up, fumbled in a basket and produced a bottle of Bull's Blood. With much glass-clashing we toasted the Empress, mother of twelve children and, substantially, the founder of the Austro-Hungarian empire.

Good wine tends to evaporate. We carried something more than a litre of Chianti and food including Parma ham, mortadella, long rolls and various cheeses. Fritzi weighed in with thin slices of braised wild boar, some cognac and I forget what else. On the whole we did rather well. He told us how he had acquired the whiskers in his hat from the private parts (he patted his own) of an old wild boar. You had to hit them fast (*Abknallen*), he said, and to show how they did it with a Magnum .375 he snatched up one of our long rolls and put a shot clean through the head of a ticket inspector who just happened to be walking through the corridor.

In simple English and execrable German I tried to tell him how, from glimpses of wild boar (*Wildschwein*) in the Ardennes and the *Schwarzwald* I had got the impression they were not democratic animals. They felt far more at home under sporty *Herrenvolk* with land and trees and thickets and only limited time in which to shoot. They fled at the mere sound of the word Republic, the practical peasantry having no scruples whatever about exterminating pests which grub up their crops.

How much of this came over I don't know. It didn't really matter. We lifted our glasses to the *Wildschwein* everywhere, then to his family, to our families and to his success in the forests of Rosenbach north of Ljubljana. By the time we reached that station it took some time to decant the fellow on to the platform. Lest stone-throwing about intemperance sounds priggish, I'm obliged to admit that we had some argument about the basic mechanisms of pulling out our couchettes. And then we slept. We slept deep while the diesels thundered through the night, across the Sava Plain, towards Zagreb and Belgrade.

Came dawn, an ominous grey dawn with a rim of red light on the mountains above. We were on a single track in a deep gorge. I felt distinctly out of sorts but without disturbing Katie on the bunk above I couldn't get at the mineral water. I smelt coffee. Pulling on a shirt and a pair of pants I traced it to source, the steward at the end of the coach, talking to another passenger in what I took to be Serbo-Croat. They both smiled, greeted me in Greek and the steward asked if he could be of service.

Unable to recall the Greek for water I fell back on a smattering of German. *"Wasser, bitte. Kalt wasser und Kaffee."*

No, I wasn't a German I assured him. *Engländer.* In the very essence of polyglot I did my best to explain that we were travelling to Athens to start a big journey, *grosse reise,* a *safari m'kubwa.* At those last two words in the kitchen Swahili to which I had become accustomed among natives during months in North Kenya he stared at me, open-eyed.

"You speak Kiswahili!"

I said yes, but I wasn't too good at it nowadays.

He grasped both my hands in warm greeting. *"Jambo, jambo sana!"* he said and laughed. Where had I picked it up? I told him. His name, he said, was Andriko. Unasked for, a generous brandy was poured into my coffee. It came out that like so many of his fellow-countrymen he'd spent fifteen years in a well paid but unpopular job in slaughter-houses in Nairobi and Kampala. He admitted that he'd come home with quite a lot of money.

What did his father do? He was a travelling shepherd.

"But from what country?" He smiled and shrugged his shoulders again. His parents came from many countries. North of Greece, I gathered, somewhere in the Balkans. I left it at that.

Silence for perhaps half a minute before Andriko said in a curiously slow and quiet voice, as if ashamed of his origins, "*Va him Vlachos.*" I wasn't too sure about the verb but that one word, that collective noun *Vlachos* rang like the first tremendous chime from Big Ben before the nine o'clock news.

Andriko and his family were Vlachs or Wallachians, descendants of many thousands of semi-nomadic Aromanians throughout the Balkans who used to migrate twice yearly between villages and their upland grazing-grounds. They speak a Latin-based language of their own which is akin to Romanian but as different from Greek as the Welsh language is from English. The very word "Vlach" stems from the same root as Welsh and Walloon. It means foreigner or stranger.

At this point I am borrowing freely from the works of Patrick Leigh Fermor, especially *Roumeli* from which I learnt almost all I know about these extraordinary "self-appointed Ishmaels" variously known as the Black Departers or the *Adespotoi*, those who refused to be mastered. Andriko looked at me anxiously. "*Sijui?*" he asked. Had I understood what he said?

I tried to assure him that it was a privilege to have

talked to a Vlach. At this he seemed hugely pleased and reached for the brandy. I shook my head but said I'd like to take one back with a coffee for my wife.

Since Kiswahili in its crudest form is a kitchen language based, as somebody once put it, on the Ten Commandments and the Thirty-Nine Articles it would be tedious to translate the ins and outs of our elliptical talk together. Among other matters he wanted me to know that on the train, not far from our compartment, we should find the Big Chief of the Macedonian Vlachs. Nacu Zdru, he said, was his *koumbaros*, his greatly respected godfather. Perhaps I'd care to meet him? He spoke English since he lived for most of the year in California where he published a *gazetti*, a bilingual news-sheet for emigrant Vlachs.

A pleasure, I said. On previous visits to Greece especially in the Pindos and mountains of Epirus we had seen the Black Departers, usually in clapped-out furniture vans, full of sheep, travelling at night. Paddy Leigh Fermor described them as "Boojums to a man, who have perfected the art of Snark-like vanishing at the approach of trouble."

When I was leaving, Andriko asked me if I would come back at eleven o'clock. Asked why, he glanced at his watch. "There's trouble ahead," he said, but didn't tell me what. At that his boss, the guard, wearing a cap decorated with a tattered strip of gilt, looked in. He had a worried expression and a large rail map. I left them to it.

All this took time to explain to a somewhat anxious Katie who said she'd begun to think I might have been left behind at Zagreb. Over breakfast we watched townships and villages with strange Slavonian names slip past; Baǒka Palanka, Vincovci and Sid Sabak. The Adriatic shoreline of Yugoslavia is flanked by superb islands and coastal resorts, as I knew from boat trips from the Piraeus to Venice. But inland the country is thinly populated and looks wretchedly poor.

On a single track we swept into yet another gorge and the diesels throbbed as they hauled us out again into mountains as wild as any I've seen in Central Europe — dense forests of Caucasian pine and fir, waterfalls plunging down cliffs and rivers that looked treacherous. Good hunting country for our Austrian friend but not a place to bring up a family on a terraced holding hacked from a cliff. Somebody knocked on our corridor window, gently.

Enter M. Nacu Zdru from Kendrona in Macedonia. A well-dressed fellow, more than a shade overweight, who carried a large and expensive briefcase (Gucci). Speaking in the monotonic English of a Greek who had spent much time abroad, he seemed disinclined to tell us much about where he was born, or how or where he lived, except that it was on the coast just outside Los Angeles, but on one subject he exhibited the passionate dedication of a Jehovah's Witness and that was *Carti Vlaha-Engleza*, his news-sheets including bits of a dictionary and hundreds of simple phrases. He gave me a handful, over two dozen sheets. Two or three of them, I noticed, were sub-titled *NEDREPTATI* (Injustice). *Candu un poplu isi Chiari Limba, Poplu Atelu easti Mortu* — "When a People loses its Ethnic Language that People has Died".

Ever since Paddy Leigh Fermor whetted my curiosity

11

about the Departers these were just what I had been looking for. Leigh Fermor breathes scholarship. He has lived in many parts of Greece; he can unravel their dialects and knows the Greeks themselves as well as any man can, but when he first tried to unravel the language and origins of the Vlachs or Wallachians more than thirty years ago even he was obliged to admit that almost everything he touched was hedged about with question marks.

As the route through Greece we had plotted would take us (we hoped) through Vlach country, it now seemed likely that we should be able to speak to them. Greeks tend to despise them, not least because of their clipped language. Later — when we had had time to learn quite a number of words and phrases — it seemed that there was much Latin, or neo-Latin, in their vocabulary. Perhaps I am romantically attached to the theory that they picked it up from Roman legionaries who guarded the passes through those worn out barriers of ancient mountains. Thus goodbye is *Oarâ-bunâ*; snow is *alba*; "lemons are sour" is *acra easti limonia*; dog is *canili*; a goat *capra*; two goats *daua capri*. One of my favourite trees, the stream-shading alder, the *alnus* of Virgil, is *aluni* in the common talk of the *Adespotoi*.

After about an hour of somewhat one-sided conversation it became clear that Nacu was glad to meet someone interested in his fellow-countrymen. He rose to go. He had business in Belgrade and had other people to talk to before he got there.

"Just a minute," I said. "What's all this talk about big trouble ahead?"

"So Andriko told you?"

"Yes, but he didn't say what except that it was bad."

Vlachs keep their cards close to their chests. "*Panagia*," he said, invoking the name of the All-Holy Mother of God. "It won't affect us."

In one of my smatterings of Greek I hoped that his journey would be a good one. "Goodbye," I said, adding in his own language, "*Oarâ-bunâ*."

An hour before high sun we moved down to Andriko's dispensary where he and two officials were looking through the window, anxiously. Monotonous countryside. Ten minutes passed. Almost nothing was said. Small drinks appeared. The roar of the diesels sank to a murmur. The sirens wailed. We were moving dead-slow. Andriko grabbed my arm and pointed. "*Tazana! Tazana!*" he said. "Look! Look!"

Katie said afterwards that at first she thought we were passing a scrapyard where cars are crushed into blocks. Heavy cranes on the adjacent track were lifting up the tortured remains of coaches. Pieces of metal, wheels and pieces of wood fit only for a bonfire littered the ground. In the middle of the wreckage were two scarcely recognizable diesel engines. They had met, head on.

One was the prostrate skeleton of the *Flying Tortoise*, the train we didn't catch in Venice. The other, presumably from Athens, had half mounted her in a frightful caricature of copulation. Nacu reappeared. He shrugged his shoulders. Nobody could or would tell him what had happened or how many passengers had died.

13

I said we should almost certainly get the facts from the Greek newspapers. "No you won't," he said. "At least, not from officials in *this* country." Katie said firmly that we were getting off in Thessaloniki, "and we're *not* getting back. No more trains. We'll take the bus down the Greek coast to Athens."

Our diesels began to gather speed, slowly. We moved back to our empty apartment. There wasn't much to be said. But for the spin of a coin . . .

Down to the Start

What, until the advent of conceptual thought, had been a genuine oral tradition is now preserved in the aspic of tourism. For thousands of years there have been shrines to Zeus in many places as far apart as Dodona in Epirus to Mount Ida in Crete, but until we got off the train at Thessaloniki we knew of no temples on the heights of Mount Olympos, the ancestral home of the begetters of gods and heroes, and our eventual destination. So we were interested to learn from a week-old copy of *The Times* that on the very summit of the Olympian massif a team of archaeologists under the distinguished Professor Dimitrios Pantermalis was hard at work excavating not only a temple there, but also several others lower down, and were finding coins, inscriptions and the remains of animal sacrifices.

Thessaloniki, the second largest city in Greece, is rich in the remains of historic and prehistoric treasure. It was named after the half-sister of Alexander the Great, Aristotle's most famous pupil. Described as the "lion-headed" man because "his hair stood up from his forehead", he came near to conquering the whole of the known world.

Later, much later, to preach in the synagogue of Thessaloniki, a Christian convert called Paul walked there along The Street called Straight, the *Via Egnatia* from Damascus and showed commendable restraint at the reception he received from his fellow-Jews when he remonstrated with them. Apparently the gospel of peace and goodwill towards all men had its ups and downs. Another convert, the Emperor Theodosius, slipped from grace by promptly ordering the massacre of 7,000 Thessalonians at a public festival in the Circus on the grounds that they had murdered one of his generals.

The story of all this and more, including the archaeological sites, the relics of outstanding battles with the weaponry and costumes of the combatants, are to be found in four well laid-out museums. I tried them all. In the absence of Professor Pantermalis I wanted to know what else had been found among the six peaks that marked the home of the Immortals. Their answers in French no better than my own were politely evasive: I might have been asking about the disposition of airfields on their Albanian and Bulgarian frontiers, which are very sensitive subjects anywhere in Greece.

A plain-speaking geologist from Massachusetts blew the gaff. With coloured felt-tips Jack (Jacques), on leave from MIT, was putting the final touches to a large-scale stratigraphic diagram of the whole Olympos range. We exchanged pleasantries and then he left me to admire his handiwork, saying he'd be back in five minutes as he'd promised to phone his girlfriend at ten o'clock.

The ground floor of the gods is more than a mountain, it's a fault-scarped massif riven by a huge gorge resembling the keystone of an enormous bridge which collapsed, leaving broken supports on either side. The serrations are what remains of the shared holiday homes of the landlord Zeus, Poseidon, Hades, Hestia called

16

Vesta by the Romans, Demeter, Hera, wife and sister of the Gatherer of Clouds, and likeable Hephaestus, lame but with large lusty biceps, the super-craftsman, the smith-god revered among magicians and makers of ingenious things. Among his best pieces, his collection as they would call it nowadays, were the armour of Achilles, Harmonia's irresistible necklace and the sceptre of Agamemnon. So much for the heavenly crew.

Among competitive mountain climbers, *les conquérants de l'inutile* — those who seem to get their kicks from defying gravity — the peaks seen from left to right are Kalogeras, Antonios, Skolion, Skala, Mytikas (the throne of Zeus, the highest of all, 2,917 m) with Stefani, Toumba and Ilias only a few hundred metres below.

Jack came back, smiling. "How's it going?" I asked.

"Sure thing," he said. "Maria's a Turkish Cypriot who wants to go to Paris. I'm teaching her French. It used to be my first language. Papa had a business in Quebec before we moved to Concord, and she's giving me lessons in Greek. What are you doing here?"

I told him and asked him the same question. "Plate tectonics," he answered. "I'm here for three months hoping to get a doctorate out of the structure of the Olympos range."

"Complicated?"

"Sure is. The trouble is there's next to no literature. I'm having to do my own field work. Now if only they'd found oil or even asbestos in them thar hills I'd be home and dry in a month. Almost the whole range is anomalous. The rocks on the top of the highest peaks are far older than those below them. It should be the other way round."

To demonstrate what he meant he held his pen in a horizontal position and slowly tilted it to an angle of about forty-five degrees. "That's what happened," he said. "A sort of see-saw effect. When the Aegean sank to its present level it shoved Olympos up in the air, far higher than it is today. My notion is that some of the uppermost rocks have been completely overturned."

I steered the conversation round to the discovery of the temples. He said he'd heard about them but knew next to nothing about archaeology. I suggested that pilgrims and shepherds had been walking over the ridge for thousands of years. Why hadn't anybody noticed the temples before now?

He pointed towards his coloured map. "I can tell you what I know and also what I think. In addition to one huge fault between the major peaks the whole massif is unstable; it's riddled with fissures. Earthquakes are quite common. The range is trying to settle down. They tell me that two or three years ago there were spectacular cataracts in cracks where previously the peaks were covered in snow all the year round. The water brought down millions of tons of mud. Some of that mud, I think, had covered the graves which are now exposed. After all, it happened with ash at Pompeii. At phenomenal moments in time the treasures of the past can be 'frozen'."

"But why are the archaeological people next door so cagey about saying what they've found?"

"Two reasons. You don't have to live in this city for very long to discover that the Alexandrian war isn't over as far as prestige and commercialism, especially tourism, are concerned. Thessaloniki and Athens are wildly envious of each other. They are under different administrations. I suspect the city here wanted to announce the news before the festival. The other reason is that archaeological sites are haunted by ghouls in the antique business. They prey on badly paid excavators who now and again slip a piece or two into their pockets."

"About how far away is Athens from here?"

"Eight hours by bus."

"Can you see the top peaks of Olympos from the highway?"

"Yes, if you travel soon after dawn when the east face is lit up. At this time of the year you're up against clouds and heat-haze after ten o'clock. The first bus leaves about seven. Slip the driver a couple of hundred drachs and ask him to stop or slow down at the turn-off to Litohoro, the nearest village to the slopes." Valuable information. We parted warmly. Jack asked me to give him a ring if we reached the peaks. By then, he said, he hoped to be sharing his pad with Maria.

Katie had been spending an hour or two in Odos Mitropoleos and Tsimski where the best and most expensive shops hugely enlarge covetousness. Before we retired to our lodgings behind the old port we had booked seats in the first Greek equivalent of a Greyhound bus to leave town the next day. We had also walked the length of Vassileos Konstandinou, the splendid promenade facing the Aegean, that evening a wine-dark sea scarcely wrinkled by the lightest of breezes.

We swung west an hour after dawn. From seats immediately behind the driver and his mate we looked down on an enormous expanse of reedy rivers and fields of millet and rice. All Greek buses are comfortable and the long-distance runners are luxurious. As they overtake and weave around smaller users of the four-lane highways their drivers exude an air of ineffable confidence. They might be at the helm of a cruise ship among a medley of bum-boats and little freighters. Not for them, unfortunately, the cheerful chatter, the camaraderie between passengers and crew as we'd experienced it among the mountains of some of the Greek islands.

In such places the transport of freight in labelled parcels, baskets of fruit and vegetables, dressed chickens, hares and on one occasion an excitable kid goat makes for amusement all round, a running commentary on rural affairs. There is a small charge for unaccompanied freight which is not always adhered to. Katie recalled the solemn old man with a sack of broad beans. Before he put them down between the driver and the conductor he pulled out a handful, and we were all given one pod each before he got off at the back without saying a word. My memory is of a frail soul in black who handed the driver a large basket of eggs together with a small bunch of violets for his dashboard, that area in which bus drivers take to the road under the protection of a picture of the Blessed Virgin, generally a statuette of Her Son on the cross, and rosaries surrounded by photographs of their wives and families.

We struck south and purred down to that shamble of

narrow streets, the market town of Katerini, all business and huckstering. On both sides of the highway were new marquees, as might be the eve of Agincourt. Notices said "Archaeological Sites". In addition to the temples of Zeus the Greeks were unearthing what they believed to be the grave of Philip II of Macedon, father of the great Alexander. Interesting, certainly, but I felt tense. I had eyes only for the vast massif over my right shoulder. The horizons looked misty, tinged here and there with points of light as the crests caught the rising sun.

"How far is the *onomasti apopsi*?" — the famous vista — I asked the driver. "Three kilometres," he said. It felt like ten before he pulled up on the seaward side of the lane to Litohoro. Towering above the village the topmost crest of Olympos, the abode of the gods, broke through a veil of clouds. They slipped off her shoulders slowly, as if in a strip-tease act. Suddenly the light intensified to polished bronze and the highest mountain in Greece stood revealed in its majesty. The whole ridge remained coldly poised for perhaps two or three minutes, and then gradually faded from view. The sheer height of the escarpment looked spectacular and formidable. What were the chances of our being able to reach it? "It's a cert," said Katie, "and now you'd better have a sandwich."

During the long hours it took us to reach Athens classical names and places flickered past irrationally, like a video-tape spooled backwards. Ossa, you might say, was piled on Pelion — we slid round it before Olympos had slipped out of sight, an uninspiring mountain some miles to the south-east, with Turkish forts on nearby promontories. One of them, an American told us, is a resort for old voyeurs known nowadays as naturists. Pelion itself lay off our route.

We lunched at Lamia under a very untidy nest of storks and storklings on an old cartwheel, but saw little of the town as the bus stations of central Greece are built in unaccommodating places outside busy streets. Similarly about an hour later we'd hoped to get at least a glimpse of Thermopylae, literally the "Hot Gates", but like Thebes, the home of that unruly fellow Oedipus, meaning Swollen Foot, the highway is miles away from what attracts the tourists. "No matter," said Katie, "with any luck we shall be walking through the place next week."

Aspects of Attica

Athens and its depressing suburbs have a resident population of two or three millions. In the Liossion area they swarm around the super-highway north. To the south-east the modern Panagi Tsaldari has been blasted through unregenerate slums to the port of Piraeus. But in central Athens, that concentration of culture, there are highly superior districts sandwiched in between the great monuments of antiquity. By far the most elegant is the Kolonaki at the foot of Lycabettus, the Hill of the Wolves, that immense mound of pink-grey limestone nearly a thousand feet in height. Here are superb apartments, art galleries, antique dealers, luxury shops, pastry-cooks, restaurants and cafés with terraces where the cream of Athenian youth meets for a chat. Since the age of Pericles Athens has been known as the town of gossips.

At the top of a street so narrow, so steep, is a former embassy of a dozen rooms or more now tenanted by an old and most hospitable friend of ours whom, from his diplomatic associations, we call Our Man in Athens. A founder of the Eton College Archaeological Society, his interests after Christ Church, Oxford, first took him to the Middle East where he studied Arabic and Persian. Now retired from official appointments he writes intricate elegiac poetry.

After a day and a half in a train and eight hours in

a bus lugging packs, we felt like ill-dressed pedlars in that well appointed suite. A bath and a change, and we rejoined our host on the vine-shaded terrace which almost encircles his floors. The panorama is superb. On all but the worst of days it stands above the smog. Nearby the eye is immediately caught by the Acropolis, lightly floodlit after dark amid points of light like a box of jewellery. To the east and north are the rims of the principal mountain peaks: Hymettus, the Pendeli and the massive bulk of Parnis.

Much had to be done before we tramped off into the hills and most of it had to do with maps and judicious enquiries about no-go military areas markedly unmarked on anything that could be bought or even looked at briefly. A few days elapsed before we discovered that large tracts of government forestry often screened political prisons patrolled by characters with automatic weaponry. Officials in the map dispensary near the Flea Market in Monastiraki sold us sheets (1:250,000) which were almost useless and quite inaccurate.

The business of the Hellenic Mountaineering and Skiing Federation was strictly limited to the heights used by those sports and how to get there by bus and funicular. What with one frustration after another, including a fruitless visit to the principal tourist office, we agreed to turn our backs on the town of gossips the next morning, and spent the rest of the day between the university and the luxury of the Kolonaki, largely for nostalgic reasons.

When peace broke out in 1945 the Greeks remained at each others' throats for almost another twenty years.

Towards the end of totalitarian rule an international organization,* now part of the World Wildlife Fund (as it used to be called), decided to hold a conference in Athens with the hazy idea — which never came to anything — of turning Delphi, the navel, the *omphalos* of the classical world, into a permanent cultural centre with the emphasis on studying ecology throughout the world. As European science correspondent for the *New York Times* I volunteered to act as honorary Press and Information Officer to the whole affair, and soon wished I had stuck to my own business.

Events became mildly chaotic from the start. At eleven o'clock on the first night a German delegate from the Bundesrepublik, who had been billeted in Athens in 1943, beat on the front door of the home of my Greek liaison officer, Peter Petriades, a young professor of biology. With insensitivity almost beyond comprehension, the German wanted to show his wife where he had acted as *führer*. As he'd been implicated in atrocities which resulted in the death of a member of Peter's family it was not surprising that he was hit on the nose, hard. Apparently he didn't know whose home he'd partly ransacked when he and the occupying force fled. This caused a marked degree of tension among some noteworthy delegates.

We had mustered 300, most of them reckoned to be their country's leading ecologists, from twenty nations ranging from the United States to China, which was represented by the diminutive figure of Dr Te-Chee Poo

*The IUCN, International Union for Conservation.

25

and his wife. At a banquet in the Grande Bretagne hotel on the second night a group of Russians were unduly serious and uncommunicative until they discovered that ouzo from Lesbos was stronger and more palatable than their best vodka. Before the evening was over two of them had to be restrained by the management from Cossack dancing and throwing crystal goblets on the chairman's table.

During the opening session when our beribboned president and his inner council were engaged in cascades of French rhetoric, I sat as lonely as a cloud in a back room of the main university building, surrounded by foot-high piles of translations of the principal papers. About a dozen pressmen wandered in, led by two shrewd characters from Reuters and UPI. In English and imperfect French I tried to sell the ecological idea of a prosperous world fit to live in and good to look at.

Had the threat of extinction to the Javan rhinoceros, the Asiatic lion and the Crested coot anything to do with hungry nations, I was asked. I managed to fend that one off but slipped up badly by mentioning the idea of a cultural centre in Delphi. That brought me head up against the return of the Elgin Marbles: what did Britain intend to do about them? Had King Paul approached Harold Macmillan, I was asked. I simply didn't know and yearned for the arrival of Peter Petriades. He was cooling off somewhere or other, talking to his Greek colleagues.

"You should put that question to the British cultural attaché," said an attractive silvery-haired woman who had walked in unnoticed by me but not the local press.

Knowing I knew precious little about Greek politics after the Civil War, Madame Iphigenia, wife of a general and doyenne of our local Ladies' Committee, effectively took over the briefing by translating and making suggestions, without in any way impairing my slender authority. I discovered afterwards that she and her husband, a former Foreign Minister, lived in a château above the Gulf with an apartment in Kolonaki. They belonged to that rich Athenian set who could say of almost everybody in a succession of cabinets: *"Vous savez, mon cher, il est un de mes cousins."* On that morning, putting stuff across to the press and radio, and thereafter socially, I owed a great deal to her. "Phone this number," she would say, handing me her card, "and give Gregor my compliments." It was the Minister of Communications, a tyrant.

The next day Peter, with his knuckles bandaged, and three other speakers gave short papers during a plenary session on the subject of erosion, a dramatic occasion which brought us more publicity than anything else that week. After a sweltering hot morning a cold wind started to blow from the north. It became curiously dark. Lightning flickered over the city. After one gunshot-like crash of thunder our lights went out. The caretaker, I knew, lived nearby and I went out to look for him. All traffic had come to a standstill. The road-surface of Venizelos looked steamy under a rainstorm of tropical violence. The gutters were blocked with brownish silt. The caretaker said it was the *meltemi* and hurried back to start the emergency generators. I scooped up a few spoonsful of the slush in my handkerchief and went back to the lecture theatre.

A dull but diligent fellow from the Peabody Museum at Yale was droning on about siltation problems in the storage dams of South Dakota. I caught Peter's eye, beckoned to him and showed him what I'd brought back. He rubbed some grains between his fingers, smelt it and said: "That's *just* what we want. The *meltemi* is the wind that's helping to destroy Greece." Within minutes he'd brought back a microscope and a projector from his laboratory.

His extempore address on "The Fate of Arcadia" brought the press and radio back within an hour. Sketching rapidly with chalk on a blackboard, he showed how the furious wind had picked up the sun-baked soil of the north and hurled it down into Attica, where clouds of dust sparked off electric storms. That's why, he explained, their mountain tops were bare and the eastern Mediterranean was rich in humus which became fish food. "Overgraze the land and think only of this year's crop and not what your children will inherit, and you'll be left with what you'll see on tomorrow's tour of Mount Parnassos — bare mountains. That's the message," he said.

I sat up until midnight, answering telephone calls from the radio, the press and news agencies. It became front page news in several national newspapers.

Verbal snapshots of Greece flicker in and out of the diaries which have accompanied me since I first began to travel abroad. There was Anastasia, our guide during regular bus tours of the city. Her knowledge was as remarkable as the laconic way in which she put it across. She stood with her back to the driver whilst we cruised round the Kendriki Agora. "On the left", she said through the microphone, "there is a statue attributed perhaps wrongly to Praxiteles and on the right there is an accident."

In the company of Mme Iphigenia and the wives of some delegates we walked round Syntagma Square. Assuming from her faultless accent that she was English, a gravel-voiced American woman, a stranger, asked her some questions about the palace guards, the *evzones* in their distinctive kilt and pom-pom shoes who perform a sort of military ballet. She answered her courteously and in some detail. The American stared at her hair. "Say!" she said in admiration. "How d'ya get a hairdo like that in this dump?" Mme Iphigenia smiled. "At Christian's in the Kolonaki," she said. "Perhaps you'd care to give them my card?"

Until I mentioned the incident to my friend Peter I couldn't understand why one of the best-known socialites in the city hadn't betrayed at least a touch of asperity in replying to a downright rude woman. "Because she's a diplomat and the wife and daughter of a diplomat," he said. "Her husband Stephanos, a nephew of King Paul, goes shooting with the King. To have acted otherwise would have gone against the ritualism attached to our national conception of *philotomo* which is stronger than the Oriental notion of 'face'. We Greeks are a kindly people at heart. But kindliness doesn't neutralize an occasional streak of ferocity. The same could be said for your Irish and a helluva lot of those bloody Germans."

Keeping *philotomo* in mind it became possible to speak more intimately to my graceful companion. Apart from her social obligations, how did she spend her time, I asked her. "*Mon cher*," she said, "in a dozen different ways. Mostly gossiping and taking short walks with nice young men." Stephanos, I learnt later, had similar preoccupations with an unquestionable emphasis on the latter pursuit, a Greek frailty to which were added the opportunities of a former Foreign Minister.

Towards the end of our conference Iphigenia invited me to dine with them at their villa overlooking the Gulf of Corinth. Three kings had stayed there. I can't recall what sumptuosity was laid out, but there was one notable lapse from grace on this party's part. Before the fish Stephanos asked what wine I fancied and I said that I had developed a taste for retsina. A moment's silence ensued before he said no doubt they could find some, suggesting it was normally tippled by his chauffeur. Dinner over and brandy served, Madame took my hand and the three of us stood together on their terrace overlooking the Gulf freckled with the lights of shipping. As I stood between them in the velvety dark, close, I could scarcely distinguish my hosts. To my surprise a hand lightly stroked my backside. I hadn't realized she thought that much about me. Alas, the hand was not hers.

Nearly forty years later Katie and I wandered up through the Kolonaki, past the bell-booming church of St George the Martyr and through a path alongside the funicular to the summit of the Hill of Wolves. When Lycabettus was more remote from the walled town of gossips than Hampstead Heath is from Piccadilly Circus, Pausanias tells us that the wolves constantly menaced shepherds and their flocks. Old soldiers with bows were hired to keep them at bay. Today the track is bounded by vicious cactus and Caucasian pines. We talked about how we should weave through the labyrinth of Liossion. Tomorrow and tomorrow . . .

Apart from the effluent traffic at six o'clock in the morning on even the back roads out of town, the day dawned like any other. Unfortunately we'd overlooked the fact that 1 May would be a national holiday when gregarious Greeks take to the country in their family cars and drive nose to tail, like migratory lemmings, intent on a meal of roast lamb in the open air.

Our reason for starting walks from the centre of cities instead of taking some form of transport to their outermost suburbs is immoderate pride in the phrase "journey on foot". In Athens we were obliged to pick our way through the rundown area of the Patissia. Even in its heyday — that is, what Osbert Lancaster called the "early Compton Mackenzie" period — it could never have been rated above the shabby-genteel whilst after the German Occupation it became the stamping-ground of the cheaper sort of whores and the starting-place for all the more violent Communist demonstrations.

Osbert Lancaster's explanation for what happened in the Patissia and, indeed, in the long monotonous streets around the National Archaeological Museum is "a remarkable demonstration of that rugged individualism which makes the Greek planners' lot so hard". Apparently it had been intended by the city fathers that the future development of Athens should be an orderly southward

31

expansion, eventually linking the city with the Piraeus, and plans to that effect had been drawn up. However, before they could be carried out a shrewd Athenian of that period, the grandfather of the eminent publicist, George "Colossus" Katsimbalis, operating along lines exactly opposed to those which have been so successfully pursued by land speculators in our own country, bought up all the land he could lay his hands on to the north of the town. As he had anticipated, the moment it was suggested to the Athenian public by the planners that they should dwell to the south, they rushed out and bought building sites in exactly the opposite direction, and the psychologist's fortune was made.

By many a turn and twist to avoid the main roads we trudged through as rich a variety of contrasts as ever you can find on either side of London's north-western highway, the Finchley Road.

Between Iraklion Street and Philadelphia there are a few run-down mansions that smack of the poorer Bavarian relatives of the Greek King Otto, but the peeling white stucco looks leprous, often carbonized by the fumes from the repair shops for clapped-out trucks and motor-bikes on the ground floor. Withered relics of a vine or bougainvillaea are sole witnesses to former greatness.

The buildings to the north tend to become more and more commercial, relieved only by brave little houses with cascades of pendulous geraniums rooted in white-painted petrol cans. A feature of the domestic architecture is that few blocks of small apartments are completely roofed over: they are topped by tubular scaffolding, the framework of yet another floor for which there are taxation concessions. A common pattern of development is for cousin Spiros to return from fifteen years' exile in Australia, Germany or the States with more money than he has ever earned before. His biggest problem is to buy land in a country where the strict laws of inheritance may have ensured continuity of tenure for a hundred years or more. This sometimes results in an elderly grandmother with the tenacity of a hermit crab occupying two rooms in a building part of which has been twice pulled down and rebuilt. But once Spiros has acquired his plot he starts to build two floors, one for himself and his family with a lodger or tenant upstairs whose rent pays for more development.

The sight one day of a truly weird machine resembling an enormous vacuum cleaner that roars as it vomits liquid concrete between wooden moulds on the third apartment-to-be shows the whole neighbourhood that the prodigal son is both physically and metaphorically on the way up. Spiros has another financial card up his sleeve before he fulfils his dream of retiring to lead the life of Larry on the island of Mykonos where his grandmother's health and estate management are anxiously watched by her grandchildren. Within a month of getting his first job in, let us say, Chicago Spiros started to subscribe to Illinois Mutual from which a pension, small by US standards, is worth a great deal more when transferred into drachmas.

Beyond the small circle of the exceptionally rich, land for building purposes in Greece is not bought for the isolation it affords. Sociability is the rule. The majority of Greeks who like to live high in the physical sense of the word are not so much concerned about who might overlook their activities as consumed by insatiable curiosity about the goings-on of their neighbours.

We trudged on and swung left down a promising side street only to find ourselves confronted by a bewildering complex which included the super-highway to Thessaloniki, a railway line and three other roads one of which led up into the heights of Mount Parnis, mostly for the winter ski-runs. Lost in Liossion after only two hours' walking, we thrashed about until we met a genial old fellow leading a donkey who, when we managed to make it clear that we were making for Kamatero at the foot of the hills, guided us through the cat's cradle of stone and tar. The walls of ruined warehouses still bore the almost obliterated graffiti of bygone battles in the streets. The ominous word ΘΑΝΑΤΟΣ (death) and the symbol of a man swinging from a gibbet had been sprayed on the blue crown of the monarchists. ΔΕΜΟΚΡΑΤΙΑ (democracy) was almost self-explanatory, likewise KKE and a red hammer and sickle but I doubt whether we could have worked out ΖΗΤΟ ΣΤΑΛΙΝ if our guide hadn't grinned, clenched his fist and said, "Stalin".

We shook hands, warmly, and parted on the extension of Liossion Street, the road to Kamatero. "*Kalo taxidi,*" he said — may your journey be a good one — but he shook his head slowly as he tested the weight of our rucksacks. Already we knew they were too heavy.

The Athenians were taking to the hills. By ten o'clock the stream of cars had risen to a cataract. Family cars raced past us in scores, some of them trailing multi-coloured ribbons, their occupants hooting and waving. The bonnets of most of the vehicles were decorated with bunches of yellow flowers which at first I took to be gorse but from a stationary minibus with an impressive geyser hissing from its radiator I recognized broom, *Planta genista*, symbol of our kings from Henry II to Richard III, a plant of many virtues, medicinal, magical, amorous and domestic since the tough stems can be used for sweeping up. The plant is associated with lovers, witchcraft and veniality. It relieves the bladder and promotes drowsiness, a state in which much can be accomplished. A medieval poet wrote:

> Tell me, O being in the broom,
> Teach me what to do
> That my husband
> Love me true.

The holidaymakers were intent on whooping it up. We had some difficulty in dodging them and when we got to Kamatero, the first village, we disliked the place from the start. The sole tavern-keeper with an open door and sounds of music within said, with scant regard for logic, that it was closed. Probably in our haste to get away from the place we took a wrong turning with confidence. Voltaire says that doubt is not a pleasant condition, but over-certainty is an impossible one.

The rural road wriggled about like a wounded snake and when from a rocky knoll we took our bearings, we saw we need not rely on the compass. Far away to the west there appeared the Gulf of Corinth. In scrubby country where all mounds look much alike we were close to ninety degrees off course. We sighed, turned round slowly and started a cross-country diagonal, over ditches, through groves of ancient olives, around fields of withered corn and the terraced ruins of vineyards. No paths worth the name. That zealous fell-walker, Alfred Wainwright, said that path-finding in cultivated country is more prone to error and exasperation than among desolate mountains anywhere. The air felt both hot and moist. You could push it with your hand. We were climbing fairly steeply. One recompense for tackling parallel ridges is that you can hope for encouragement on the crest above. Maybe another false crest or a glimpse of the promised land.

The sudden appearance of a lurcher under the ruins of a cart gave cause for apprehension: an uncommonly large and hairy dog which did nothing except slowly sink to the ground with ears lowered and gaze fixed, I imagined, on my bare ankles. It didn't bark, another bad sign. Edward Lear, in his walk through southern Greece a century ago, hired unemployed men with *kourbachi*, horsehide whips to beat off vagrant hounds, the descendants, in his opinion, of the Spartan dogs of war. His party repelled attacks several times and he relates how an ancient shepherd "with a face like a door-knocker" nearly suffered the fate of Actaeon when, at the sound of Lear's gunshot, a pack of six turned round and fell on the man who had been urging them on.

The lurcher, if such it was, disappeared during our elaborate detour but turned up again on the next ridge, lying on its back and wriggling, an old bitch in need of a little affection. With more confidence than I had, Katie scratched it between the ears and, with an opportunity for taking off our packs, we gave it some biscuits. We set off again, trying to make it plain to the animal that we'd had enough of it.

The last ridge disclosed first the top of a thunderhead of Zeus, the Gatherer of Clouds, an almighty anvil-shaped mass of cumulo-nimbus with, partly obscured below, the blue-grey summits of the Parnis range beset by racing cloud shadows. As we quickened step down a steep path a ribbon-shaped village appeared from which arose curious plumes of smoke as if a tribe of red-men were sending out urgent signals.

At three o'clock in the afternoon we reached Phyle where whole flocks of lambs were being sacrificed and spit-roasted. Scores of trippers had settled on the village. In addition to two overcrowded tavernas there were family parties and community parties with roasts on glowing beds of charcoal from which arose plumes of thyme-scented smoke which united in one pale blue cloud above the defile. We had relied on being able to order a meal but waiters scurrying between tables made it clear that they were booked up for at least two hours.

"Good day, friends. What's the problem?"

Despina had the compassionate, the almost ethereal face of a young girl who had learnt to live with a deformity, a fearfully twisted leg — a car accident, she told us. A librarian in Melbourne, she had come back to Thebes, her birthplace, on her first visit since she had left at the age of eighteen to marry an Australian doctor. Next to her sat Granny, an old lady with brown, deeply lined features, unquenchable curiosity and wit although she scarcely spoke more than a few words of English. Despina translated. She called a waiter with an order for two more portions to be added to their own and there began the first of two memorable encounters on our first day out.

In addition to the Greek's passion for company is a way of putting wholly uninhibited questions to strangers to which we had become accustomed in our wanderings around the Peloponnese and the islands. One's immediate and future business, one's age, health, income, marital status and views about the Greek way of life, are all matters in which they take a burning and perfectly genuine interest and on which deliberately to withhold information would be considered churlish. Whether the grand-daughter would have been equally forthright is difficult to say.

After we had gone over the nuts and bolts of our intentions, Granny abruptly asked *why*?

"Curiosity," I said to Despina.

It took two sentences to interpret that one word. Sensing we were rather enjoying the quiz-game, our interpreter said: "Granny wants to know who pays you."

"Books and articles," I said.

Granny turned the matter over as she slowly dissected a titbit from the charred shoulders of the lamb. Eventually, wiping her mouth with a tired carnation which had fallen to the table, she asked how old I was. I told her. She nodded, apparently satisfied and munched away before saying, in translation: "You are fortunate. You will have a good journey. We Greeks respect old men."

A silence in which I poured another round of light Demestica, from which Despina refrained since she intended to drive Granny home. A little matter of property was involved. Opening her eyes as if from profound thought, the old lady asked whether my wife always wore jeans. I said no, she always carried a formal dress but we had walked from Athens that morning and intended to spend the night in a tent. Translating slowly as if dissociating herself from the comment, Despina replied: "She says, 'Good. In a skirt, the Mother of God (*Panagia*) will always protect her. Especially in the mountains'." She added something else in Greek which I took to be a mild reproof. "My family", Despina explained, "are rather old-fashioned Boeotians. They have a reputation for kindliness but don't take to modern ways. Hard-working but slow. Perhaps it's the air over the plains, which you'll find is heavy and without movement. Good for growing vegetables."

Not for the first time that day we had some difficulty in refusing an offer of a lift up into the hills. It was difficult to explain briefly and graciously the pride we took in trying to walk every foot of the way. If up into the hills, why not on to Thebes, or even further? It can't have been easy to translate to the old lady who asked, predictably, why we couldn't enjoy ourselves in one of the comfortable buses lined up to ferry the holidaymakers home.

Attempts at a reasonable answer were cut short by a muscular and bare-chested Greek youth who wove his way somewhat unsteadily to our table since, as I understood it, he knew our elderly Boeotian friend. He went through the pleasant rituals of touching his forehead and bowing to all of us. Despina said: "He wants to know if you'd accept a drink from a lover of the British people and might he, please, try to lift your huge pack?" He meant both packs. Machismo.

He bowed again, took a deep breath and picked up one in each hand in the manner of a Japanese wrestler poised for the first grapple. He fell, or at least he staggered backwards where he bumped his bottom against the next table and knocked over two or three glasses of wine. He lowered our packs and looked aghast at the dripping surface.

They each said something, loudly. A confrontation? The man at the table stood up, put his arms round the other's shoulders and kissed him on both cheeks. What had he said? "He has assured him that every action has its charm," said Despina. And the young man? "He will be indebted to him for life. The difference", she added dryly, "between a man from Athens and a man from Thebes."

Our young friend had studied Greek history, and before we parted she told us that for ancient Attica, Phyle was of tremendous importance. It used to be the central pass of the great wall of the Parnis range, forming a natural and easily defensible frontier against their enemies, the Boeotians. The other passes were Eleftherae to the west and Dekelea to the east. The latter gained fearful notoriety when it was betrayed to the Spartans by Alcibiades, the pupil and intimate friend of Socrates. Fearful lest they should also lose the Phyle pass, the Athenians sought divine help. During thundery weather they posted augurs on the towers above the gorge who at the first flash of lightning were instructed to send messengers to Delphi to make suitable sacrifices to the Lord of Storms. "They would have been busy this evening," Despina said, looking out at the ominous sky. "Are you sure you wouldn't like a lift?"

Lightning flickered as we climbed up the Gorge of the Virgin, the Panagia Kliston, topped by a monastery — not in forks or bright sparklets but dully as might be from a faulty fluorescent tube. The cars of a few holidaymakers growled down in low gear. We could hear them coming from somewhere in the gloom above. Impossible to guess how high we were and how long it would take to reach a recommended tavern near the summit, since contours on Greek maps are haphazard and never disfigured by numbers. I had reckoned on a walk of five or six miles and assumed that a gorge was a gorge and not a staircase of twisting roads.

An hour passed. More heavily buttressed bends in the narrow road of the kind known in France as *lancettes*. In vain I combed the air for evidence of life, the sight of a bat or the call of a bird. We heard only the sound of our feet on the gritty surface.

We discussed the questions that had been put to us and I wondered why I hadn't given a straight answer to the one about being burdened like Balaam's ass.

The answer surely was that with a tent on our backs we could stop for the night anywhere and in any sort of weather. Or could we? As we were to discover often in the ensuing weeks, even the toughest groundsheet affords no protection against the prickly scrub of the Mediterranean. It left no alternative but the road and the hazards of wheeled traffic.

Another hour passed. From somewhere on the almost flat and almost parallel road just above came the increasingly loud noise of falling water until, after swinging round the next bend, we peered over the parapet of a cataract that fell thirty or forty feet before plunging into a hidden defile: overhanging trees and protrusive boulders amid a tangle of thorny vegetation marked its visible course. Nowhere could we have placed our bedding down there.

The mist thinned, two more *lancettes* appeared above our heads and gradually we came out into groves of juniper and Cephalonian pine. We had emerged from the top of a thin bank of cloud. A signpost pointed on the one side to the Monastery of the Virgin and on the other to Thebes. Not very helpful. The lightning flickered again. Under such circumstances, we are told, Socrates accepted the fatal cup.

Few signs could have been more welcome than a board nailed to a tree which pointed up a heavily churned-up dirt track and simply said *Taverna 100m*. We walked down to a clearing and found a huge wooden shed in which four men staggered about, washing trestle tables and piling them up around a garbage-littered floor scavenged by a host of quarrelsome cats. Brothers Megaros were so tired they didn't even seem surprised to see two rather elderly English walkers appear out of the storm. They were almost totally exhausted after serving, one of them told us, more than 1,000 hungry visitors that day. At the mention of drink — we felt we'd earned a strong one — and perhaps a little food, the youngest of them clicked his tongue, closed his eyes, tilted back his head and slowly lifted up his arms, palms uppermost, which requires no explanation from the Romanian border to the Peloponnese. Speaking very basic Greek, Katie pointed to two empty chairs and a table and asked if we might sit down for a little while as we had walked a long way. That seemed to be all right, and as if walking in his sleep the man turned round and carried on sweeping.

Silence on our part. Bats snapped up huge moths around the butane lamps. With no enthusiasm I thought of our emergency supplies: instant coffee, packets of dehydrated food and vitaminized fudge, the latter particularly useful for making friends with dogs of uncertain temper.

Katie said this wasn't the time to keep going on about the stiff one — I tend to go on about all sorts of things — but just to be a little patient until they'd caught up with things. She might have been overheard. The banging and clattering ceased. Laughter, snatches of song and a short burst of recorded music. We felt abandoned, but not for long. They all came over. One of them put a woven shawl around Katie's shoulders, another a basket of bread on the table whilst the third carried plates of cold meat. It looked as if we were being offered a laid-aside portion of their own meal.

They over-poured glasses of warmish red wine, a strong local vintage which was more than acceptable, and we invited them to share it.

The cup had gone round three or four times before a flash of pale-blue light and the crash of what could have been a shot from a twenty-five pounder echoed from the roof of Karampola. Huge spots of rain. Clearly the time had come to leave. Where could we sleep? On padded chairs in the dining-room, they suggested. Then on the grass of their car-park, they said, obviously puzzled.

I could do nothing about the reckoning which in drachmas came to the equivalent of about two pounds, and amid embraces all round we left to put up our tent in the pouring dark just out of sight of their windows.

Whilst shoving the telescopic ribs of our hemisphere into seams below the outer fly sheet we got pretty wet, but once that's done there are physically no strings to it and we can crawl into our igloo as if under the shell of a tortoise. Then we can peg down the wafer-thin inner fly and groundsheet all in one, in relative comfort, zip our sleeping-bags together and arrange all our bits and pieces around us.

With half a dozen pegs between her teeth Katie muttered: "Why on earth couldn't we have stayed under their roof?"

"The party showed signs of going on for another two hours," I said. "We can probably be up and away before seven o'clock. There's nothing better than independence."

"With or without water?" she asked quietly, thinking about our dehydrated breakfast.

The hiss of rain subsided. Within twenty minutes it had stopped. Feeling no end of a fool I pulled out the canvas water-bag and returned to the kitchen where they were lolling back with their legs on a table looking rather the worse for wear. Water? Hadn't we seen the tap in their car-park? But water needed to be flavoured — and they pushed a tin mug of Metaxas into my hand.

We sipped it in the warm dark of the tent where I found Katie looking out through the unzipped outer fly. Somewhere nearby a frog belched, to be answered almost immediately by cork-popping noises and trills in different keys by many others. As we slipped off to sleep the chorus rose and fell, making about as much sense to our ears as a flute concerto by Schoenberg.

Two against Thebes

We opened our eyes early, or at least one of us did. It needed a kiss on the shoulder and a gentle shove lower down to bring Katie back from dreams of West Hampstead to the realities of outermost Attica. "Wha' time's it?" she asked, and on hearing that she had lost near half a day in sleep — wholly untrue — she woke with what alacrity could be expected.

Towels were exchanged as we shivered under the car-park tap; plastic mugs were brought out, the butane burner roared. Nescafé spiked with the last thimbleful of Metaxas gave slight heart for a shared packet of dehydrated beef and vegetables and we started to pull our portable igloo to portable size.

Even with the latest equipment this is a dispiriting exercise on a wet morning. Whilst shaking ice-cold droplets from the outer fly we decided against an idea that it was warm enough in Greece to allow us to leave the inner skin on the doorstep of our generous hosts. We rammed down our possessions into gaping rucksacks, ensuring all the heavy stuff sat on our shoulders and so on.

Unquestionably overloaded, we wondered whether to sacrifice our heavily annotated copy of Pausanias, the Michelin Guide or an illustrated work on the flowers of Greece, but all these were trivial compared with the weight of the Pentax and its zoom lenses, the spare tin of liquid gas and an all-purpose skinning-knife I had carried from Yorkshire to North Kenya. In the end we took them all along.

The last look round. No litter, no combined tin-opener and corkscrew left in the rank grass. And then, pause, I gripped Katie's pack under the shoulder straps, lifted it on to my right shoulder and hooked it over her upheld arms. It felt dreadfully heavy, the curse of Atlas. Mine too, but with all stowed away we set off for another long haul.

The small road from the taverna lapsed into a well-trodden track bordered with shy flowers in the ditches, especially wild orchids: that handsome commoner, the Butterfly orchid with large pinkish bracts and her cousin with her green wings in a loose spike, and *Dactylorches*, too, with flowers graded from violet to the colour of Cornish butter. Here seemed all we had been promised for high Attica in the season of flowers.

The path from the road, unmapped of course on the government sheet, narrowed and then suddenly disappeared. Not in a flurry of options or because of some obstruction but peremptorily, as if banished by state decree. Only a small pile of stones and the ruins of a truck marked its sudden abdication. This left us puzzled and indignant. By what authority had the wayleave, fortified by the local knowledge of our hosts, been withdrawn? Apparently we had crossed the unmarked boundary between the prefectures of Attica and Boeotia, the first one rich and the other relatively poor. In my imagination I can now see the leading citizens of Athens and Thebes at last agreeing on a piece of infertile land on which nobody was prepared to settle, a rocky place, deficient in calcium and phosphorus, fit only for some Boeotian Esau.

Ahead lay a waste of rock and mica-glinting sand thickly-populated by clumps of *Quercus coccinea*, the foot-tripping scrub oak, only ankle high but seemingly devil-deep. Here and there were ghostly drifts of asphodel which, inexplicably, is reputed to flourish in the Elysian fields, a stiff unlovable lily which according to Anthony Huxley is often a sign of derelict ungrazed ground. The plant is not usually eaten by animals. Its tubers, rich in starch, are used to make glue for shoemakers and book-binders. Huxley notes that the flowers of two sorts, white and yellow, "are sometimes planted around graves because the roots were thought to nourish the spirits of the dead". Understandable. Our daffodil is a corruption of the ancient Greek word associated with gloom and glue.

Between eight o'clock and high sun we saw not a single soul among those lightly clothed ridges of red earth with tares and thorns that put us in mind of illustrations of the biblical wilderness, but we gained what comfort we could from the fact that our march north-west by north was matched by a line of huge pylons which, we assumed, were carrying Athenian power to Thebes. Katie as usual endured the harsh landscape with better grace than I did, and when the arid plants and a few birds, mostly Crested larks and squeaky creatures like small partridges, probably quail, failed to hold our attention for long, we exercised our imagination. I discovered a Lost City. Not perhaps a city, scarcely a village with the ruins of walls and gates almost covered with prickly oak and blanched vines, and I'm not sure it was lost, but we told ourselves that it might have been the last defence line of ancient Boeotians against their traditional enemies, the Plataeans who lived to the north of the Gulf of Corinth.

Because of the ridge-and-furrow nature of the terrain we couldn't see the pylons from the hollows but from the crests they appeared to be slipping out of sight. Clearly we were throwing away altitude hard gained the previous night, and were glad of it. Patches of corn appeared. Hardly worth harvesting, I should have thought, since in places the meagre crop could scarcely be seen for spikes of purple gladiolus and acrid euphorbia bloated with poisonous sap. From the top of one steep crest we looked down on an extensive marsh with pools that winked like watery eyes. Here, surely, were the outliers of those famous Boeotian swamps into which invaders were fatally beguiled, the mother of rich crops and malaria?

For us it presented an outstanding problem: how could we cross the depression? The friendly pylons swung even further away to where, in the distance, we could just see vehicles racing along the great northern highway.

Predictably unmarked on our maps were narrow roads and polders above the feeding-grounds of plovers, waders on stilts, sandpipers, oyster-catchers and dense flocks of small skittery marsh-hunters such as sanderlings that rose like smoke, uniformly turning and twisting in mid-air as if under a master command. High-speed photography attests there are many matters which, fortunately, we know next to nothing about. Man appeared, the first of its species we had seen that morning. He literally popped up on a very ancient motor-cycle propelled by one asthmatic cylinder. A friendly but rather fearsome-looking fellow with grey, black and gold teeth and a huge sack of beans strapped to his back. He switched off and all but fell off as he grasped my hands. To him, no doubt, we were also a rare if not entirely new species in that deserted country.

Good-days were exchanged before the ritual: where from? Where to? To the recommended *kafeneion* at Skourta, we said — had we the right road? His assurance was expressed as if by an exaggerated signing of the Cross, with the downstroke giving us a visible bearing and the right to left, fortified by an agonized mime, indicating those paths which were to be *wholly* ignored. We were also promised a good and easy journey. He pointed to some birds, probably storks, flying high over a line of dead trees. From a chance meeting with an art-dealer in Thebes a day or two later I learnt that this classical form of divination still heralds good fortune to some country people.

Drinking mugs of tea brewed in the shade of a plane tree I thumbed through Pausanias' *Guide to Greece*. This doctor from Greek Asia Minor devoted nearly fifteen years to travelling in mainland Greece during and after the reign of Hadrian in the second century AD, "the brief Golden Age of the Roman Empire". Almost all that I know about this marvellously obsessed commentator comes from the translation and scholarly introduction by Peter Levi to the two-volume edition which, in his search for copious footnotes and what conditions are like today, suggest that he travelled as far as Pausanias did. As for the man who "believed a ruined building was hardly worth mentioning", Mr Levi tells us that Pausanias belonged in Athens to a circle of almost professional antiquaries; he worked in great libraries; he consulted the sacred officials and city guides whom Plutarch describes at Delphi and who existed in every city. He appears to have been almost incessantly asking questions and writing, beginning when he had already passed middle age. In late life he became addicted to bird-watching and complained about steep hills and bad roads. Mr Levi suggests that his scholarship — he wrote in Greek for Roman philhellenes — and encyclopaedic curiosity were a burden undertaken in an attempt to satisfy a deeper anxiety which had been apprehended in religious terms. "The collapse of ancient religion or some deeper collapse was the unspoken object of his studies. If this anxiety had not ridden him as it did, or had he been a less patient and learned traveller, modern archaeology would be immeasurably poorer" — and we should not have had such an informative travelling companion.

Pausanias says that the old kingdom of Boeotia, now a *nomos* or prefecture, was named after Boeotus, legendary son of Itonos by the nymph Melannipe who, according to another source, when she found herself with child by Aeolus, fled to Mount Pelion and was there metamorphosed by Artemis into a mare. The indefatigable doctor describes the rise and fall of Plataea to the south and between them the meandering of river Asopus which at one period divided the two kingdoms.

He mentions sacred springs and divine objects called *daidala* made from oak wood. Five hundred years after the event, he writes of the crushing of the Spartan invaders at Leuctra by Boeotians under the mighty Epaminondas, and the decline of that war-ingrained race who, I suspect — on no good authority — took their name from the Spanish broom, *Sparteum junceum* which seems to have been as common in the Peloponnese as *Planta genista* in Anjou. Perhaps unknown to themselves, might not present-day Athenians still be celebrating the defeat of their traditional enemies by adorning their vehicles with bunches of broom on 1 May? Pausanias also writes of the building of the Seven Gates of Thebes to the sound of singing and the sweet noise of lyre and flutes. At the word "singing" I heard, as if from long ago, a poignant aria which I have known since my father played the disc on his hand-cranked gramophone.

In his tuneful — if highly imaginative — version of *Orpheus in the Underworld*, Offenbach introduces King John who, among the shades below, catches a glimpse of Eurydice and immediately falls in love with her. But what can he offer a girl who is as dead as he is?

When I was King of Boeotia
All my men were men of war.
But then, alas, one day I died
And all I owned were lost besides.
Yet I can't pretend I really miss them.
What in this place I really regret
Is that I didn't choose you for bride.
But then, as I've said, alas I died.

If I were still King of Boeotia,
Upon my word you would be Queen.
But now you're offered in image only
All my royal power, yet
The finest shade, my darling,
Can offer you no more . . .

Poignant, but as I sang it under that Boeotian plane
tree and apostrophized Katie in those last two lingering
lines, a critical soul might have thought she seemed
over-anxious to be off and away lest I sang it again.

The day wore on, slowly. No especial trauma at the
village of Skourta if you are prepared to accept being
rooked the equivalent of £5 for a plate of vegetables and
a huge mound of what I suspect was goat liver. Why
should we complain? We had asked neither the price
nor the weight of the meat the fellow recommended.
Fortunately we ate what we could in the open air where
our presence attracted first one and then a horde of vicious
cats who squabbled over the rubbery gobbets we were
most anxious to be rid of.

To allow both the sun and our rumbling stomachs
to lose their fervour we took a siesta in the shade of
a jumble of rocks, and then were off again towards
a distant horizon which could well have overlooked
the sea. There is something that can almost always
be said for the Greek scene and that is the abruptness
with which it changes. Events were to prove that
no matter whether we traced the rims of mountains
or silently cursed the heat of a plain, we were

constantly surprised by what could not be visually anticipated.

As we approached the cliff edge of our imagination the horizon dissolved into a series of indefinable ridges until immediately below us stood a well-built farmhouse with outbuildings, beehives on a raised platform and an almost new tractor and a truck in a shed. We circled the house with its open doors. With dogs in mind we called out, loudly, but nobody answered, no dogs appeared. Handsome-looking horses grazed in an open held with a scampering of foals around the mares. Could this be the hamlet of Daphnoula, the only place marked on the map?

Mr Levi tells us that: "almost all maps except old hoarded military staff sheets get you into more trouble than they get you out of." However the road clearly ended at Daphnoula; it appeared to lead somewhere along our line of march and we followed its generous curves. We began to lose height, gradually. In a depression marked by an arc of reeds and sinuous willows, some diligent fellow, perhaps the owner of the horses with winter fodder in mind, had planted an extensive field of lucerne which had been invaded by poppies, vetches and other plants I couldn't recognize.

The field shimmered in the fierce light. The colour came from the soft gradations of violet and blue punctuated by the blood-red poppies, but the wonderful movement arose from undulations of hosts of butterflies, mostly members of the Blue family wholly at home on leguminous plants. Accustomed as we are to the scarcity of these beautiful creatures on the poisoned soils of post-war Britain, we were favoured, it seemed, by a glimpse of a prelapsarian state of affairs. In their urge to copulate, innumerable spires of the Least blue (*Cupido minimus*) arose and fell like will-o'-the-wisps; the Osiris blue (*C. osiris*) seemed more intent on laying eggs on the trefoil leaves of the lucerne than sipping nectar from the short spikes of its flowers.

By far the commonest species was that butterfly so rarely seen nowadays on the English Downs, the fast-flying Long-tailed blue (*Lampides boeticus*) which can be identified only between its urgent migrations. Large and Small coppers (*Lycaena*), Clouded yellows (*Colias*) and large numbers of Cabbage whites (*Pieris*) hovered over the huge thistles, daisies and miniature chrysanthemums around the lucerne. On the bark of a pink-flowered Judas tree I caught a glimpse of that spectacular butterfly with lace-edged wings, the Camberwell Beauty (*Nymphalis antiope*) once known as the Great Surprise because of its unexpected and striking appearance.

That afternoon I seemed touched by the wand of youth as I recalled days absorbed by the pursuit of insects in our northern dales. By unravelling the scientific names of creatures brought home alive in match-boxes and the celluloid tubes of the manufacturers of Beecham's pills I picked up a nodding acquaintanceship with the classics, since the names of most insects were taken from Greek or Latin mythology. Carl von Linné (1707–78) introduced the foreshortened, the scientific binomial. When his predecessor, John Ray (1627–1705), wished to allude to the Peacock butterfly he had been obliged to describe it as *"Papilio elegantissima ad Urticarium accedens, singulis alis singulis maculis oculos imitantibus perbelle depictis"*. "A most handsome butterfly that frequents stinging nettles with a spot painted most beautifully on each wing so as to resemble an eye". Thereafter, in order to make his meaning quite clear, he went on to mention the name or descriptions given by Petiver, Mouffet and Goedart, and also the English name. For the man who Latinized his name to Linnaeus, a bare two words sufficed, *Nymphalis io*, which, however irrelevantly, commemorates the daughter of an otherwise forgotten King of Argos.

Similarly, the scientific name of the Least blue (*Cupido minimus*) is derived from Cupid or Eros, the trouble-making son of Aphrodite; the Long-tailed blue carries the suggestion of its flame-like quality, *Lampides* meaning a torch or flambeau. I can't imagine what the coppers, both large and small (*Lycaena*), have to do with the she-wolf: the word is probably Lucaios, a town in Arcadia; whilst many of the Whites (*Pieris*) are named after the Muses who were reputedly born in Pieria under Mount Olympos. Pedantic perhaps, but *Pieris* sounds better than Cabbage White.

After another three hours of walking our meandering road led us to the village of Pili where, more tired than we should have been, we sought comfort in a noisy though hospitable tavern. More than anything else we had a mind to sit quietly over a bottle of wine. It didn't work out that way. No sooner had the good woman of the house put down the retsina and the usual titbits, biscuits, olives and the like, than a precocious little moppet put her head round the door. Seeing we were alone she shouted and skipped in with her friends. We made polite gestures of disapproval. Imagining them to be some form of greeting they imitated my upraised hands and ferocious grin. The first moppet said, "Me English spik. Me from Thivai [Thebes] come." Not wishing to be outclassed the rest of the children danced round our table chanting first the English alphabet and then fragments of our multiplication tables.

In the midst of the hullabaloo an old man walked in, dismissed the children with a few sharp words which it would have been wise to have memorized, sat down and began to interrogate us in a wheezy voice. He was joined by a priest and the village blacksmith, Nicos, who had spent ten years on Clydeside. It came out that the oldster, a professional soldier, had fought the Germans under the name of the National Liberation Front, EAM. "Where?" I asked. "First here," said Nicos, translating, "and then on Mount Parnis. I was only quite young when the bastards came in with an infantry patrol, two armoured cars and a light tank." Had I been a soldier? I nodded. He spoke rapidly to the old man. They beckoned me outside where, by pointing out landmarks with his stick, the old soldier — over eighty — described how with advance warning they had mined the road in several places, overturned the armour and killed or wounded most of the infantry before he and his neighbours took to the hills. Reprisals followed. Among several adolescents who had never handled a rifle, three of his relatives were lined up against a wall and shot. "We were lucky," Nicos said. "Father took us up to the Kliston *monastiri* above Phyle."

Before we returned to our table I asked Nicos whether the priest had joined the *Andartes*, the Resistance fighters. He hesitated before replying. "No," he said with echoes of Maryhill and Sauchiehall Street in his voice. "He wasn't a *papas* until the Germans were kicked out. He was a young novice in the monastery during the invasion. After that . . ." He shrugged his shoulders.

With a murmured blessing and hopes for a good journey the priest left us. The old man followed him. Katie walked through to the kitchen for a word with our hostess about food, leaving me to talk to Nicos alone. I wanted to unravel the ground plan of that terrible affair, the civil war when brothers in divided villages fought against each other, and wondered how to begin. As if reading my thoughts he asked about the strength of the Communist Party in Britain. Weak in numbers, I said, but the big unions had small if influential groups of what we called the Hard Left, and I added, "unfortunately". He half rose and banged the table with his fist. "It's the same everywhere," he said, his voice rising. "We are still contaminated."

Within minutes I learnt that he supported Papandreou and PASOK, the Pan Hellenic Socialist Movement. He would have preferred Mitsotakis, the leader of New Democracy: "A tough Cretan who doesn't try to please everybody," he said. Before Katie returned with our supper wrapped up in a Theban newspaper, he gave me local examples of how the Resistance movement, EAM, developed on Russian lines with Russian arms and became an organized army (ELAS) and even a navy (ELAN). The Communists formed their own trade union organization (EEAM), a Youth Movement (EPON), a Cooperative Society (EA), a Secret Police (OPLA) and a Civil Guard (EP). In Greece there are not a few passionate politicians. They are all passionate politicians.

I returned to the subject of priests actually carrying arms. Nicos grinned. In his opinion there were more rifles in monasteries than anywhere else. On the island of Chios the most successful guerrilla force was raised, organized and led by a priest. According to Osbert Lancaster, many years ago, in the notoriously violent Mani country, the participation of priests in blood feuds was governed by certain well-defined laws. As he put it: "Thus while Holy Orders were not in themselves regarded as sufficient to remove a priest from the category of fair game, the Man of God could not be potted while actually officiating behind the iconostasis. On the other hand he was obliged to remove whatever firearms he carried beneath his cope before approaching the altar."

Nicos asked us where we intended to spend the night. My turn to shrug. Why not above his foundry, he asked. We could then have breakfast together and meet the man who led the local Resistance. I was obliged to go through the ritual excuses about getting away early but he did give us valuable advice about a track to head for the next day. With our supper in the newspaper and another bottle of wine the colour of honey, price about twenty-five pence, we walked out into the murky dusk. What turns everything to majesty in Greece is the sunlight; when that goes everything seems to shrivel in the dark.

We might have slept under the stars if we had realized how warm it was. The inner fly started to perspire. Cold drops of water fell on us until we took the sheet down in the dark. Then came a mysterious scratching noise. Something appeared to be moving under my portion of the sleeping-bag. A mole cricket, I thought, or maybe a field mouse. Katie woke up as I tried to locate the creature. Nothing visible by torch light. We slept, fitfully, until she woke me again saying that something seemed to be moving under the waterproofs and a cloth that served as her pillow. Whenever we moved the scratching noise ceased and we tried to ignore it.

From that morning onwards we usually packed our gear after a frugal sponging down, postponing coffee and something to eat until we had limbered up and got into the swing of things. The sight of a river meandering under the early-morning sun looked tempting and to the sound of more frogs than I have ever heard before we stopped for breakfast.

I lifted Katie's pack off her shoulders, winced at the weight of it, and inched off my own. Too heavy by far. Mentally running over what could be left behind at Thebes I turned at her half-suppressed cry. As she pulled out the cloth wrapped round the butane stove, a red centipede, the biggest I have seen, a flat creature about eight inches in length, fell to the ground and scuttled off. At the time, that is between lighting the cooker and enjoying the fried bacon, bread and coffee, I thought it best not to say too much about the thing, not least because I know the species can bite if provoked. Centipedes have never been among my familiars but frogs now, there's as merry a crew as ever brightened me up when affairs haven't been at their best. A professional observer, Dr Archie Carr, once wrote: "I like the faces of frogs. I like their outlook and especially the way they get together in warm wet places and sing about sex."

Among the reedy shallows of the meandering Asopus, a classical stream much written about by Pausanias as the boundary between inter-Boeotian rivals, Thebes and Plataea, a legion of multi-coloured frogs were at an amphibian version of the "Hallelujah Chorus". They leaped from beneath our footsteps on a marshy bank strewn with purple iris and saffron-eyed daisies; they splashed down among their fellows with their forelegs interlocked under the bellies of fertilized females: gloriously green frogs, goggle-eyed and seemingly grinning frogs, acrobatic frogs with two — sometimes three — mates struggling to get down to copulation. *Kama Sutra*? Not for nothing have these inter-graded hybrids been given the scientific name of *Rana epierotica.*

The chorus defies easy description. Enough to say that through the cheeps, peeps and tremolos came the belchy bass notes which haven't changed since Aristophanes described the noise over 2,000 years ago in his bawdy and vastly entertaining comedy, *The Frogs*: *Brekeke-kex-ko-ax, ko-ax*. Behind the vulgarities his theme is a serious one. As a recent translator, David Barrett describes the scene: "In January 405 BC Athens was not a cheerful city. At Dekelea, only a few miles away, the Spartans lay encamped. Not many months before, they had marched right up to the city walls,

61

30,000 strong, and the Athenians had only just managed to man the defences in time. And now Lysander, the Spartan admiral, supported by Cyrus the Persian, was preparing for the spring offensive in which he hoped to inflict the final blow on the Athenian fleet."

Behind the mask of the comedian, Aristophanes creates a completely farcical situation which begins on the outskirts of Athens and ends in Hades, suggesting that during that crucial period the two realms weren't all that far apart. One by one the characters, both the living and the dead, the mythical and the real, including Euripides, Charon, Aeschylus, Pluto and Dionysus, the patron god of drama, engage in mock-serious debate derided by the chorus of frogs: *Brekeke-kex-ko-ax, ko-ax* — which might be put across today as *Blah Blah Blah*! Dionysus tells them to shut up.

> Now listen, you musical twerps,
> I don't give a damn for your burps!

He is exhausted. He has rowed across the lake.

> What a sweat! I'm all wet! What a bore!
> I'm so raw! I'm so sore! And what's more,
> Some blisters have come on my delicate bum
> Where I've never had blisters before.*

With enormous skill Aristophanes blends uncommon

*Aristophanes, The Wasps, The Poet and The Women, The Frogs, David Barrett, Penguin Books, 1964.

sense with outrageous slapstick. What he is really getting at, says Mr Barrett, is that the City is in great danger. Unless the Athenians can find advisers who are both wise and moral and not merely clever fellows they will perish, swallowed by a system which hasn't worked. With little profit to the State they have listened to politicians and orators: isn't it about time they listened to other advisers? What about the poets? In that much quoted line Aristophanes says: "Schoolboys have a master to teach them, grown-ups have the poets."

With the pocket-recorder and field glasses at the ready we clung to the Asopus for mile after mile to get the best of the sounds and riotous scenes in the river below. Various warblers and orioles contributed to the chorus but they were as nought by comparison with that massive frolic of frogdom. It led us astray. By following a wayward tributary we all but missed the city of Thebes and were obliged to retrace our steps by some three or four miles, much of it through calf-deep mud on a flood plain.

Down an inconspicuous side lane we squelched up to the predictably unmapped hamlet of Neohoraki devoted almost entirely, as far as we could make out, to the growth, extraction and transport of wayside alps of pink potatoes in the process of being shovelled up by some very friendly natives. Shouts of welcome. Handshakes all round. The innkeeper's apologies for not being able to offer us more than a dollop of the for-ever-simmering cauldron of mutton stew were interrupted by the arrival of a van-load of sardines, loudly proclaimed by bursts of recorded bouzouki music audible, we reckoned, at a radius of half a mile. Mildly deafened but satisfied by grilled fish, fried potatoes and immoderate flasks of retsina, we rested awhile before soldiering on through landscapes of Boeotian spuds.

The tracks were far from straightforward since the Neohorakians made it clear that anybody in their right mind would head for the main road just visible on the horizon. Some fibrous roots tripped me up, twice. An overladen man stumbles easily. Katie's ankles were deeply scratched by heavily armoured thistles. In short, we were up against Ventre's stark dictum that *les choses sont contre nous*. Resistentialism. No matter. We struck a tolerably surfaced side road and quickened pace when a signpost half promised that we were within two kilometres of sacred Thebes of the Seven Gates, birthplace of Dionysus, Hercules and all that lot.

The dramatic moments of life are apt to fall singularly flat. Neither of us had been to Thebes before. On several occasions I had been driven to Delphi but it had always been by chartered buses or the equivalent of American Greyhounds which bypass the town by two miles on their way to Livadia and the roller-coaster road to Delphi. Had I spent more time on Pausanias and less on the flora and geology of Greece we should not have been so disappointed by the rather shabby quarter of a rather shabby town. For years I had been carried away by the prospect of the Seven Gates first mentioned by Homer in the eleventh book of *The Odyssey*, the Book of the Dead. The world's first story-teller and, surely, one of the greatest in the world, relates how Athena,

Goddess of the Flashing Eyes and Circe, Mistress of the Magic Arts gave Odysseus of the Nimble Wits precise instructions about how to reach the Shades below where, he was told, he could assuage the enmity of Poseidon, the Earth-shaker, brother of Zeus who had for so long kept Odysseus in exile, unable to return home to Ithaca and the faithful bed of his bride, Penelope, beseiged in her own home by a horde of amorous and ambitious princelings.

The Earth-shaker has always seemed to me to be a petty, broody fellow and it doesn't require Freud to explain what Homer knew by instinct — that Poseidon should suffer from nephew resentment, not least because the Gatherer of Clouds had described the gallant young wanderer as "not only the bravest man alive but the one most generous to the immortals who live in heaven". I used the first three words of a poem by Andrew Lang for the title of the first book I ever wrote*, the reminiscences of a youthful fisherman.

> Within the Streams, Pausanias sayeth,
> That down the Cocytus valley flow,
> Girdling the grey domain of death,
> The spectral fishes come and go;
> The ghosts of trout flit to and fro.
> Persephone, fulfil my wish,
> And grant that in the shades below
> My ghost may catch the ghosts of fish.

*Within the Streams, Harvey and Blyth, London, 1949.

Horace, in his old age and on a well-deserved pension from Maecenas, wrote: "Often on a work of grave purpose and high promise is tacked a purple patch or two to give an effect of colour."

The story is that Odysseus brought his blue-prowed ship into the deep-flowing River of Ocean, the frontier of the world where the fog-bound Cimmerians live in the City of Perpetual Mist and dreadful Night has spread her mantle over the heads of that unhappy crew. There the wanderer, exiled son of Laertes, encountered first his old companion Elpenor and then the spirit of blind Tiresias, most famous of the Theban prophets who told him how he might overcome fearful obstacles on his way back to Ithaca and what he should do when he arrived there. Odysseus thanked him. He admitted that the threads of destiny could not be cut since the gods themselves had spun them. Yet he begged to be allowed to speak to the spirit of his dead mother, Anticlea, wife of Laertes, who had been in good health when he sailed for Troy, and also to other high-born souls with the ability to tell him something about the strange relationship between the gods and men and the cities they built — such as Thebes when she ruled the greater part of Greece.

His royal mother wept at the sight of her grievously travel-worn son, not least because being a spirit without sinews and bones to hold her flesh together she could not embrace him. Yet she told him how she had died out of heart-ache for her shining first-born and she comforted him with news of his resolute wife, Penelope and their son, Telemachus, ever-watchful and constantly at her call.

We said very little as we climbed up a steep hill towards what should have been the Hypsistai Gate on the southern approach to the Kadmeia at the centre of the city reputedly founded by Cadmus the Phoenician. Not a gate, not a tower in sight. We were in a nondescript quarter devoted mostly to the sale of meat, vegetables and bathroom appliances. With fantasies mildly encouraged we struck along Pindarou Street — once the home, possibly, of Pindar, one of the greatest lyric poets of Greece whose house was spared when Alexander sacked the city. Enthusiasms were stirred slightly when we crossed Dirkis Street for this, surely, was associated with that unfortunate woman Dirce who, for some reason I have forgotten, was killed by Amphion and Zethus who tied her to the horns of a bull understandably enraged by having its balls interfered with.

On what we hoped were more certain grounds we passed Oedipus Street on our left and another to the right named after his daughter, Antigone (O shades of Sophocles), who led her incestuous and self-blinded father to Colonus where she buried him before taking her own life. Can one be surprised that to the name of no other city of antiquity does there cling so romantic and so ominous an aura as that praised by Homer for its gates? But where were they?

I put the question to a swarthy young policeman: *Parakalo. Pou ine oi epta portes?* He looked surprised. Did we want a good restaurant with many doors? No, I said, no! *Ohi!* Clearly he didn't know what I was talking about. With the same result we tried the man with a tall wooden crucifix which fluttered with dozens of raffle tickets, a fishmonger and a waiter in a small bar who motioned us to an outside table and returned with an old man to interpret.

At my elaborate explanation about the great city of Thebes of a long time ago, he smiled hugely. The drachma had dropped. He pointed down Pindarou Street and said, "The museum!" But, alas, it was being made new again and would not be open for many months. We sighed. He sighed but brightened up at my suggestion that a drink might be good for all of us. As we ate a small meal there and refreshed his glass I asked about a good hotel, not too far away. At this he closed one eye and with his forefinger pointed straight up into the darkening sky. I looked at Katie and she, practical as ever, stepped into the middle of the road and looked around. "He's quite right," she said. "The Hotel Meletiouy is almost upstairs."

Within minutes we had dumped our packs, handed in our passports, braved the creaking lift, pulled off our sweaty clothes, taken a shower and sunk into what seemed centuries of sleep on a super-pneumatic bed of eider feathers.

We awoke to find the world new-made and shining. A shabby town did I say? From the street level, as we had discovered the previous evening, there are few architectural prizes to be won in modern Thebes because the best-known town in Boeotia stands on a huge mound, a natural fortress. Rusty iron stairs from our balcony led up to a flat roof where, far beyond a richly covered riot of pantiled roofs, we saw a ring of distant mountains, pale purple in the early morning light: Kithairon to the south, Helicon due west, Thourion and Chlomon to the north and Ptoon and Messapion to the north-east, relieved by sparkles of light from the Euboean Gulf.

We were far from alone. High above, like a cloud of gnats, countless hundreds of swifts screamed around us, some of them so close that we could hear the whirr of their sickle-shaped wings. We clambered down to our room, gingerly, since our underfootings were sore and lightly blistered which, to a professional walker, is as adultery in a priest. Leaving Katie with a light breakfast and three days' laundry to attend to, I suggested we should meet again in an hour or two and took a town stroll, alone but not for long.

The swarthy cop, talking to Stefano, our helpful informant, gripped my arms as if on a serious charge. Through rapid interpretation he enquired whether we found our lodgings favourable. "Very good," I said. This clearly pleased Stefano since it turned out that the wife of the patron, apparently a rich woman, was their favourite aunt on his mother's side. Greek scales of familiarity tend to be biased in favour of the prospect of a rich inheritance.

Parting from my two companions with some difficulty I walked up Epameinondou Street, north, towards the museum, fascinated by the number of shops devoted to flamboyant if not downright vulgar bathroom appliances. Baths, bidets and basins in pink marble were commonplace, eclipsed only by a big store which gave a whole window to a huge lemon-coloured jacuzzi that, the manufacturers claimed, could be filled in fifteen seconds by pressing a gilded console.

Most of the general stores in Thebes add to the

fun in the Boeotian bathroom by offering a great variety of soaps, bath salts, fragrant oils and unguents presumably supporting John Wesley's curious belief in the relationship between cleanliness and godliness.

Just off Kevitas Street is a *plateia* nicely framed by ancient planes and mulberry trees where, hearing the ringing, the almost trumpet-like call of a Golden oriole, I forgot about the museum and sat down to coffee and brittle rolls together with a shot of superior Greek brandy (Votrys) the better to digest them. Tiring of the three-day-old edition of the *International Herald Tribune* I took out the micro-recorder and whispered into it *sotto voce* much to the admiration of the waiter who thought, I suppose, that I was speaking to Athens or London by radio telephone. Why, I asked that useful little machine, were the Thebans so addicted to soap? Could it be that hygiene is the corruption of the conscience by notions about external cleanliness? Pliny the Elder wrote that the Phoenicians were the first to prepare the stuff that makes you a little lovelier each day from goats' tallow and wood ashes. Now wasn't Cadmus, who is said to have founded Thebes, a Phoenician, who might well have brought soap in addition to the first use of letters in Greece to that very Kadmeia in which I sat? Didn't he sow the dragon's teeth? By persuading commoners to soap off what their best friends wouldn't tell them, he was perhaps among the first to wash civilizations down the drain. I began to warm to the proposition. Votrys is evocative stuff.

I thought of Rome where the inhabitants became so obsessed with lying around in hot baths that they could no longer face sleeping out on cold battle-fields and thus fell prey to unwashed barbarians. I thought of modern America under the spell of J. Walter Thompson and Proctor and Gamble. Mark Twain said something to the effect that soap and education are not as sudden as massacres but they are more deadly in the long run. I wondered if during our finest hours we in Britain could have tolerated Goering's fire-raisers but for the fact that soap was rationed and we were limited to five inches of bath water.

Two splendid birds like enormous butterflies floated down from the crown of one of the plane trees. They were pinkish-brown hoopoes crested in the manner of a Mycenaean lord in battle-dress. They alighted on a patch of rough ground which they began to probe with their long curved bills. When they found something succulent, a caterpillar or a beetle perhaps, they crooned with evident delight: "*pou-pou-pou*" which is good Greek — as even I know since I had been saying it so often — for "where? where? where?" That deeply melodic call can be imitated almost precisely by blowing a gentle staccato across the mouth of an empty wine bottle.

The birds, probably a mated pair whose fledgelings had gone off on their own, were not only superior-looking, as if conscious of their fine plumes and matching gowns, sable and argent from the shoulders down, but also seemed downright *fond* of each other. They fed close together and when they weren't amicably *pou-pouing*, the male or maybe the female (since the sexes are virtually indistinguishable) would give a hiccupy *gloop* suggesting possibly that a beetle had gone down the wrong way.

Inevitably *Eupupa epops*, to give the creatures their endearing scientific name, have figured heavily if wholly improbably in Greek mythology. Tereus, son of Ares, the god of war and not to be confused with Tiresias, the bisexual soothsayer of Thebes, brought up his commandos in support of Pandion, King of Attica who had got himself into difficulties in a local shinanikin. With help from the Immortals Pandion won hands down, and in gratitude married off to Tereus his rich daughter, Procne and she bore him a son, Itys. Unfortunately for all concerned, Tereus fell in love with the voice of his sister-in-law, Philomela who resisted him. So he raped her on the side. Affairs thereafter got more than somewhat gruesome, even by classical standards.

Procne, his wife, got wind of the affair and to stop her blabbing Tereus cut out her tongue. Planning revenge on her barbarous husband, she slew their child Itys and served him up to Tereus for supper. When he rumbled what had happened, he picked up his axe and chased the sisters to Daulis on the road to Thebes. There he might have killed them both, but the gods intervened. They turned Philomela into the nightingale who forever mourns the death of Itys in her throbbing song: *"Tereu, Tereu, Itu, Itu"*; Procne into the swallow that twitters and flies round in circles but cannot speak; whilst Tereus became the hoopoe flying in pursuit of them, crying *Pou, pou, pou* — where? where?

To my mild annoyance the birds flew off at the approach of a misty-blue Mercedes, a quietly luxurious car bearing Swiss plates. It turned round in near its own length, reversed and purred to a standstill in a shadow which might have been made for it. The driver, a trim-bearded fellow in his sixties, as handsome as his car, stepped out, apparently with some difficulty. He limped over. He glanced at my copy of the *Herald Trib*, lowered his head, politely, and said, "Good morning, *M'sieur*."

Since I yearned for someone to talk to and because, too, he fitted my notion of Svengali, I suggested he might care to join me over a coffee. Within an hour I had learnt much about Thebes and a little about the intriguing activities of an exotic art-dealer.

Born in Famagusta of Turko-Jewish parents and now a naturalized citizen of Ascona, M. Théophane, to disclose only the received portion of his name, could fairly be described as an extremely knowledgeable exquisite. Wisely worldly, not the other way round. His car, dress, idiom and other lightly worn jewellery were all of a piece.

"What brings you to Thebes?" he asked.

Dressed as I was in tourist gadabouts, a respectable pullover, jeans and open sandals, I told him, briefly — we were going to Southern Macedonia on foot. We had a mind to see at least the summit of Mount Olympos. He looked down at my sandals. *"Mais c'est une grande tournée,"* he said. "There is between here and your destination some considerable difficulties. Have you experience in these matters?" I told him I had been to many countries, always on foot.

He paused before saying: *"On dit que* the man who takes long steps is obliged to turn his back on large spaces."

"Is that Islamic?"

He shook his head. "From Malaysia. I was in Borneo, among the Dyaks."

What had he been looking for? He smiled before saying, "Whatever is of value. The fetish figures, amulets of jadeite and human heads, but shrunken of course."

"Rather gruesome, eh?"

"*Peut-être, mais j'ai payé cher.*"

"How much?"

He sighed before he slapped his thigh. "With this. The polyneuritis. I was on crutches and it was three years before I could walk without a stick." I tried to turn the conversation back to Thebes, but mentally Théophane was still in the tropics. "In the Belgian Congo it was acute dysentery and in Peru yellow fever," he said. "Have you visited there?"

"To the Congo for several months — up and down the river twice in the Belgian days. But never to South America. What did you find there?"

"*Beaucoup de choses*, including this," he said, stretching out his second finger, encircled as it was by a small but exquisite ring of bright green malachite set in silver. There were deep incisions on the square face of the stone which I couldn't make out.

"That is from Cuzco, an Inca seal ring cut in the great days of Huayua Capac, *c'est à dire* before Pizarro arrived early in the sixteenth *siècle* when he began to destroy the first and probably the most successful socialistic government in the world. It lasted for three *siècles*, almost. Had I another ring like this I could buy a super-Ferrari, that is, if I wanted one. *Mais non*, I

74

prefer the ring. It has a rather curious history. Look at the engraving, like a labyrinth, no? The squares represent numbers. The Incas had some acquaintance of Pythagoras. That is of no surprise to me. So did the architects of your megalithic monuments in 2,000 BC. You can draw an immense stone circle with the equivalent of string but not a precise oval, where you are obliged to understand the properties of right-angled triangles. Only one other ring resembles this one, that I know, and that is in the museum at Ankara. One dug it up in Anatolia."

"At Çatal Hüyük?"

He laughed outright. *"Mon Dieu, non!* So you know the story of what is perhaps the oldest roofed city in the world, 6,000 BC eh? And the missing jewellery which — how shall I put it? Shall we say, implicated one of your fellow countrymen?" He laughed again. "Yes, I have been to Çatal Hüyük and nearby Hacilar in the Taurus mountains. I have good stuff from there. But I am an honest dealer, *vous savez*, not an archaeologist."

"But what's the connection between the two rings?" I asked. "Arab traders," he said. "They took their dhows across the Atlantic not long after, possibly even before the Vikings. For the purposes of barter is it not likely that they presented the Incas with mystical drawings including algebra from Byzantium? Pythagoras died in 500 BC *tout à fait* obsessed with ideas about the immortality of the soul and its transmigrations. That would appeal to the Incas. Much came from Anatolia and Phoenicia."

He stroked the ring with affection. "In the period between the second millennium and the second century before Christ, Greece gave to Europe its first poets, its first dramatists, its first architects, first historians, first philosophers and first scientists. It developed ideas on reasoning, democracy, and even the first notion of a universe composed of atoms in perpetual motion. The cultures came, *à l'origine*, from sources as far apart as Mongolia, Upper Egypt, Minoan Crete, Anatolia and Phoenicia."

"By what routes?" I asked.

He lifted his arms in an eloquent Turko-Gallic gesture. "*Je ne sais pas*," he said, "at least not with precision. But then nobody else does. If I did know I would not fly around the world like a mad magpie picking up expensive trinkets. It is for me not possible perhaps to walk for more than a few hundred metres, but movement of any kind is a substitute for making the decisions, as premiers and presidents know. It assists me to keep intellectually alive."

"What on earth did the Mongolians contribute?" I asked.

"*Beaucoup*," he said. "You have heard, *sans doute*, of the Scythians — or the Kindred-Scyths as the anthropologists call them to confuse the record in case they are challenged? They were a race or confederation of warrior-horsemen, perhaps the first to domesticate that striped wild beast named after Prewaltski. They dominated a vast crescent of the steppe which stretched from the Wall of China to the banks of the Danube. They were known to, they were feared by the great Darius, the father of Xerxes, who started the long war between Persia and Attica. He had seen samples of smelted gold in bars from a royal treasury in the Altai mountains. A Russian called Radlov found some of it about a hundred years ago. Since then there have been located and excavated several frozen tombs known as *kurgans*; one of them at Pazryk disclosed the tattooed body of an elderly warrior, probably a prince who had died of battle wounds. Alongside him lay a woman, *bien-tonne* but frigid of course, his consort slain by ceremony. Objects of *grande* value included gold-inlaid war apparatus, armour and the like, sacrificial tablets, musical instruments, portable furniture made of Chinese sandalwood, carpets, jewellery, cosmetics and hashish burners. Today, the material, including the bodies of the royal Scyths, is all in the Hermitage museum in Leningrad. I have seen it. I should like to visit the Altai mountains — but do you suppose the Russians would admit a trader who is *assez bien connu*?

"The Scyths attained the Balkans where they clashed with and were beaten by the Thracians who absorbed much of their culture, in particular in what today is Bulgaria. Herodotus tells us that the Thracians were a people made for war who, if they had been united under a single king, would have been invincible. He says also that each man who could afford the luxury had several wives and practised barbarous customs. When the warrior-husbands died, the women made dispute among themselves with some violence to decide which one he loved most so that she could be buried with him. The Thracians used to hold regular lotteries and the winner — if that is what one may call him — was thrown up in the air by his comrades so that he landed on upturned javelins. He was given instructions to let their great god Zalmoxis know what it was on earth that they most desired that year. If the *pauvre homme* died, they thought the god would grant their wishes. But if he did not die, at least within the few hours that they stood around and watched him in silence, they blamed him, saying he was an unreliable man, and after the rising and the setting of the moon during a certain season they drew lots to decide who should be the next hero-victim.

"The Thracians reached Greece where they were counter-attacked by veritably *tout le monde* from the Macedonians to the Romans. They had no written language but some strange ceremonials and their history was depicted on golden cups and tablets. One of them[*] shows a huge double door, *un peu entr'ouvert* to reveal the head and forearms of a terrified old man. A small group of armed warriors almost as tall as the door are advancing upon him with upraised Thracian swords and expressions of murder." He paused for a second for dramatic emphasis and slowly lifted his forefinger. "*Écoutez*, could not that be the story of the Seven Against Thebes?"

"Do you think the huge door could be one of the seven gates?" I asked.

"*Non*. I do not believe there were ever seven gates to this city."

"But Homer talks about them in the Book of the Dead and Pausanias claims he saw them. We have brought Levi's translation with us."

---

[*]Part of the Penagurishte treasure in Sofia.

"I suggest you reread it with more care," he said. "Seven Gates has the sound of mythology. Seven is a mystical number: the Seven Heavens, the Seven Sacraments, the Seven Joys of Mary, the Seven Liberal Arts, the Gods of Luck, the Hills of Rome, Seven Seas, Seven Sleepers, the Seven Deadly Sins — I could make it twelve. Seven Gates would be very difficult to defend, but three would have offered access to their principal roads: north to Thessaly including the port of Vathi from which we believe the fleet sailed for Troy; south to Athens; and west to Delphi along the Sacred Way. How do you propose to get there, might I ask?"

"Tomorrow we shall head for the southern rim of Mount Helicon and then west to the port of Itea below Delphi," I said.

He sighed. "Even if my legs were in good condition I should prefer the comfort of my car. I think there is little of the noble and virtuous in the cultivation of blisters. No matter. Nietzsche is of your opinion. His thought was that a sedentary life is the real sin against the Holy Spirit. He says our finest thoughts come to us when we push one foot in front of the other, slowly, as we are thinking."

He rose to go and held out his hand. "*M'sieur*, it has been a privilege to talk to you. But I have business here. The key to much that has happened in the past still lies in this town, but do you suppose Thebans with their minds of commerce are prepared to let people burrow like moles for the chance of finding a few objects which are likely to be carried off to the museum in Athens? *Heureusement*, there are a few who have embraced archaeology for non-scholastic reasons and I am one of their patrons. My respects to Madame in her heroic exercise, and good luck to you both." He limped towards his mist-blue car. He waved briefly from the side window and drove off.

Katie sat on the balcony surrounded by our almost dry laundry. Before I could tell her much about the dealer from Ascona she said: "I have news for you. In one of his footnotes to Pausanias, your friend Mr Levi suggests that the Seven Gates were not the gates to classical Thebes but to the Kadmeia, the ancient acropolis, a sort of shrine within a city. And perhaps there were only three. The others might have been invented by Aeschylus. I have looked him up. It fits in nicely with his *Seven Against Thebes*."

Fruits of the earth

We were alone again but not for long. Half a mile beyond the city limits I found that I had carried off the huge brass key to our hotel bedroom and, worse, I'd forgotten to pick up our passports. Taking off that heavy sack and leaving Katie with a book in the sanctuary of a mosque-like church, I strode back, peevishly, to the hotel receptionist, a pretty chubby girl whose Danish name sounded something like Moll Flanders, a fanciful notion heightened by her truly hypertrophic bosom which had put one of us in mind of the famous snake goddess in topless garb I'd seen in pictures of Knossos. I walked there and back far too fast, and felt out of sorts when we set off again.

Our friends, including the helpful cop, had assured us that our little road, not unlike an open lane in Devon, would take us to the steep southern flanks of Mount Helicon which plunge into the Gulf of Corinth. The carefully tended fields devoted to foraging flocks, ancient olives, vines pruned to within two feet of the red soil, vegetables various and a pale green haze of newly emerging corn were refreshed by whirling sprays that clicked and hissed above the screech of young starlings. Not my favourite bird. Among the furrows they made me think of lice in the seams of a tramp's clothing.

Here and there, usually in the vicinity of whitewashed farmsteads, could be seen the dark green foliage of mulberry trees on which, for many centuries, the Boeotians fed their silkworms. There is reasonable evidence that in the seventh century those industrious caterpillars were smuggled into the Byzantine empire from China by two monks who combined religious zealotry with a practical devotion to the principles of free trade. Until the Bulgarians sacked the city in 1040, Thebes could be regarded as the Lyons of the Eastern Mediterranean. After its resurrection by the lordly Burgundians and Franks, Theban silk became a staple probably more widely known, certainly no less valuable than Cistercian wool.

No silk is now produced there but, as I learnt from the knowledgeable M. Théophane, the fertile plain around the city is still known to oldsters as the Morocampus and the surviving trees, mostly *Morus alba*, could well be the descendants of the purple-encased seeds sown at the beginning of the Theban Renaissance under Nicholas de St Omer and his youthful liege lord, the extremely well-connected Duke of Athens. Thickly clothed mulberries make efficient windbreaks, the leaves are used for feeding livestock, but most trees are cherished, I suspect, because the fruit is the source of a bootleg liquor known as *moru*.

For some botanical reason beyond easy comprehension the raspberry-like mulberry is a fairly close relative of the fig. They are gastronomically neglected since they combine the extremes of squashiness and pippiness, though the flavour, searchingly sour and hauntingly sweet, comes out best in the liqueur. In a stylish restaurant it should be asked for by tapping your lower lip and saying with quiet authority: *"Thelo na soo mileeso moru, parakalo."*

The morning wore on and when we began to gain height, almost imperceptibly, the soil looked stony and less fertile. The terraced vines appeared to be fighting for survival. Patches of corn and parched vegetables were protected from itinerant goats by formidable palisades of cactus, the prickly pear. From the numbers of highly poisonous plants thereabouts, such as *Hyoscyamus*, the white henbane; *Mandragora* or mandrake which was supposed to shriek when dug up, "a noyse that spells death to incautious delvers": and Datura or thorn apple, with its white trumpet-shaped flowers, I wondered if that particular soil was contaminated, possibly by arsenic.

A curious thing about many poisonous plants is that, even to those innocent of their lethal properties, they look downright unpleasant. Who, for example, would pluck and chew the black cherries of the Deadly Nightshade not uncommon in our chalk quarries in company with Old Man's Beard, the wild clematis? Yet my old friend the Alchemist* assured me that a fearful outbreak of poisoning causing several deaths occurred in London in the last century when the fruit was offered for sale under the novelty name of Nettleberries by an urban vendor who was either ignorant or without a conscience, or both, since the plant has been known as Dwale, Doleful Bells or the Devil's Cherries. He was subsequently convicted of manslaughter.

Few trees could be seen except the pink-flowered

---

*See *John Hillaby's London*, Constable, 1987.

Cercis or Judas tree on which the Iscariot is said to have hanged himself. According to legend, the flowers still blush. The junipers clung to the ground and olives had reverted to their wild form. They were fruitful but when, once and for all time, I bit into one they were as bitter and tongue-tingling as something between aloes and sloes. I should have known better. They were festooned with small yellowish-white flowers: I had sampled one of the berries of the previous year.

Huge boulders littered the flanks of small hills. Flocks of bell-tinkling goats were carefully watched by seemingly motionless old men and women leaning on crooks taller than themselves. What their animals fed on amidst that riot of scrub, I couldn't make out. And what were their minders thinking about, day after day, week after week? Could it be that they were not so much watching as *listening* for an occasional stray?

From behind the shelter of an old wall I looked back through glasses at a man who, as far as we could make out, hadn't moved for at least a quarter of an hour. A Vlach if ever I saw one. As I focused more intensely, the better to make out his rough coat and floppy hat, he turned round, looked in our direction and slowly raised his right hand. I felt almost certain we couldn't be seen. Was he employing some paranormal sense of watchfulness? Or was it that, even on the soft verge, the sound of our footsteps had suddenly stopped?

We wore floppy canvas hats ourselves, heavily peaked and nicely aerated with muslin on top. They were to prove the most useful objects bought *en route*. We pulled them down over our eyes and strode on, cautiously admitting that we were gaining momentum and that our packs were becoming at least tolerable.

Ahead of us rose the usual false crest pierced by a row of almost cylindrical peaks, rounded at the top like the heads of giants watching our approach. Slowly they rose higher and higher. What could they be? They resembled the plugs of volcanoes. I took a compass fix: near due west. Mount Helicon? Almost impossible. That massif some thirty miles away — as I knew from notes made in London — was composed of sandstones and shales folded on sedimentary limestones, nothing plutonic. The map, of course, told us virtually nothing. We were again conscious of moving in a fog of ignorance. What did it matter? Not for the first or the last time we clung to the light-hearted notion that we were invincible.

In a series of generous curves our good-mannered road sauntered up to a small plateau beyond the crest. Up there all appeared desolate, a rocky defile fit only for vultures and brigandage. Cyclopean blocks of sandstone tinted bright green and reddish-orange from algae and ferrous compounds lay on top of each other in confusion, as if in some bygone age a cathedral had collapsed.

Our road narrowed but never wavered. It knew what it was about and inside a mile we were looking down on a fertile and far-reaching plain chequered with smallholdings. By some trick of perspective our volcanic plugs — if such they were — seemed to have shifted some thirty degrees to the north of our westering, but we couldn't make out whether their phallic shapes stood above clouds of heat-haze or behind another range, possibly far-distant Parnassus. We never did find out and thereabouts we cared not at all for we stood above the village of Melissohori at the chiming of the Angelus. Pretty fair going, we thought, since we'd left Thebes an hour after Prime.

The name of that village, perhaps only a hamlet — because it appeared to have no purposive roads beyond the one that led us there — enlarged our vocabulary by one golden word: Melissohori, the resort of the bees, remembered thereafter for a certain brand of golden lager* which, ingested under heat and stress, has no fellow. It comes close to indefectibility, a liquid such as Athena pressed on Penelope to ensure her constant affection. The name rolls over the tongue. I can taste it now. Within three-quarters of an hour — to the marked interest of the locals — we had emptied four bottles. Par for our dehydrated course. A genial place.

Four very senior citizens in fustian dress sat alongside the retsina bench addressing themselves to a common jug which held about two litres. Two of them greeted us with a circular hand wave, palm outwards and a muttered "*Yass*" short for *Yiasou*. Surprisingly no questions were asked about what we were up to but they were obviously fascinated by our packs parked against a whitewashed wall. Under pretext of studying our almost useless map we tried to correlate their vigorous sign-language with the few words we heard and understood.

The signs, which are probably older than proto-Greek if not sentient mankind, are mostly expressed with the right hand either clenched or with vigorous movements of

---

*Amstel.

the upraised or waggled index finger. In the terminology of music, the left hand may be regarded as *continuo* or figured bass, supplemented by engaging whirls of their worry beads. In serious argument, especially during backgammon, both hands are used vigorously, as in deaf and dumb or the tick-tack language of bookmakers.

The two who greeted us — we shall call them Pano and Stefano — were either trying to sell something, a mercantile matter, or else it had to do with village politics. They were as one with each other. *"Hronoi prin,"* — it had all happened before, one of them said, "many years ago". He confirmed the matter by raising his right palm and flicking it backwards as if throwing a coin over his shoulder.

The other two, let us say, Carlos and Joanni, were of a different opinion. Their spokesman, the one with a fearful scar over his eye, crossed his forefingers over his mouth and kissed them before letting out an explosive *"Ohi! No! Ma to Theo!"* which means "By God! I'm telling the truth."

About what? We never discovered. An old but agile *papas,* a priest entered the bar in a rustle of a somewhat superior brand of cloth. He turned to us and smiled as I stood up. *"Kalos orissate stin Melissohori."* He was pleased to welcome us to his village. Would I please sit down. *"Kathise, parakalo,"* he said, extending his palm downwards and agitating his fingers as if patting an imaginary dog.

He greeted his parishioners, glanced into the wine jug, blessed it and helped himself to a modest measure. Glasses were raised: *"Kalee kairee."* Thereafter they put their heads together, physically, and the argument resumed, loudly, passionately on the part of the laity. The priest spoke quietly, judiciously as if seeking approval for some disputed course of action. Eventually he sighed, shrugged his shoulders, picked up an empty cigarette packet and tore it open so that he could scribble on the blank surface. Scribble *what*? A draft letter to their bishop? The odds on a horse at Corinth? How best to get another subsidy from Athens? Katie, ever charitable, suggested a Bible class or a meeting of the parish church council. Entering into the spirit of the occasion I whispered, *"Then andecho pia,"* I'm damned if I know. You can never be sure with a village *papas*.

Most of them are ill-educated and drawn from the ranks of the secular clergy. They are permitted to marry but on doing so forfeit all chance of preferment. With their often begrudged free meals, they tend to be regarded as a bit of a joke, as one of the village features together with the horse-dealer, the rural guard and the tavern keeper, but as man not as priest. Recall what we heard about those gun-toting clerics at Pili, on our second day out of Athens? Our *papas* could have been of their persuasion.

We were hungry. I stood up and put the matter to the priest as best I could. *"Papas, parakalo. May kovi lortha,"* and went through the motions of sawing my stomach in two. He smiled and shouted to someone downstairs to be answered by a subterranean and wholly incomprehensible screech. He pointed to a door behind two wine barrels and gave a thumbs down sign and a down-going motion with two fingers on his knee.

The stone stairs were as steep as hell and I felt like Orpheus in the Underworld. In a corner of the cellar a very old woman stood with her back to me, vigorously pumping air from leather bellows into the glowing ashes of a wood fire. There ensued an eruption of sparks in the manner of a firework remembered from youth as Golden Rain. She couldn't hear a thing I tried to say, and I climbed back to the parish council.

In a right paternal gesture the priest, his beard a foot from mine, put a hand on my shoulder and said, "*Danske?*" I shook my head and said, "No, *ohi*, we are English," and waved towards Katie. "My wife," I said. This appeared to please him and he nodded in her direction. Re-enter Scarface, left, puffing, slightly. Greeks who spend most of their time in taverns, like their English counterparts, get fat at forty. Some seem to have been born fat. Their active agrarian kinsfolk, especially meditative watchers of goats, for no metabolic reason I can think of are as skinny and tough as whips. To him that hath . . . Scarface had great news. He smacked his lips, noisily. "*Kotopoulo!*" To ensure there could be no misunderstanding he flapped his arms vigorously and vented that noise as Peter heard it, thrice.

I awoke very slowly. It seemed curiously dark. My newly purchased and much valued cap had slipped over my eyes. Katie lay beside me snoring, gently, her head on her prostrate rucksack. I could hear the melodious hum of bees. We had gone to sleep near three or four brightly painted blue, white and scarlet hives. I woke her up. "Where are we?" she asked. I said I didn't know but could tell from the westering sun that we were alongside the little road that led towards our destination that night, the small township of Elopia.

We both stood up, somewhat unsteadily and tried to reconstruct what little we could recall. Katie remembered that the priest helped to put on her rucksack but it took two men, both laughing uproariously, to lift up mine, pretending they were saddling a horse. But what happened after that? I shook my head. "Don't you remember the bridge?" she asked. "You thought it would cool you off if you waded through the stream and I had to pull you back."

I couldn't remember the stream but I had a hazy memory of a signpost pointing in the right direction. Had we paid our dues? Katie nodded. "I did," she said. "You bought them another jug of wine and later they insisted we should drink with them, first retsina and then brandy. Huge ones, about a cupful. You drank half mine. That's what did it. I don't think we should go back to Melissohori on this trip. A pity. That old priest's eye opened and glowed when he spoke. Scarface had been to London. He was in the merchant navy."

"He couldn't speak English, could he?" I asked anxiously. She shook her head. "None of them could. I asked them in Greek and you gave them a short lesson in English which they seemed to like. They wrote some words down." No comment on my part.

The time, nearly half-past four. As far as I could make out, we had walked for an hour after lunch, miraculously, and slept for an hour or thereabouts in the bee-loud glade, choosing a gentle depression carpeted with wild thyme in an orchard of old citrus trees. The marvel is that, apart from temporary amnesia and my sunburnt nose, we felt more energetic than we had any right to. Our packs were laid out, neatly; they were shouldered up and off we went, along a partly macadamized road with broad verges which were easy on the feet.

Almost everywhere, it seemed, we were in the company of bees. *Protinus aerii mellis coelestia dona exsequar* . . .

> Let me sweeten my poem with honey for its theme, the gift of the sky.
> Permit me now, Maecenas, to present for your entertainment a miniature state;
> I will give you an account of its fierce-hearted leaders,
> Its orderly tribes, their manners, their pursuits, their wars.
> Is the subject too slight? Who will slight a poet's pains
> If the gods do not grudge him and Apollo hears his call?

Thus the opening lines of Virgil's *Georgics*, Book IV, as translated and introduced by Robert Wells. Both in our heather-covered moorland garden and on many long walks together, Katie has patiently endured some of the forty or more lines from the *Georgics* remembered from school days. They were physically thrashed into me by an elderly Latinist who invited his favourite scholars into his bedroom study at the end of our dormitory. With unruly red hair, buck teeth and a marked tendency towards insolence, I wasn't among the chosen few. Although I've never had the slightest difficulty with binomials, the scientific names of plants and animals, especially insects, I hated that red-faced Glaswegian and some of us thought he had complicated the intricacies of Latin grammar and syntax to make our life almost intolerable.

One day I managed to buy a cheap second-hand parallel translation of the *Georgics*, probably a Loeb edition, and marvelled at the descriptions of animals I knew quite a lot about. "First seek a settled home for your bees . . . place not their hives where the butting heifers can assault them. Let the spangled lizard with his scaly back be also a stranger to the rich stalls. Beware the bee-eater and Procne, the swallow with breast marked by bloodstained hands."

Unfortunately I had picked up a very free translation and one, of course, well-known to the resident catamite of Vintner House, whose aberrations were as opaque to me as the pluperfect and the future perfect indicative active. With rasping irony he bade me unravel the meaning and syntax of the lines, word for word. More sadistic slaps on my bare backside after dark with a slipper. Since we were obliged to take a shower every night, I wondered why he was so concerned about the hygiene of my genitals. *O hominem impurum! Heu me infelicem!* The accusative of exclamation.

To go back to the evocative treasure in the work of Robert Wells: he says what Virgil seeks to do is to break his subject open, to till it and make it more fruitful. He wrote towards the end of devastating civil wars:

"Caesar against Pompey; Octavian and Antony against the murderers of Caesar; Octavian against Antony . . . Octavian promised an end to the guilt, a world no longer at odds with itself and a new peaceful beginning." Virgil (70–19 BC) draws a parallel between his own nine-year-long struggle with the niceties of the *Georgics* — a word which means earth (*ge*) and work (*ergon*) — and that of the victorious Master of the Empire.

Notwithstanding the indiscretions of our lunchtime break Katie and I were knocking along at what we call a pretty fair lick, hugely encouraged by a signpost which promised that Elopia was no more than twelve kilometres away. The well-tilled soil intersected by irrigation canals and boundary-markers of pink and white oleander and dwarf cypress looked rich and humid enough to nourish crops of bananas.

With some time on our hands we throttled down to a modest pace, the better to take stock of veritable garlands of wild flowers. Some like fragrant jasmine and the electric-blue sepals of *lithospernum* made basket-work out of the stems of their taller sisters; others, especially a riot of orchids, most of which were entirely new to us, favoured the sloping but deep-cut banks of the water channels. We wondered who kept stock of the communal supply since, with a few greedy spadefuls taken out here and there, it would be an easy matter, we thought, to deplete the whole system.

By far the most charming aspect of the landscape was the integration of beekeeping with the density and variety of both the wild and cultivated flora. Most of the clusters of the three- and four-tiered hives reflected good husbandry, they were well cared for. Yet even in olive groves some errant swarms had built their clammy cells in natural fissures in the hard wood. The fissures had been either enlarged or cut away to provide the bees with landing platforms. Below these boughs, or around the parent trunks of the trees, thoughtful apiarists had put a necklet of chicken wire and thick cloth to protect their charges against spangled lizards and the like.

Virgil tells us how "under the towers of Oebalia's citadel" — which is to say at Tarentum in Italian Calabria — he saw an old peasant "who had a few acres of unclaimed land, a soil not rich enough for bullock's ploughing, unfitted for the flock and unkindly to the vine. Yet, as he planted herbs here and there among the bushes, with white lilies about and verlane and slender poppy, he matched in contentment the wealth of kings and, returning home in the late evening, would load his board with unbought dainties."

T. E. Page remarks that "to Virgil nature is not a dead thing but living and sentient. He constantly speaks of things as possessing almost human feeling." This is echoed by Robert Wells who recalls Osip Mandelstam's trenchant line: "We live deaf to the land beneath us." Virgil had seen "the empty fields running to waste" and "the plough dishonoured".

As we walked through the harmony of orchards, cereals, vegetables and vines tended with such care by labourers often working back to back, we thought about the inhuman, remorseless agriculture of depopulated areas of the Yorkshire Wolds and East Anglia. Did those get-rich-quick Eurofarmers ever set foot on their own land except to shoot game? Did they care a damn about other birds, bees, wild flowers, hedges, ditches and unpolluted streams? And yet . . .

According to the melancholic Robert Burton, "No rule is so general as that which admits of some exceptions." A few marvels can be accomplished with next to nothing in the way of human effort. This came home to me hard on a long walk which ended at Nice.* After cresting the Bonette, that great pass on the fringe of the maritime Alps, all became downhill. The geometry is flowing and it flowed south, into *la grande chaleur* in the season of cicadas.

At St Auron or it may have been St Sauveur in the Gorges de Valabres, I settled down for one thrice-blessed night of luxury in a wayside tavern, almost exhausted. M. le patron, a sophisticated fellow, heard out my tale of where I had come from (Holland) with a marked lack of enthusiasm. "Idleness", he said, "is an appendix to nobility," and to support this effrontery he told me how, many years before, he had been amongst the hard-drinking fishermen at Cannes. One of his fellows, a certain Auguste Célestin, retired to the hills where, from his mother, he had inherited a house, a little vineyard and one big *brusc*, a primitive beehive. Since Célestin knew nothing about hives or Virgil's philosophy a neighbour would extract the honey for him. Feckless Célestin never fed his bees, nor cleared the hive; never gave them water, never cut out the queen cells, never killed an old queen and never put in a new one. He did just nothing every

Journey through Europe, Constable, 1972.

year, and with no labour whatever he would be supplied with twelve to fifteen pounds of honey.

Another visitor, a fruit-grower from somewhere down the valley, listened to the story with marked interest. He shook his head. "You are lucky", he said "that you had only one *fainéant* [drone] like M. Célestin."

The twelve kilometres might be likened to an Irish mile or the length of a piece of string. Elopia, when we eventually got there, turned out to be a one-horse village. We saw the horse, a skinny beast tethered to a tree in the *plateia*. Over an ouzo in a crowded bar we asked our host first where, *parakalo*, we could erect our little tent and, second, the lip-touching question about our interest in food.

He scratched his head, said something almost inaudible above the Niagara of noise of TV pop music and pointed through the window. Katie who had managed to catch a word or two said we were being invited to join the horse that night and that there was something in the kitchen. She sniffed. "It's mutton," she said.

Difficult to refuse both offers politely, though we were already fed up with mutton and were averse to sleeping in the local equivalent of Trafalgar Square. A customer with a smattering of English invited us to follow him. He lived at the back of the pub where with the pride of an estate owner he pointed to a concrete yard and then to his hen run, already tenanted by chickens on perches. Stalemate. More apologies on our part.

The outcome, briefly, was that one of a small band of really sympathetic youngsters led us to the spacious grounds of their locked-up schoolhouse where, after a word with the caretaker, with endearing enthusiasm they helped us to put up the tent under a huge cypress tree. As a bonus they pointed to a tap in an unlocked shed.

We reciprocated with lollipops all round from a very superior-looking *zaharoplastio*, the Greek equivalent of a *pâtisserie*, which unfortunately sold only coffee, sweets and delicious-looking sticky buns. The children waved, we waved and went back to the taverna.

Adequate rather than superior, but made memorable by the company and Katie's striking up a warm relationship with Mama Elena who was both the cook and the grandmother of the young boss — Aristotle, we imagine, but referred to by all the company as Ari. The place was packed. He pointed to two rickety stools at the bar and bade us wait there. Drinks? I resisted the idea of ouzo, feeling that after our over-indulgence earlier we ought to be reformed characters, so we ordered *krassi* (wine) *aspro* (white) *aretsinatos* (non-resinated). Katie is not over fond of retsina and in rural areas they usually serve it unless asked for something else.

Around us the sound of excited human voices fortified by electronic bouzouki bounced back from the crudely plastered walls and ceiling, and noise enveloped us. We were obliged to shout.

Before long Ari appeared from the kitchen and with the silent authority of a traffic cop waved Katie back there to order food, and me towards two empty chairs between two fat men at a table normally for six.

"What do you want?" Katie shouted.

"Best there is," I shouted back, "but no damned

moussaka." If overcooked it resembles dried-up shepherd's pie, the bane of my school dinners.

I couldn't decide whether my table companions were more interested in me or in our wine bottle. Perhaps both. All six, three men and three women, gave me a hearty welcome. *"Aspropato"*, they shouted, which means "White bottoms", the Greek equivalent of "Bottoms up". Six small glasses went up in the air, and three were banged down empty.

We went through the standard catechism and I gave very cautious answers — we had come from Thebes, we were going to Delphi, but I let slip the fact that we were on foot. Incredulous looks. I'm telling the truth, *"ma to Theo"* and I pointed to my dusty boots.

A few minutes before Katie returned I offered our bottle all round. It was seized upon by the menfolk for three brim-fillers and something close to a cheer. It became common property but they gestured vigorously towards their own almost full jugs. Much clashing of glasses and some apprehension on the part of this would-be penitent.

Greeks are among the most generous people in Europe but possibly through some inborn trading instinct they dispense their generosity in a ritualized manner. They are not to be taken for a ride. It's up to the stranger to make the first move. Thereafter they usually can't do too much for you. It came out later to our slight embarrassment that they were paying for everything we drank.

The company fell about when Katie appeared. Seats were rearranged so that she sat between me and one of their wives, a handsome well-dressed woman. A good arrangement since Katie has more than twice my grasp of linguistic essentials. She lifted her eyebrows at the sight of our almost empty bottle. "Not me," I said, defensively. "I'll get another one."

She shook her head. "Make it a half," she said. "Remember Melissohori. Granny Elena is a darling, we got on fine. Grandson isn't married. She's a bit worried. You may have noticed he wears a ring through his ear."

"But what about food?"

"The choice is between rather dry moussaka, an omelette or lamb stew, *arni kapana*. For *arni* read stringy mutton. Looks as if it's been simmering for days. We put our heads together. I found tomatoes, red peppers and aubergines which could be chopped up for a dressing. She seemed delighted, you'd have thought I'd just invented *boeuf Bourgignon*. Looks as if they'll all get it tonight."

I introduced "Katerina" and she met Toula, Thea, Antonio and Paris, each one accompanied by strange relationships we couldn't make out. A kiss for Katie, a hand-grasp and a mild thump on the chest for me.

Enter Ari and Granny proudly carrying a wooden stretcher bearing more wine and eight plates of *arni katerina*. Loud cheers. "Looks like Breughel's *Wedding Feast*," whispered Katie. Granny made a little speech and pointed to her. More cheers. Clink, clink.

Underneath the lightly braised vegetables the mutton stew tasted much as it does the length of the Balkans. The Greeks pride themselves on their cooking and say it has slowly evolved from Homeric feasts. Others say this is absolute nonsense, it's a mixture of Turkish and Italian dishes — despite the fact that there still exists in former Greek Sicily a temple dedicated to Adephagia, the Greek goddess of good eating and merriment. Perhaps under divine guidance she invented mutton stew.

A neighbour of ours, a much travelled architect and ecologist, claims that fundamentally there are only three ways of preparing local food: French, Indian and Chinese. But try explaining that to those whose culinary dream is of prime roast and Yorkshire pud, Thanksgiving turkey and apple pie like momma made, or even Hungarian goulash.

By feeble torchlight we circled the *plateia*, said goodnight to a farting horse, the first Elopian we had met, and took the wrong turning. A clear sight of the Plough and Polaris showed we were completely off course on a road back to Thebes. We turned round and saw the schoolhouse at the foot of a rustic track.

The tent looked inviting but we were far from alone. At our approach sparrows arose from a cypress and flew off with much twittering and whirling of wings. It sounded like distant applause. They circled overhead before settling on the schoolhouse and adjacent trees where the clamour died away except for a few birds which kept up a repeated *chur-tit-tit, chur-tit-tit*, the sparrows' alarm call.

Because the birds almost invariably assemble and fly in at dusk when their breeding season is over and done with, we could not have foreseen that we had camped out under a heavily populated roost. Unlike starlings which spend their nights on ledges in orderly lines, equally gregarious sparrows quarrel and tumble over each other in a confused mass, chirruping until they settle down. Roosts of up to 100,000 birds have been reported from several countries. Katie and I know vast assemblies on Hampstead Heath, and once in November we found that every tree in the fashionable Avenue Bourguiba in Tunis was so thickly covered that the tables for tourists had to be moved out of excremental range.

In Elopia we were tired and promptly slept until two in the morning when to our annoyance we were awakened by those damned birds. Above the twittering and excitement we could hear a musical *pee-oo, pee-oo* repeated softly at regular intervals for about twenty minutes. An owl, surely, but which owl? At dusk the next day we both heard and saw the slim little chap, Scops owl, only a few inches in height. The commotion died away and we slept again until the village awoke at the slow chiming of one bell. Prime in Ascension-tide.

We got away at a more civilized hour. It took time to wash our white-spotted tent under that invaluable tap. We packed up the better to enjoy a pint of strong tea with Granny Elena's parting gift, a packet of cheese and some fruit. All chores done, we strode along towards the distant flanks of Mount Helicon.

We were still on a narrowing plain of less rich soil, trimly laid out with lines of almond trees and olives interplanted with vines. Friendly labourers, always with covered heads and arms, greeted us with a loud *"Yass"*, and waggled their mattocks

101

and rakes, resting awhile until we were out of sight.

Damned hard work, it seemed. Some more lines from the Georgics came back: *Multum adeo, rastris glaebas cui frangit inertis vimineasque* . . . "Yea, and much service does he do the land who with mattock breaks up the sluggish clods . . . nor is it for nought that golden Ceres views him from high Olympos with favour." Presumably PASOK has laid down labour rates, but are they paid in outlying regions? Most of the workers were noticeably old folk. We guessed that their children and grandchildren were working in the cities.

By walking through the avenues of trees we could see more flowers than on the little road. Greece has a flora of at least 6,000 species, near twice the number to be found in Britain, wild bees including a huge blue creature were commonplace but relatively few domesticated species. Although we could hear the echoing *croomp* of men abroad with shotguns, the glades throbbed with birdsong. On most patches of waste ground we found at intervals of about a hundred paces the most vociferous of nightingales still deploring the violent adultery of Tereus and the fate of poor Itys. Many other birds are common, too: several different kinds of warblers whose songs could not be disentangled; the *chink* and stammer of tits and finches busy destroying fruit blossom; and the metallic rattle of rollers, sky-blue in flight and as large as jays.

And then a curious thing happened. All the glorious sound ceased. Not *tout à coup* but as if under electronic volume control — diminuendo, or cross-faded in studio jargon.

The sight of shotgunners? No! The birds had seen that fork-tailed predator the Black kite which swept across our path a few feet above the ground, buoyantly with long glides and slow wing-beats. It passed us almost overhead and the glorious sound was resumed.

On the road we came across the gunners dressed to kill: camouflage battle-dress, waisted with plaited leather belts to hold their twelve-bore shells and American-style peaked caps incongruously decorated with *tiroler* tufts of boar fur or pheasant feathers in the manner of the chorus from *The White Horse Inn*. Around their necks they carried silver or chromium-plated bird-callers which at intervals they *pou-poued* like an amorous hoopoe, apparently to attract small doves, a specimen of which was carried by only one man, their sole triumph. I tried to ask about the Black kite, a species which I knew carried off farmyard chickens and goslings, and finished up by a makeshift imitation of the bird. I crouched and waggled my arms backwards but suspected from their serious expressions that they thought I wanted a toilet, since they pointed towards some bushes.

At hourly intervals, strictly speaking at twenty past the hour, church bells chimed. From behind us we could recognize, by a small crack in its voice, our own sanctuary away back in Elopia. It was echoed by an alto triplet *ping-pong-pang* from an unseen village in the hills to the south and, with increasing volume, a carillon pealed out due ahead. We had forgotten it was not only Sunday but that especially sacred one within the octave of Ascension-tide.

Half an hour passed. During a fine avian oratorio on

all sides the bell-tower in front of us spoke plainly. The sound and its echo died away and, to our huge surprise, we heard, although at first faintly, a *kyrie* sung in plain chant with a stress *basso profundo* on the second line.

Kyrie, Kyrie
KYRIE ELEISON

Within an hour we stood outside the Church of Our Lady, the Panagia herself, a basilica of pink granite blocks under copper-green pendentives at the heart of the hamlet of Xironomi.

Groups outside as if at a synagogue on the morning of Sabbath — "the cessation of labour" — greeted us like old friends. Without a head-shawl and wearing jeans, Katie felt she couldn't go in. I left her with a family dimly remembered from the night before, and entered a mystery: the service of the Orthodox Panagia, Mary the sanctified successor of the old Demeter transformed — Ceres of the Romans, protectress of man and of all the fruits of the earth.

The church was packed, the service somewhat confusing but the singing superb. Worshippers came and went, crossing themselves right to left, kissing one or more icons just inside the narthex. One very old lady, wholly in black, wept as she knelt before the stiff portrait of the Panagia; a good soul obliged to walk with a stick paused in front of an icon of the Last Judgement. She lowered her head, said a prayer audibly, and with a tremulous finger lightly touched a recumbent figure at the foot of the painting. After she had limped away I saw that she had touched the head of the Prince of Darkness, proud Lucifer cast down. I could make nothing of her simple gesture.

Orthodoxy has retained the basic simplicity of the earliest known churches. Only the priests and their deacons are permitted to walk behind the iconostasis, the high screen of icons which separates the sanctuary from the nave. The belief of this enormously popular and widespread religion is that Byzantine iconography excels realistic painting as a means to meditation. There are no statues within the church; they are reckoned to be impious relics of the polytheism of the pre-Christian era.

In between three hours of prayers and the reading of sacred literature there is much wholly unaccompanied chanting and singing, led by the clergy and by cantors of a vocal quality comparable only to that heard in High Anglican churches and cathedrals. I came out of the basilica strangely moved.

Katie had heard part of the service through the loud-speakers which had attracted us to the church. Better still, with a diplomacy which I wish I could emulate, she had approached several groups waiting outside and asked, politely, if they knew of anyone who spoke English. She introduced me to Georgios who had done his fifteen years overseas making and selling bread in the Bronx. He had interpreted part of the service for her although, as he put it, "Shit! I haven't been on my knees since I left Xironomi." He ran his father's farm nearby and drove his mother to church for the four great festivals.

I asked if he could explain the action of the old lady

who had blessed the Devil. "Don't know, but I'll ask Mamma when she gets off her knee-bending."

With her twinkling eyes and ready smile, Ma was pretty spritely for her seventy years. He explained the situation rapidly. "She don't know either," he said. "She don't go to church that often but she'll ask the old lady if you'll point her out."

I saw her at once and nodded, and promptly regretted the action when I caught Katie's disapproving look. But too late, too late. The two old ladies were talking and, thank God, smiling. Apparently they were friends if not close neighbours.

Georgios' mother returned and with small gestures, as if she were blessing him, spoke benevolently. He translated slowly. "Mamma says Dora thought no one else seems to be praying for him and surely he needs prayers for forgiveness more than anyone else in the world."

We felt peckish. Our friends left by car after giving us meticulous instructions about how to reach their favourite *kafenio* at the far side of the village, fortunately *en route*. Why couldn't they drop us there, he asked. Hard to explain that one briefly, but we knew the routine: we'd been going through it for nearly a week. We waved them goodbye, promising to mention their name to the *patron*.

Among the three or four locals was a fellow noisily slopping up yoghurt, a word which we couldn't pronounce easily (*yahourti*), but by saying who we had just seen and pointing politely we were given two generous portions topped by an inch of honey, the man behind the till pointing out his hives and the milk churns.

Katie stirred hers vigorously but paused over the last spoonful. She picked something off her tongue and handed it to me on her forefinger. "What", she said, "are these?" Two creatures the size of caraway seeds. Now as a Fellow of the Royal Entomological Society I knew damn well what they were: *aphodius*, a small dung beetle, which we shall shortly meet again. "A tiny insect," I said. "They're common around here. They are probably good for you. Harmless."

The man behind the till wouldn't take any money for our yoghurt, coffee and a packet of biscuits. "Georgios," he said with a theatrical wink, and on we went, on and on during a long, long day which ended that night in a hell-deep gorge on Mount Helicon.

The countryside hilly, mixed agrarian and pastoral on progressively hillier slopes. The great range ahead looked ominous, a lop-sided massif with its left shoulder on our line of approach leaning south towards the invisible Gulf of Corinth. Few labourers about and fewer still when, on Georgios' advice, we struck right beyond a burnt-out church, at the old road — literally the *asprodhromos*, the white track. Up and up, in that fog of ignorance.

We rested, briefly, in the shadow of a shieling, the ruins of a house of somebody's grandfather. The huckling of hens, busy beehives and two open churns of milk wrapped about with moist rags, tomorrow's yoghurt under an old mulberry tree. We peered inside them. Many small insects, moths, flying ants and beetles, including *aphodius*, moved freely on the creamy surface of the milk.

"Is that what I nearly ate at lunchtime?" Katie asked.

"I think so," I said, adding mendaciously, "That's why Boeotian yoghurt is so famous. It's another flavour, like banana or pineapple." She didn't say any more.

The white track seemed to go on for ever.

As an abode of the gods Mount Helicon has been sung about for over 3,000 years. The Muses were reputed to have spent part of each year in a sanctuary up there. It lies behind Thespiae where there are the remains of a theatre, statues and an Ionic temple erected in their honour. Presumably the famous Nine used the place as a sort of shared holiday home. We wondered how Zeus and the rest of his improbable company got on at the top of so many feet of snow.

We have much of this in *The Theogony* or birth of the gods by Hesiod who, although born at Cyme in Aeolis, retreated, together with his unsuccessful father and his ambitious brother Perses, to the village of Ascra some miles to our north.

Hesiod, together with Homer from whom he probably borrowed extensively, sketched out the basic *Who's Who* of classical literature, but whence came this truly remarkable mythology? Simple answer: oral tradition, source wholly unknown. It still exists, or certainly did into this century.

More years ago than I care to remember, my brother Joe, an historian, and I crossed a little market-place near the superb Greek temple of Segesta near Palermo in west Sicily. According to Thucydides its ruins date from the third century BC. To an attentive audience of about a dozen villagers, a ragged old man who gestured with a thick baton was telling the history of the village in the tradition of the ancient "mimes". He spoke in a curious droning voice. He had got as far as the arrival of the Saracens in the ninth century when we arrived. By the time we returned about two hours later he was deep into the Pharos and the Knights of St John. My brother who has a fair grasp of Italian said that the narrator was pretty near the historical mark.

Wandering about in Attica and Boeotia somewhere around 750 BC is presumably how Hesiod acquired his extensive information whilst his brother wasted his patrimony and ultimately came to want. Hesiod relates how he lived the life of an industrious farmer (questionable) until the Muses met him as he was tending his sheep on Mount Helicon and taught him, like Caedmon of Whitby, "a glorious song". This was almost certainly the *Works and Days* and *The Theogony*. Glorious perhaps in showing from what meagre threads Homer wove the plumes and golden garments of his mighty armies. Hesiod's distinctive title to a high place in Greek literature lies in the very fact of his freedom from classic form and his serious yet child-like outlook upon the world. A near exact translation reads as though some amateur had tried to present Milton in the language of John Clare, the Northamptonshire peasant. Banalities abound.

Call your friend to a feast but leave your enemy alone and specially call him who lives near you . . . A bad neighbour is a great plague . . . not even an ox would die for him. . . . Be friendly with the friendly and visit him who visits you . . . Do not let a flaunting woman coax and cozen. She is after your barn . . .

Looking back I don't think we missed much in turning our backs on Ascra and Hesiod who in Quintilian's opinion "rarely rises to great heights". Even his name might be a literary twist on the Greek for "the Guide". As for his claim to have challenged and beaten Homer in a singing competition as related in the *Cypria*, I am at one with Jonathan Swift who, on the subject of classical poetry, wrote:

> As learned commentators view
> In Homer, more than Homer knew.

Herodotus maintained that Hesiod and Homer lived not more than 400 years before his own time, consequently not much before 850 BC. From his controversial tone it is evident that others had made Homer more ancient. What seems indisputable is that nobody knows when Homer actually lived.

The day seemed endless, the sunlight ferocious, the track confusing. We came across canals with steep concrete banks which we could see, from general bearings, wandered off in the wrong direction. We were very thirsty. We tried to fish for water by tying a length of cord to the neck of our plastic container — a precarious exercise. The water, when we managed to haul up about a pint, looked ominously discoloured.

We began to climb. We saw nobody except a shepherd too far away to be of any assistance. Katie sighed gently and murmured, *"Les choses . . ."* They were indeed *contre nous*. We tried to think of something to think about. The curious absence of bird life except those Crested larks. The heat haze. The horizons shimmered. Without saying a word I looked at them with mild consternation. They not only shimmered but a portion of a crest far away to the north appeared to detach itself from the general lie of the land. A mirage? *Le cafard?* Or perhaps, far worse, the onset of hyperthermia, heat exhaustion? The Psalmist's sickness that destroyeth in the noon-day. I had encountered it in the desert, often. We needed salt. We carried salt tablets but without water they bite. We had to find at least a cupful.

Under various pretences I probed every steep gully, overturned large stones for a glimpse of moisture. God be praised we found a freshet, a mere trickle but with the addition of two saccharin-sized tablets it tasted like iced Bollinger. A metabolic explosion. We pressed on.

About an hour later we entered another low defile where the tracks divided as decisively as the Y-forked hazel twig of a water diviner. Should we go right or left?

"Packs off" I said. "You go left and I'll go right. It'll only take us a few minutes to see what's ahead." I had a notion that I was literally right.

I hadn't got half-way up my slope when Katie gave

a great shout: *"Thalatta! Thalatta!"* The sea! The sea!

Stumbling up to her with both packs I saw the Gulf of Corinth stretching into infinity. In the blazing white sunshine it was wrinkled like beaten pewter.

Coastal encounters

With scarcely enough water left to brew a mugful of tea
we took to the shade of another ruined farmhouse which,
to judge from concrete apertures and walls pock-marked
by spent bullets, had been used as a military strongpoint.
Inside it felt pretty warm but tolerable. Leaving Katie
to make a temporary divan out of sleeping-bags on a
fallen door propped up with bricks, I made for a rift, a
depression in the slope of Helicon marked by a Golgotha
of pink-flowered Judas trees.

Flood debris at their feet still felt moist. Like a questing
hound I moved down the depression, first to a sprinkling
of iris and asphodel where I thought I heard the belch of
frogs. O blessed sight! A reed-ringed pool of clear water
over which flew electric-blue dragonflies! I half-filled
our plastic carrier, screwed it tight and returned to Katie
claiming I had found the Fountain of Hippocrene. She
seemed, I thought, singularly unimpressed. Whilst the
butane burner hissed I scanned the landscape through
glasses from the Gulf below us up to the highest peak
of the range above.

On the map the coastline of the Gulf of Corinth
thereabouts has a somewhat dissipated appearance beset
by small bays and long wedge-shaped promontories
which hang down like the dugs of a nanny-goat. In
our constant efforts to cling to hard-won altitude they
were to be avoided at all costs. But surely only one bay

could boast of three small islands — the Dombrenis group — and there they were, due south, about a mile in length and twice that distance offshore. Surely even Greek maps couldn't be off-course by a day's march? The peak to the west of Ascra must be Motsara where Hesiod claimed to have received divine inspiration from the Muses, those nubile immortals who danced round their swimming-pool, Hippocrene. Maybe I wasn't all that far out in saying where the solvent of our tea had come from. This stuff, said I, taking immoderate gulps, contains the very essence of inspiration.

For the first time since we left Elopia with its bees, its hospitality and the field of the farting horse, we knew precisely where we had got to. How to get to Prodromos, the next place in the right direction on our miserable map, was still covered in question marks. We were surrounded by that ubiquitous prickly stuff.

An old but vigorous fellow seemed anxious to help but was busy trying, unsuccessfully, to control a herd of anarchic goats with blasphemous shrieks. Apparently he hadn't heard of Prodromos — rural Greek villages often changed their names during the Civil War. But at the word *paleohoro*, the old village, and a wave towards the north-west, he resorted to vigorous sign-language. Up there, on to the hill and then down, down steeply towards the left.

Relatively easy, until we got to the boulder-strewn summit of the hill he'd indicated where tracks wandered off in various directions but not the one we wanted.

Then very faintly, from afar, we heard the familiar, the dreadful noise that donkeys make when they imagine

114

themselves unloved. Within half an hour we reached the tavern in the steep hill village of Prodromos.

Almost nobody about. What on earth were they all up to? Except for a muttered *"Yiasou"* in the tavern, little sound but grunts, the triumphant slap of a winning card and the rattle of boxed dice. We were so accustomed to being greeted loudly and promptly cross-examined that we felt obliged to speak in whispers.

No matter. We had found what had been on our minds for some hours: ice-cold Amstel beer which we drank outside in the company of an old dog who scratched himself excessively. Somebody observed that fleas are good for a dog: they stop him from brooding over being a dog. The atmosphere intrigued us. We sensed tension, waiting, as for a solemn thing about to happen. It began with the slow, the distant tolling of a bell. The old men inside rose to their feet and stayed there holding their caps in both hands. The man of the house came out pulling on his jacket. He shouted at the dog as a cortège climbed the hill. We inclined our heads as the procession approached.

First four priests, their lips moving in inaudible prayer, then the black-sashed bearer of a huge cross inlaid with silver. Then a battered van with an open coffin protruding from the tailboard. Inside could be seen half-shrouded shoulders and bare head of a very old man, his mouth agape as if in an arrested scream, fearful to look at. Then followed a long trail of relatives and other mourners, perhaps the whole village. They passed out of sight round a bend of the road. We sat down. We were alone in the forecourt except for the dog which had slunk back.

Half an hour elapsed before the whole company returned in a far from funereal mood. Certainly two or three women wept quietly, but they were kissed and hugged. Jugs of wine and little glasses of liquor on trays were handed round. A young man came up and in flawless English said: "My name is Spiro. Momma thanks you for your respect. Will you please take a drink with us?" Saying that he would be back in a moment he returned to the company who were intent on exorcizing the stark fact of death with secular festivities: upraised glasses. With hands round each others' shoulders they talked as if at a wedding. The tops of tables were wet with wine. A bouzouki combo struck up. Mock fights broke out and ended quickly with much back-slapping. All part of the ambiguities of Hellenism: violence and compassion, a capacity for survival and an ability to see things as they really are.

As our new friend Thomas Spiro, a well-to-do Cretan put it: "This is how we are all going to end up, so we might as well have a good time at the rehearsals." He said that the dead man was an old-guard Marxist and had probably left a small fortune. "That's practical politics. During the Occupation he took most of the village up into shacks on Helicon where he lost an arm during raids. For the last twenty years he damn well ran this place. Anybody who stood up to him got chucked out or a warning shot in the leg. Pity he can't see what's going on now. *Endaxi*, eh? All kiss and make up, but in a few days' time they'll be at each others' throats again. To hell with it. We'll be back in Iraklion."

As to our roundabout route to Delphi via Kirra and

the Sacred Way, he couldn't understand why we didn't take the direct route through the hills to Distoma; we'd be there in half the time. We tried to explain. He shrugged and lifted his glass saying, "White bottom." I lifted my own and said, "*Aspro-pato* and thank you, all of you. Our blessings on your house, may it stand forever." He bowed to Katie. His huge moustache brushed my cheek. We waved to the company, they shouted back cheerfully, and once more we were off again.

What had he said? Skirt the back of the village through their vineyard. Ignore the road. Keep to the track until we could see the sea and one small island. Look out for an old signpost that pointed up a track to the monastery, a steep hill but it could be trusted. He had known the place since he had worn short pants.

No doubts, no misgivings until, feeling tired out, we came to the hill. It wasn't a hill, it was a stony goat track up a steep cliff. We puffed and grunted. Hard going.

On the hill of the Holy Brethren we found the stream Spiro told us about. The last there was, he'd warned us. Musical water that tasted like Perrier. We filled up a stoppered plastic udder — enough for supper, a catlick wash, and breakfast. Near two litres. Heavy even when half full, and we were still trudging up and up to a steep rocky defile that twice echoed this uncertain path-finder's shout down to Katie.

"Enough," she shouted back, "let's stop here." "Here," said the echo. "*Here*," whispered another. I agreed with them. We'd stop, but where? The perennial, the ever-to-be-faced problem at sundown: where to doss down in that riot of rocks, thorns and tares entangled?

117

Why the Desert Fathers sought holiness and hardships in Lower Egypt I could never make out: by comparison with what we were up against in the ruins of Arcadia, sand would have been luxurious, and mere pebbles tolerable.

With a womanly eye to exterior decoration Katie homed in on a large pink-flowered Cistus, high-arched enough to be crawled under. "Roses round the door," she said, not noticing, I suspect, that at the back a rounded lump of limestone stuck out like a partly submerged porpoise.

"Not quite our place," I said, but quickly added that if she sat down I'd scout around on my own. She looked tired. Eventually we settled for a hollow in a bank which smelt of wild thyme and could, with imagination, be described as mossy. Behind it an aromatic herb, probably rosemary, symbol of fidelity. Newly-weds used to roll on it.

With tent up, supper on the boil and a shot of Metaxas as an aperitif we felt we could relax. A small prick-eared owl greeted us with a gentle *pee-oo* (pause) *pee-oo* before floating off on fairy wings.

Katie began to lay out supper of reconstituted Turkey Creole — whatever that is — but in a necklet of chopped-up walnuts and figs it went down all right. We lolled back with our heads on our packs recalling incidents of a day that had begun well and ended not too badly.

To ensure that we knew where we were heading for the next day I replayed my recorded instructions about how to reach the monastery. For a minute or two Spiro's voice came through loud and clear, and the sequence ended in fond farewells and sounds of revelry at the end of that tape. I turned it over and put the little machine away.

As a dog stands up and turns round before it settles down for the night I suggested we should wander round for a few minutes in the almost dark. Far below, pewtered in the unearthly light, we caught a glimpse of the cold and ancient gristle of the sea. The moon sailed through a sea of wrack. As the lightest of cat's-paw winds shifted a little to the east and then counterwise to the west the warm air bore the aroma of all-abundant honeysuckle and oleander. Faintly, far away from somewhere in the depths of the gorge a nightingale jug-jugged and chirruped at intervals, hesitantly as a concert flautist might moisten his lips and play a few bars before the conductor raises his baton. Its song cannot be reduced to the phonetics of bird watchers. Izaak Walton caught the spirit of it: "Such sweet loud music they breathe that it maketh mankind to think that miracles are not ceased."

Suddenly we seemed to hear music, vaguely familiar. Was there witchery abroad, such as Falstaff heard in Windsor Forest at midnight? With mock-severity Spiro had warned us that in that gorge, despite the proximity of the holy brethren, there were *daoutis*, evil spirits. The music grew louder. As we approached the tent we recognized Stravinsky's *The Rite of Spring*. The wild Bacchanale before the sacrifice of the maiden. Hypnotic percussion from the bass viols. In our minds' eye we could see the *corps de ballet*, those knock-kneed Lolitas with long braided hair.

The music came from my micro-recorder: in putting it away apparently I'd turned it on again. Until I spooled the tape back I couldn't understand why we hadn't heard the music before we took our stroll. Then all became comprehensible: a silence of about three or four minutes before part of one movement of the Stravinsky began. The recording was part of a series of hour-long BBC programmes called "Man of Action" in which a few of us such as walkers, solo yachtsmen, mountain climbers and glider pilots were asked to select music that ran through our heads in moments of exhilaration and stress. The tape, an old one, sounded tinny but it meant we were carrying a little less than an hour's private concert with us. We spooled on and settled down to the harmony of violins in the final diminuendo of Mozart's "Ave Verum Corpus".

That darned nightingale turned up again after midnight, this time about twenty yards below us, where it encountered invincible rivals, the echoes in the gorge of its own voice. In vain it chattered and trilled until it flew away, whimpering. But a resolute nightingale: it came back twice during the night when, heartily tired of rolling over on top of each other, we got up and re-aligned our sleeping-bag so that on the slope we were able to rest feet downwards.

An hour before dawn we heard the whinny of a horse, the bleat of sheep and goats and the bark of dogs on the track below our shelf. Who were they? Vlachs? We hoped we couldn't be seen. At first light we could still hear the dogs at a distance and decided to pack up soon, leaving breakfast until we reached the elusive monastery. As a dog deterrent I whittled down a gnarled branch of a Judas tree with my skinning knife for as effective a shillelagh as ever you saw.

Before we set off I fished out a couple of sheets of Vlach expressions from the fellow we had met on the train. On a small hilltop overlooking the plain we spotted a piratical-looking rider on a fine grey. He wore a dark goatskin cape surmounted, arrogantly, by a bright red knitted sock.

Leaving Katie I walked towards him slowly. Two or three lean curs bounded up, aggressively. He reduced them to belly-crawling submission by terrific shouts. Leigh Fermor says that, from shouting to each other across the windy tops of their hills, Vlachs are almost incapable of quiet speech in the open air. He watched my approach with contrived indifference. A middle-aged fellow but heavily bearded, an adornment which, apart from those on priests, is relatively rare in Greece. Red-sock bore a rich growth in which a pair of sparrows could have nested. Holding up my arms in greeting I bawled *"Yass"*. He shouted something similar and spurred his nag towards me. In basic Greek I said my wife and I were English; we were walking down to Kirra on the Gulf; where, please, is the monastery? There followed something in gruff speech and sign language I couldn't understand. I tried a different tack: *"Bunâ dzua! Dukesku! Paree Kalo Z'burask. Eshti Vlachos?"* At that fragment of Wallachian he smiled hugely, dropped his reins and with hands on pommel vaulted to the ground in one acrobatic movement.

"Bunâ dzua!" he said with evident satisfaction. Seeing

121

comes before words. The child looks and recognizes before it can speak. There is what Dylan Thomas called an international flavour in most if not all European languages but Red-sock and I didn't get very far in terms of verbal communication.

He was a Vlach called Janos; I was an Englishman Yanni, married (*hiu sura*) and there she was, I said, pointing to my bed-mate (*mulliari*) Katerina under a tree. I waved, she waved, he waved. To her I held my arms out laterally as if about to fly which, in our sign language, means, "I'm fine. Stay where you are." Thereafter only two things I learnt, one distinctly negative: I couldn't put across where we were heading for. I tried *monastiera* and *basiliki*. He looked puzzled. I put the tips of my fingers together in the manner of the Hindu greeting. I crossed myself, looked up at the sky and murmured *papas*. He shook his head. Perhaps he thought we weren't too sure about the weather.

After scratching his head he pointed to the hills to the north and said something out of which I managed to abstract only one word: *Arachova*. The village on the main road between Livadia and Delphi.

I smiled hugely and said, "*Graz, graz*," thank you but no! "*Nu, nu. Pou ine Antikira?*" Where was that little port on the Gulf?

His turn to look pleased. He swung his arm round, first to the south and then to the west. "*Ashits, ashits. Dukesku Antikira.*" Yes, yes he knew the place.

With a glance at my notes on Wallachian I could have told him that his dog (*canili*) was barking (*alatra*) and the house (*casa*) was old (*easti veacli*) but without them my vocabulary was limited to about twenty memorized phrases and incantatory words such as numerals and the present, past and future tenses of the verbs "to be" and "to have". Not the stuff of intimacy. Two men (*doi barbata*) on donkeys (*gumari*) were working their way up to us driving their sheep and goats. Time to go, but Janos wouldn't have it. He asked me, as they all did, how old I was. This threw me. I knew only the words from one (*un*) to ten (*tsats*). Slowly I lifted up my open-fingered hands seven (*shapte*) times. He started and said something incomprehensible. Did it mean "What a splendid fellow" or "Silly old sod"? I shall never know. As far as I could make out from similar gestures on his part he was about thirty-five. He gripped my shoulders. We said "*Mulza ardio*" several times and I made my way back to Katie who, with her head on her rucksack and eyes closed, was enjoying what the travel packagers sell to uncritical indolents as the joys of the Mediterranean littoral.

"Were they really Vlachs? What did you say to him?"

"Precious little. As far as I could make out he didn't know much Greek and I couldn't remember Vlach phrases until I glanced at my prompt."

"Where are we heading for?"

"Back to the sea, I'm afraid. He indicated there's a track there to Antikira."

"Why there?"

"It's near Kirra. Old Red-sock had actually heard of the place and it's marked on the map."

* * *

Down we went, on to a small road where, hidden among trees, we found two trucks, the rear doors webbed with knotted rope. One looked like a very old army vehicle crudely camouflaged in a mosaic of dark green, brown and sickly yellow paint; the other was covered in faintly blue threadbare canvas. The trucks were double-deckers. There were two floors, one above the other and both were inches deep in sheep and goat droppings. Fresh donkey dung fouled the tailboard to which, presumably, the beasts were strapped in transit. So this is how they travelled at night from one grazing ground to another, the Black Departers. We had twice seen small convoys of similar trucks very early in the morning, and had assumed they were farmers taking their stock to market.

With his usual lucidity Patrick Leigh Fermor says; "Ordinary Greeks approve of their [Vlachs'] Greekness, their freedom, admire their primeval severity of life but despise their primitive ways. 'They never wash,' they say, 'from the day of their birth till the day of their death.' Their aloofness promotes distrust. Plainsmen speculate about their buried and supposititious wealth. They regard them as sly opponents and the two are often at loggerheads when nomad flocks encroach on their grazing ground."

Later on, in the Agrapha Mountains, those hostile peaks to the north-west, we found that the Vlachs were the only temporary inhabitants to practise transhumation, the custom of driving flocks up into pockets of high grazing-ground in the burning heat of summer and returning to hutments on the plains before inhospitable winter set in.

* * *

To reach the coast we took to the banks of a canal which appeared to run parallel to the line of the shore, and had to abandon it when it veered inland. The going became steep: a goat track down through a landslide of rocks. It led us to an almost deserted fishing village unmarked on our map but remarkable for the carcases of caiques and a ramshackle tavern supported on the seaward side by wave-worn stilts.

The company of four included a Master Mariner who knew precisely where he was and what we might expect when we again ventured inland. The man of the house served us with Amstel, bread and hot mutton broth, and in between mouthfuls we were again thoroughly examined.

At the question: "Where have you come from?" we produced our maps, easier than explanations. The Master spoke with authority: *"Alla tara poro simera?"* — Where next today? I shrugged my shoulders. If I could have put across the irony in Greek I would have said: "We have nowhere to go but everywhere." I pointed to Antikira on Sheet 2, *Nomos Phokis*. He clicked his tongue. *"Simera?"* A long way, he said, about twenty-five kilometres. He picked the map up, holding one corner between two fingers as one might the tail of a rotting fish. We knew just what he felt. We were bidden to wait.

Within minutes he came back wearing a navy-blue cap with threads of gold around the peak. On the table he spread out the equivalent of an Admiralty chart with a section of the coastline. "You are here," he said, stabbing a small appendix to the Bay of Zaltsas with his forefinger.

Their own village, Panagia, lay a little to the west.

Briefly the fog of ignorance was dispersed. But to Antikira there were neither paths nor small roads that we could make out, unless we went back on our tracks and up to Arachova.

The Master took my sheet and drew a decisive line up into the nearby hills, an *asprodhromos*, a white road, a very ancient track, the one they used during the war. Within an hour we were up and away, climbing steadily through hamlets with names.

Unlike our helter-skelter down the goat trail, the upland track rarely rose or fell with anything that irregulated a steady pace. It bore the spirit of antiquity, a purposive ongoing quality, a gradual ascent that followed contours and old terraces near the very end of their productive tenure, and we blessed the Master who had pointed it out.

On a staircase of ruined terraces we heard fearful screams. In a state of manic fury an old man thrashed the bloodstained flanks of a donkey in his efforts to drive the iron shoe of his plough into a forty-five degree slope. The flayed beast, with a fearfully visible cage of ribs, stumbled and fell to its knees. The old fellow stopped for a moment to prise out a large rock before he resumed his screaming and thrashing. Sisyphean labour. To what end? To hack out a path or a springwater channel from the small carpet of greenery above him, perhaps his sole holding in that wilderness. It seemed hopeless, the last despairing gesture of husbandry at the end of its tether.

Perhaps not entirely hopeless. On the highest slopes,

within the shadow of the Helicon ridge, stood herdsmen as immobile figures, each with his own wardship. From our ongoing track we tried to pace out their small patches: a linear mile or less. They depended on skindeep soil, barely capable of sustaining and providing anchorage for goats' fodder. The question remained: What on earth were those silent wardens thinking about?

Towards sundown we faced up to finding water and somewhere to bed down with less than Spartan rigour. Doubt about the merits or otherwise of an inexplicable platform of fractured concrete in a depression were resolved by leaving our rucksacks there and setting off on our own to look for more comfortable lodgings.

I gave up within five minutes and rejoined Katie on the platform to find our packs beset by columns of small red ants which bit us painfully when we brushed them off. She had found what was probably a holiday home of a rich Theban merchant. Apart from the superb view across the Gulf, we couldn't make out why anybody had built a modern bungalow in almost complete isolation except for a track down to a small bay. We knocked on the door. Somebody shouted what presumably meant, "Who's there?" Katie shouted back, "Good evening. We are on foot. We need water. Can you help us?"

A bearded middle-aged man with dark, deep-set eyes appeared from the patio on the seaward side of the bungalow. He nodded, sympathetically and said something we couldn't understand but he lifted up his finger which we took to mean that we should wait. We heard him talking to a woman, rapidly and in a language we guessed was Serbo-Croat, then they came out together, smiling somewhat fixed smiles: she, a gypsy-like woman whose nervous eyes never left ours. We were shown the water tap and invited to take a drink with them on the patio. Then there began one of the most puzzling and intriguing hours we ever spent under a Greek roof.

The only verbal communication was between Katie and the woman of the house, whose Greek was only a little better than her own. The couple were hospitable. Eventually they gave us, two complete strangers, a meal and offered us a bed in a small room, but they were suspicious of every move we made to the extent of standing outside the lavatory door until we emerged. The man, Karol, watched me closely when I took off my jacket and shirt and washed in the kitchen sink. Both he and his companion Magda treated Katie in the same way. These moves were embarrassing but we couldn't do anything about it. What were they so concerned about?

Karol and I passed the partly open door of a room lined with books. He closed the door a little too quickly for decorum, but not before I caught a glimpse of the deck of a modern radio transmitter. From hooks alongside their double-bolted door hung a canvas game-bag, very curious leather straps, a holster and a bandolier for shotgun ammunition. Alongside on a shelf were boxes of twelve-bore cartridges and small taped-up cartons labelled Biretta 9 mm. So that's what he carried in that under-arm harness.

Shotguns are for sport but with a 9 millimetre slug you could blow a hole through a church door. I felt mildly alarmed. Why on earth had they let us in? If we could have got out under some pretext, Katie would have been the first through their bolted front door, but try as I did, I couldn't speak to her privately.

Tension is contagious. Choosing a deep chair on the patio, Katie all but sat on a very superior cat, a Burmese which became air-borne. At its howl I rose to my feet apologetically and knocked over a carafe of wine, which did nothing to improve the situation. Supper, a good supper, was served and eaten punctuated by polite platitudes between Magda and Katie. In an effort to bring a little warmth to the table, she talked of our home in *Londino*, our children, and our travels in Greece. Then, *"Apo pou ine?"* Where did they come from, she asked conversationally. The question seemed to freeze in mid-air. A short silence before Magda spoke rapidly in their own language, and then in Greek translated what Karol replied. Katie turned to me. "She says that like ourselves they travel a great deal."

"What next?" I asked with an expansive and wholly hypocritical smile. "We are going to bed as soon as we decently can," she said.

We slept for nine hours and were up and away by seven o'clock. Our hosts gave the impression that they hadn't been to bed.

By following the line pencilled on our map by the Master it took us two days of hard slog to reach the foot of the Sacred Way. It entailed climbing up the seaward face of Mount Helicon and — almost certainly in error — climbing down again through a steep boulder-strewn gorge. This put us back, painfully, for half a day. But there were compensations, especially the folk we met who were as helpful and straightforward as the two of the previous night had been mysteriously suspicious about everything we did. Even their external gear abounded in question marks. Surely a couple with intricate aerials and a powerful spotlight on the flat roof of a bungalow wouldn't get far as secret agents?

We didn't discover until we replayed all our micro-recordings several weeks later that the curious incidents we discussed *sotto voce* in our hosts' bedroom were irregularly overlaid and sometimes obliterated by electronic noise.

At midday we stared with no enthusiasm across a barren plateau bounded to the north and a little to the west by the snow-clad summits of Helicon and Mount Parnassus. On that plateau the old road split into a variety of tracks, as if uncertain where to go next, so we made for a distant procession of power pylons. Each of the nearest three was inhabited some half-way up by an amiable villain doing something to the metalwork. The first fellow seemed hugely amused by our arrival. He waved, he shouted something to his mate on the ground in the language we had heard the night before: staccato consonants and deep-throated auxiliary vowels as in *Brezhnev*.

I looked up and shouted: *"Parakalo. Theloome to voeethema."* We needed his help, a phrase at which I had become adept.

"*Angleekee?*" he asked. I nodded. He called to the man on the other side of the pylon. In the manner of a character from Damon Runyon he asked "Whad'ya want?"

"The old track down to Antikira," I said.

"Jesus! If ya wanna kill yourselves, climb that hill and make for the shack you can see from the top. Mama Anoula's place. She'll make ya coffee. Don't reach for ya pocket or she'll go bananas. Say you're friends of Gregor's. Ask her to point out the Devil's Arse (*kolos too thiavolo*), a river bed. It's dry now but filled with goddam rocks. It'll bring you to the bauxite plant at a shit-heap called Paralia; there's a road from there to Antikira."

"You from round here?" I asked.

"Us? Jeez no! *Voulgarous*, Bulgarians. I mean we wuz before the bastards started to shoot each other. Now we're Greeks. No goddammed work in Sofia. We come here by truck from Livadia each day."

We did what he suggested. Impossible to guess Mama Anoula's age. A very active old lady, her skin wrinkled but her eyes bright and shining. She took Katie's hand as if her favourite grandchild had come home. After driving out a flock of indignant fowls she dragged us into her wooden hut with its iron stove and an array of pots for making cheese. Coffee? Impossible to refuse. She was grinding the beans. We drank it on a bench outside. We talked awhile, mostly murmuring pleasantries, then, leaving to Katie the problem of how to reach the *kolos too thiavolo*, I walked round the small-holding with map and compass, peering down, trying to work out where we'd got to. Discouraging.

Several tracks disappeared in the shimmer of heat. We had strayed off the Master's line.

Katie called, "Time to be off. Granny says it'll take us about an hour to reach the gorge." Fond farewells, embraces and off we went.

Within ten minutes an eagle-like shriek pulled us up. Far back we could just make out Granny bounding down towards us with the agility of a goat. She stopped and pointed decisively with her right arm. We were on the wrong track. We swung to the right, she urged us on with upward movement of both arms. We found a much wider track. Apparently satisfied, Granny waved and trudged back. A wonderful old lady. She had given us abounding affection, coffee, and before we left she wrapped up a huge piece of feta cheese which we nibbled for days.

Soon afterwards I discovered that on my short foray alone I had lost a map, a compass and my snap-on sunglasses. The first two didn't matter: we were close to the next map sheet and, as usual, a small spare compass had been sewn into the pocket of Katie's rucksack. But my eyes ached from the westering sun.

Despite what Gregor said about the Devil's Arse, it didn't look particularly difficult: silvery sand between rounded slopes. A meandering but, as we were to discover, a very deceptive gorge. Within half a mile our complacency evaporated. Beyond the first right-angled bend we came to the ruins of a massive land-slip which had all but blocked the defile. From there the going worsened to a point where I wondered whether we should be able to get through without trying some real mountaineering. The slopes became cliffs with here and there an ominous overhang. The gorge narrowed, the stones became a torrent of boulders and in scrambling around them we sweated profusely.

At the appearance of yet another bend I left Katie to rest in the shade whilst I rounded the thing, hoping at best for a sight of the sea below. At worst I could judge whether we could get through slowly, with care. Instead I found a promising length of gravel. At this I tootled merrily on my whistle *staccatissimo*.

At critical points our packs tended to throw us off balance. The air became hotter and more still. I made vulgar jokes about the nether anatomy of His Unholiness. I contended, imaginatively, that we'd already got through the worst half of the whole damned cave.

"What cave?" Katie asked, looking up at the narrow band of skylight.

"This one," I said. "When the great ice melted thousands of years ago the plateau below Granny's place became the shore-line of a huge lake not far from the sea. Remember that silvery sand? The water rose higher and higher. The side pressures must have been enormous. The lake burst through the walls of the cave and brought the roof down. These rocks have been polished by ancient cataracts, not seasonal rains."

Katie has become accustomed to Sermons on the Mount. "But what's that," she asked, "a volcano?" — pointing to a plume of smoke rising from behind yet another bend. I didn't know.

Forgetting what the Bulgarians had told us, we were surprised to look down on the enormous bauxite plant at Paralia on the Gulf of Antikira. After the hours of eerie silence in the gorge we were taken aback by the squalor and noise. Workmen were excavating with pneumatic drills and pile-drivers. Among fuel stores, dumps and railyards bells clanged and small engines whistled as they shunted trucks of grey-white clay into the furnace sheds. Activity on all sides.

Threading our way through the debris we made for a harbour of sorts and settled down at the foot of a blockhouse heavily protected by barbed wire. Notices said we were in danger of death from high explosives. Pretty soon we had rehydrated and then boiled the contents of two packets of Caribbean Sweet Beef with Chillies, accompanied by a pint of coffee as a poor substitute for that Greek elixir of life, Amstel. Nutritious as it probably was, after several spoonsful of the unappetizing mess I decided to award the *Cordon Noir* to Dr Sydney Schwartz, one of the prime begetters of these dehydrated foodstuffs designed originally for astronauts and then mountaineers and long-distance walkers. That assassin of good food, a scientist in the pay of the US Space Agency, went one better and devised what he had the impertinence to call "edible structural material". This meant that after take-off the dispensable parts of a man-carrying rocket could be eaten by those prepared to tolerate the ultimate in gastronomic crime.

"More coffee, please," I said. "At least it takes the taste away."

"Hold it," said Katie. "Here comes Nemesis."

A camouflage-painted jeep bounced down towards us. It stopped. An elderly man stepped out, locked the door and approached with the swinging gait of a guardsman. A shrewd fellow with a clipped moustache, and cornflower-blue eyes under a semi-military kepi. He wore a tight-buttoned jacket notable for a little gold ribbon on the collar.

He stopped, saluted and said in clipped French, *"Monsieur et madame, Lieutenant Perouse, Chef de Securité. Vos cartes, s'il vous plaît."*

He went through our travel-worn passports page by page, pausing over the stamps, Tunisia, Morocco, France, Cyprus and Russia — *"Pourquoi avez-vous visité la Russie?"*

We were travellers, I told him, interested in seeing as much of the world as we could, on foot. Experience has taught me that admissions about being an author or, worse still, a journalist are distinctly unwise in the presence of officialdom.

"So you are British, *monsieur et madame?*"

Almost imperceptibly his shoulders stiffened. *"Moi, je suis Légionnaire."* With pride he held out his own discharge: *"Lt. Ramond Perouse, Régiment de Marche de la Légion Étrangère, Sidi bel Abbes, Algérie, 1962."*

"But, monsieur, Algeria gained its independence that year."

"That is true," he said. "We blew up our barracks in Zeralda and were allowed four months in which to transport our sacred possessions, including fifteen banners, from Sidi bel Abbes to Camp de la Demande near Aubagne in Provence. The Eternal Family will never die. I have a different occupation now, but what does it matter? You may be too young to be a Légionnaire, but with luck never too old."

After accepting a cup of coffee our much-decorated friend did his best to persuade us to spend the night with him. He lived nearby. We assured him he was *très très gentil*, but alas, it was not possible. We still had far to go that evening.

"But *pourquoi? Pourquoi?*" he protested. When I told him, incautiously, that I had served in France, briefly, after Dunkirk, he seized my hand. "But we have so much to discuss," he said. I shook my head, sadly. At this he went back to his jeep and returned with a bottle of marc.

After more coffee and much more marc than we drank, the dedicated warrior told us he was on the brink of his seventieth birthday. Before the war he had served in the High Atlas from central Morocco to Tunisia. In May 1940, as a *Sergeant-Chef* under Colonel Monclar, his battalion captured Narvik and returned to France, and eventually Port Soudan via Brest. After battle honours in ill-fated Indo-China, his active service ended in Zaralda. His opinion of Vichy was "a government of folly". As for *Le bon Charlie* (de Gaulle), he considered him an unapproachable man. He looked down on things. It would have been easier to be on intimate terms with the Eiffel Tower.

Before we said goodbye he reproached us again, gently, for being in such a hurry but admitted he felt a little unsteady. "*Je vous donnerai une phrase employée par mes anciens camarades dans les circonstances similaires: à moi les murs. La terre m'abandonne.*"

On the last stage of that seemingly endless day we

mulled over fragments of what our friend had told us about the brigades in what he referred to affectionately as The Eternal Family. He said the ranks of the Foreign Legion, even their commanders had been drawn from over a dozen nationalities including many Germans and would-be Beau Gestes from Britain. Surely no other army in the history of the world could be compared with them? I thought of Alexander the Great, and of thirty Roman legions with their swarms of auxiliaries pressed into service from Spain to Pontica on the shores of the Black Sea, but had no wish to dispute with a proud and honourable soldier.

Little can be said about the appearance, the history and economic importance of Antikira since, after a shore-line walk, we arrived there at dusk and left before dawn. What's certain is that, with energy flagging, we found it a most hospitable place. All the action seemed to be centred on the tree-lined and lamp-lit square flanked by shops. Everyone had something to say to us. It didn't matter what they said, their nods, their smiles and chatter were of the very essence of goodwill. Compare this with crowded Oxford Street or the Strand, where you wouldn't get a squeak out of a stranger unless you happened to tread on his toes.

We sat on a bench outside a taverna, trying to give the impression we weren't gulping down pots of Amstel. Within a few minutes up came a young good-looking fellow with curly red hair not often seen among Greeks. He was incongruously got up in bloodstained apron and laced-up cowboy boots. He held out his hand. "Hiya, folks. Nice to see you. My name's Gus, Gorgeous Gus they called me in Chicago. Guess them damn Yanks in the stockyard couldn't pronounce Giorgios. That's my butcher's shop over there."

We got the impression that Gus the Fixer just about ran Antikira, a town sung about by Homer and razed to the ground by troops under Philip of Macedon. To our surprise we were told this by Gus.

"Yeh! I used to have the job of acting as Greek interpreter at the British School of Archaeology in Athens. They was digging around here about twenty years ago. Somebody — guess it must have been a Brit, though I can't remember the guy's name — had found a temple where they worshipped Artemis. Pity the dig closed down when they ran out of money — they paid me ten bucks a day just for talking."

That generous fellow the Fixer seemed put out that he couldn't fix anything for us. Not a good little hotel, his brother's place? Wouldn't cost us a dime, he said. Food? Anything except lamb. Every lamb from Patras to the Piraeus had been slaughtered for the May Day festivities.

He paused. He lifted up his forefinger and leaned forward confidentially. "Say, what about a plate of fried mussels with a salad of black-eyed peas?" The very idea made our mouths water. Yes, we said. Would he have a drink?

He shook his head. "Guess it'll take Ma Kassotis half an hour to fix something. I'll go have a word with her an' tell you when it's on the cloth." He walked back to his shop. We heard the sound of a chopper on a block. He came out. He waved to us and walked off quickly, carrying a bloodstained parcel of meat. Barter is fairly common in small country towns.

And generous barter it was for one of the best meals we'd eaten in days. Ma Kassotis, his great-aunt, left us with a starter of *mezedes* — olives, almonds, shrimps and hard-boiled eggs — and then went off to cook the mussels. A blessing to find a Greek restaurant well stocked with a variety of fresh dishes after the eternal lamb stew and moussaka.

She came back with mussels, dipped in batter and fried in olive oil, and served with plates of sliced vegetables dabbled with garlic sauce. We ate rather too much, and there was more to come. She put on a local speciality, almond pears and nutty balls of icing which, with a nipperkin of mulberry liqueur, slid down like meringues.

After coffee Gus turned up with a short fat man and a distinctly shifty-looking fellow. He introduced them, chatted awhile and then dismissed them, summarily. "Fatso", he said, "likes to think he's mayor. It's his wife who tries to run the place. The other bastard is a *malakismenos rouphianies*."

"A *what*?"

"A wanking pimp. Police informer. One of these days he's likely to get one between the eyes."

Time to go. The bill came to little more than the equivalent of an English pound, which we reckoned hardly covered the cost of the wine. Useless to argue. Katie embraced Ma Kassotis. Gus kissed us both, told us where to sleep on the top of the hill, and said, "May your hours be good ones."

* * *

Without putting up the tent we unzipped our double sleeping-bag and slept apart, each in a private cocoon, each on a mattress of one of the fly-sheets cushioned by towels and spare clothing. I stretched out and gripped Katie's hand. Owls called. A shooting star drew a chalky line across the immensity of the night, and we were asleep within minutes.

Somewhere around three or four in the morning I woke up. To judge from Katie's contented and scarcely audible snores hordes of frustrated mosquitoes had turned on me. I had been bitten several times around the face, neck and arms. No amount of wriggling deeper into the sleeping bag afforded protection from further attacks, heralded by that fearful near-hypersonic whine. Remembering that my mattress, the inner fly, was equipped with a ventilation panel, I tried to pull it over my face. Wholly ineffectual — the gauze couldn't be comfortably arranged. Nor could I find the unused tube of insect repellent.

A bad night, that. I wriggled about and woke Katie, too late to act on her suggestion that we should put up the inner fly. At five o'clock we were brewing tea in that Tiepolo-blue light which is the mother of dawn.

On our way to Kirra at the foot of the Sacred Way I scratched like a dog. Despite antihistamine ointment my face and arms were pink and swollen. Katie hadn't been touched. Strange, this. We both thought we were relatively resistant to mosquitoes which, to breed, are given to gorge themselves with blood — Katie because, as the widow of a tea-planter, she had spent fifteen years

140

in Ceylon. I had travelled extensively in Belgian Congo and the Canadian tundra, investigating supplies of that vital element, uranium.

All outside activities in Uranium City, a shack town of less than a thousand residents at the eastern end of Lake Athabasca, were strictly conditioned by "skeeter hours". Between six o'clock and half-past eight at night, and approximately two and half-past four in the morning, there arose a high-pitched hum, like a large dynamo heard at close quarters. It came from "the slew", a mid-town pond which couldn't be drained as a spring sprung from a marsh some twenty feet below the surface. The fearful hum came from the wing-beats of billions of "skeeters".

Uranium citizens had more than their share of problems known to those obliged to live in the outbacks of North Saskatchewan and the Territories. High among them was what to do about the slew.

They could have used soluble pesticides, or oiled the surface heavily, which would have put paid to the skeeter larvae in a matter of hours but made for problems of public utilities in a community where tolerably fresh drinking-water cost over a dollar a barrel.

All this took place in 1953 when the outcome of the Korean War couldn't be foreseen — hence American interests in Canadian uranium. When I was there the slew had begun to stink, the skeeter problem had intensified, and the chances were that if it hadn't been for regular outbreaks of arson the water would have been drained at whatever cost.

As a radio and newspaper correspondent* on the look-out for feature material, I learnt from Kurt Larsen, owner of the Uranium City hotel, the only one in town, that their wooden shacks were being fired at the rate of one or two each week. To what end? "Insurance," he said. "Everything in this town burns well and the volunteer fire brigade charges over the going rate for water." He reckoned there was one man behind it working on a percentage basis, but apparently even the Mounties didn't know which one.

Those who should have known better than to be out and about in the bush during skeeter hours were hunters and prospectors, according to Doc McDougall who, Kurt told me, hadn't been cold sober for six years. Speaking with some authority, the Doc put it down to booze. "If they strike it rich the silly buggers are apt to get a skinful, leave their tents and wander into the bush in the hope of knocking off a deer."

He said if they got lost without even the protection of smoke from wood fires they were at extreme risk, not only from dense clouds of skeeters but also from minute Black flies known to the Indians as No-see-ums. Men who got bushed had been known to tear their clothes off and, partly blinded, wade up to their chins in lakes. The Doc had seen their bloated bodies when they brought them in days later.

No-see-ums, he assured me, could kill Wood buffalo. Apparently most big game such as elk, caribou and moose were protected by thick fur, but Wood buffalo

*BBC and the *New York Times*.

were only partly acclimatized to Jack pine scrub. They were refugees from their natural habitat, the declining forests of noble conifers on the edge of the Great Plains. Their genitals were almost naked, an easy source of an unprotected meal for Black flies. Agonized by ferocious attacks the buffaloes' last resort was to run their underparts against rocks which, if unduly sharp, occasionally lacerated them to the point where they bled to death.

With a room in Kurt's hotel for ten bucks a night I made more recordings there than I should have done with limited supplies of tape. On alternate Fridays when truckloads of miners from distant syndicates swarmed in with a fortnight's pay in their pockets they raised merry hell. They diced, played cards, sold skins behind the back of the Hudson Bay Company, argued and sang bawdy songs.

On those occasions Kurt hung up a notice which said in letters two inches high that anybody who hit a man would be barred for at least a month; those who took pot shots at bottles on the bar would be thrown out for the weekend and charged five times for the liquor spilt; but if anybody bust a window or one of his huge fly screens he wouldn't be seen there for at least a year. They took skeeters seriously in Uranium City.

"But why didn't they have a go at me last night?" asked Katie.

"Simple answer: I don't know. Maybe they're particular. Nothing but the best for a high-class Greek skeeter. Could be something to do with our blood

143

groups. When I earned a living writing about science I remember a chap at the Tropical Institute studying malaria who reckoned that people in certain groups were more immune from different kinds of blood-sucking flies than others. There's also this business of skeeter hours. I can hear the damned things at a range of two or three yards but I didn't hear a single peep until they woke me up somewhere around three in the morning."

She persisted. "You say there's an ecological place in the world for everything, but what have skeeters got to offer except make an awful nuisance of themselves and breed more skeeters?"

I went on at some length about the inter-related web of life especially in the tundra where in many places there is about as much water as land. In the spring the Territories are invaded by millions of migratory birds, including at least a dozen species of flycatchers.

At this point I recalled the curious story of how a distinguished Greek, Professor George Mangakis, in a letter which he smuggled out of prison, described his affection for three mosquitoes. At that time, that is on our way to Kirra, I could recall only the bare outlines, but later I looked it up.

I would like to write about a friendship I formed the autumn before last. I think it has some significance. It shows the solidarity that can be forged between unhappy creatures. I had been kept in solitary confinement for four months. I hadn't seen a soul throughout that period. Only uniforms — inquisitors and gaol keepers. One day I noticed three mosquitoes in my cell. They were struggling hard to resist the cold that was just beginning. In the daytime they slept on the wall. At night they would come buzzing over me.

In the beginning they exasperated me. But fortunately I soon understood. I too was struggling hard to live through the cold spell. What were they asking from me? Something unimportant. A drop of blood — it would save them. I couldn't refuse. At nightfall I would bare my arm and wait for them. After some days they got used to me and they were no longer afraid. They could come to me quite naturally, openly. This trust is something I owe them. Thanks to them the world was no longer merely an inquisition chamber.

Then one day I was transferred to another prison. I never saw my mosquitoes again. This is how you are deprived of the presence of your friends in the arbitrary world of prisons. But you go on thinking of them, often.*

John Berger, who reported the foregoing, commented that animals were the first subjects in palaeolithic art, and the blood of animals was perhaps the first paint used by Man.

The day, to put it mildly, had its ups and downs. Easy stuff for the first few hours, all of it on a small but steep road. Then down towards the village of Desphina where, before we got there and after we'd turned our tired backs, regretfully, on the *plateia*, the resort of serious drinkers, we stopped and considered

Second Nature, edited by Richard Mabey, Cape, 1984.

in all their discriminatory possibilities the significance of three signposts. Experience had taught us to distrust them. The first two, both modern affairs, pointed due north to Delphi. The third, a worm-eaten piece of old pine erected, we liked to think, before Byron got there, showed some reluctance at disclosing in Greek characters that, if the dirt track due west were followed, travellers less sceptical than ourselves would reach — distance unstated — the place we'd talked about for days: Kirra. We took to it with no marked enthusiasm.

Although it couldn't be seen because of immense cliffs, below us lay the Sacred Way. The marvel is that, historically, it remained inviolate for so long.

Towards the end of the sixth century BC when Athens, ever mindful of Persia, became a dominant sea-power, Sparta, "that city without walls lying low among the rifted hills", broke the might of her Peloponnesian neighbours. All her considerable powers were directed towards violent but devious expansion. True Spartans were an élite; all lowly work was carried out by serfs. Young Spartiales were selected like favoured stallions and subjected to atrocious severities. They were marched for hours on end, trained in weaponry, flogged in initiation ceremonies until they fainted. They were encouraged to fight each other, naked, in gangs until the losers were physically laid low with broken limbs or thumb-blinded eyes. No rigours ever matched those Spartan battle courses.

Athenians, Thebans, Lydians, Scythians and Plataeans sought Sparta's aid, but she always temporized when asked for reinforcements. The moon was in the wrong quarter for immediate action; her diviners proclaimed that birds of prey had been seen flying against their interest. She could never throw herself whole-heartedly into the affairs of greater Hellas beyond her own doorstep. Elsewhere she probed, delicately, like the tentacles of an octopus. And where better than through the back door into Phokis with an enormous prize on the way; that is at Delphi where oracular supremacy was fortified by treasure for which we have no modern counterpart. Riotous indignation would break out against domination of the Sacred Way from Kirra to the shrine under the cleft of the Phaedriades. But there are back doors to your neighbour's allotment, and it seemed likely that we were on one of them.

The Sacred Way

Pausanias put it about that Homer referred to the very ancient port of Kirra as Krissa in both *The Iliad* and the *Hymn to Apollo* but Peter Levi won't have this. He says firmly that they were and are different places. Arriving at Kirra tired, hot and thirsty, we were totally underwhelmed by the information. All we wanted to know at that moment was whether the first taverna we came to served well-cooled Amstel.

A downright dull place on the lines of Peacehaven between Brighton and Beachy Head, a ribbon-developed strand of nondescript holiday homes. Few people about. No shops to speak of and nothing in the way of safe harbourage. Yet here it was, not long after Minoan times, that ships bearing merchandise and votive treasure inched their way through the western narrows. They were beached on what is now the Gulf of Itea, and a succession of invaders struck north through the gap between Parnassus and Giona into the rich plains of Boeotia and Thessaly. Here was the gateway into central Greece; herein lay the beginnings of Delphi, the navel of the classical world which for the centuries preceding the Persian Wars held a place comparable to the medieval papacy.

Itea today is the western extension of Kirra, indistinguishable from the old landing-place except that it's coming to life as a small modern port and bathing-resort instead of providing the last resting-place for a condemned fleet of rusting tankers. Hotels are springing up in the vicinity of the best restaurant within twenty miles, run by the brothers Stamatis. We ate, we slept, and when the sun poured over the peaks of Parnassus we began to climb up through an ocean of olives, one of the biggest groves in Greece.

Not the best time for tackling an unrelenting slope of six miles between the sea and the site of the oracle, except that the trees in that horticultural forest had been planted close to each other and with a little thought and much use of the compass we kept in the shade of their small, leathery grey-green leaves, silver below. They were sprinkled with greenish-white flowers which, Katie said, smelt of mignonette. She would have been of a different opinion in the last century when the ground was thickly manured with cast-off rags left to rot until the stench, it was said, could be detected by the crews of incoming ships.

Ancient agriculturists believed that the olive wouldn't do well if planted more than a few leagues from the sea. Theophrastus of Lesbos, that extraordinarily gifted if pedantic philosopher, put the limit at 300 stadia which is less than 40 miles. Simple observation shows that he was wrong, but the general principle is sound and the sea-misted crops north of Kirra are reckoned the finest in the country. Trees in good, that is to say calcareous, soils grow to a height of between twenty and thirty feet. They develop large twisted trunks covered with smooth grey bark which cracks into scales with age, and in the sun-dappled light we were fascinated by the remarkable variety of their branches. The general impression is one of angularity like the sketch of a tree by John Craxton or the winter silhouette of a horse-chestnut.

Olives attain a prodigious age. Some plantations are supposed to have existed from the time of Pliny. From those trees above Kirra we looked for clues to the land-holdings and climatic history of Phokis. Could it be that some of the oldest, the stumpiest inhabitants with vast girths and a mere crown of greenery had been planted by Byzantine serfs in the days of the redoubtable Basil the Bulgar-slayer? What of those sawn-off limbs, all at the same height on trees of the same age on the edges of south-facing clearings? A winter of furious gales not long after the Turks arrived?

Here and there we saw well-defined groves of middle-aged trees which had been not so much pruned as carefully shaped by axe and saw. Had the owners inherited a property in disrepair, or was this the product of a pandemic of beetles, olive flies or fungus? Without constant vigilance, olive trees attract hosts of pests, invertebrate and botanical.

The unanswerable question is at which period prehistoric man began to cultivate the olive from what Virgil described as "the unblessed wild plant with its bitter fruit". In the Homeric world, as depicted in *The Iliad*, olive oil is known only as a luxury of the wealthy, an exotic product prized chiefly for its value in heroic toilet; warriors anointed themselves with it after the bath. Achilles sang sadly about how the body of his bosom friend Patroclus, slain at Troy, was sprinkled with the oil, but there is no mention of it among the foodstuffs of the heroes nor does it find a place on the Achillean shield which depicts the vine. However the presence of the tree in the garden of Alcinous who befriended the wandering Odysseus and carried him home in one of his magic ships shows it to have been not uncommon when *The Odyssey* was probably first sung.

All tradition points to the limestone hills of Attica as the place where it was first cultivated on the Hellenic peninsula. When Poseidon, Girdler of the Earth and Athena of the Flashing Eyes contended for the future city, the legend is that an olive sprang from the barren rock at the bidding of the goddess. That this legend has some association with the planting of the first olive in Greece seems fairly certain from a remarkable story told by Herodotus.

When the crops of the Epidaurians of Argolis on the Saronic Gulf withered away during a drought, the citizenry sought the advice of the Delphic oracle. They were enjoined to erect statues to those symbols of fertility, Damia and Auxesia, which had to be carved from the wood of the true garden olive, then possessed only by the Athenians. The request was granted on condition that they made annual sacrifice to their patron and founder, Athena. The command of the Pythia was thus obeyed and their lands again became fertile. The sacred trees of the goddess are said to have stood for long on the Acropolis and, though destroyed in the Persian invasion, they sprouted again from the roots and suckers when they were planted around the Academy.

We strode on, always upwards, always through those

seemingly endless symbols of victory and peace until first, on a huge mound, we could see the little village of Krissa and then, high above it, the cliffs behind which, we knew, stood Delphi. Thereafter we struck a little to the east. The trees thinned and the ground became precipitous and strewn with boulders until we came to the almost dry bed of a torrent, the Pleistos which, in the season of melting snow, thunders down through a gorge immediately below the site of the Oracle.

There we sat on a spur of mica-glistening rock, drank strong local wine and munched bread, cold quail and chopped onions prepared by one of the brothers Stamatis: fare fit for an heroic landscape.

Far below we could make out Lilliputian ships heading for Itea on the Gulf. They were probably ferry-boats, colliers or the caiques of sardine-trawlers, but in our mind's eye they became full-bellied merchantmen sailing before the wind or lithe warships with rams lustily rowed by one, two, or occasionally three banks of oarsmen, according to whether they were biremes or triremes. Some were oared by up to 170 men, to the rhythm of two huge goatskin drums. Unless the ships were known or carried their home country's device, coastguards had to decide whether they were deep-laden with gold for the treasuries at Delphi. Or with armed men.

Pausanias says: "It seems that from the beginning there had been innumerable plans to invade and sack Delphi. There was this Euboean bandit and the Phlegya people some years later. Then Pyrrhus, son of Achilles attempted it; then a detachment from the forces of Xerxes, then the rulers of Phokis who made the longest and strongest attack on the wealth of the god, and then the Gaulish army."*

Throughout Greece "Phokian desperation" connoted ruthless fighting down to the last man on his feet. They were artful fighters, too. Expecting a Thessalian raid into their country they buried water jars up to their necks and covered them over with a thin layer of soil. Not knowing this, the enemy galloped over the jars; horses broke their legs and riders were thrown and promptly slaughtered. Retribution followed, but after another foray when camp faced camp at a pass into Phokis, 500 picked Phokians watched for the full moon and attacked the Thessalians at night, covered in white-washed armour. If what Pausanias was told is true, they carried out a terrible massacre against adversaries who thought "what was happening had something more of the gods about it than a night attack".

From the bone-white bed of the Pleistos we clambered up steps that led us, conveniently, to the last tavern and the last hotel on the down-slope from the village of Delphi to that riot of columns and treasuries around the inner Sanctuary.

We rested on the rails and looked across at that deep gorge bounded on the one side by the cliffs of the Phaedriades, an outlier of Mount Parnassus and on the other by Mount Kirphis, and reckoned that few if any notable sites of antiquity could be more easily defended;

*Peter Levi's translation of *Pausanias' Guide to Greece*, Penguin Classics, 1971.

indeed that gorge between a clamp of defiles had been used in the sixth century as a novel means of attack, that of chemical warfare when the uppity inhabitants of Kirra on the Gulf were physically purged by the torrent.

They became covetous over the wealth bound for Delphi, unshipped within sight of their sea-facing balconies. To the extreme dissatisfaction of the League of Neighbours, the Amphictionies, it was alleged that they had committed sacrilege against the Delphic deity, Apollo, and had stolen land from the god. War was declared against them. Commanders were appointed who in 580 BC or thereabouts brought in Solon, the celebrated Athenian legislator, as Strategic Consultant.

The top brass consulted the Oracle who, as it usually did, gave them enigmatic but, on this occasion, rather subtle advice: they wouldn't win, they were told, until the sea broke over Apollo's enclosure. So they consecrated Kirra to the god and diverted the waters of the Pleistos which ran through their city into a large reservoir. But the Kirrans still held out against the siege, drinking from shallow wells and what water the god rained on them. Whereupon Solon ordered that cart-loads of roots of hellebore, a powerful vermifuge for domestic animals, should be thrown into the reservoir, and when the water was heavily toxified he turned it back into its channel. The delighted Kirrans glutted themselves on what they had incautiously prayed for, "and the men on the walls had to abandon their positions through never-ending diarrhoea".

Over and above some badly needed rest we had much to

do in Delphi. There were clothes to be laundered, repaired or replaced; to lighten our loads everything that could be dispensed with was left with friends; we needed local information about a cross-country track to the township of Amphissa, the last place of any size before we tackled the formidable Pindos; and, most important of all, Katie had blisters which urgently needed attention.

The first chemist we came to sold us four grams of Terramycin with a polymyxin additive for the equivalent of about a pound sterling: in Greece powerful antibiotics can be bought over the counter like wine and cheese. The pros and cons of a possible path caused a deal of argument in an underground retreat near the bus station much resorted to by a self-appointed council of knowledgeable locals. Two taxi-drivers, a wholesaler of wine and a fish merchant couldn't understand, predictably, why we didn't take to the road which we knew snaked down to Krissa before losing its identity in the busy highway north-west to Lamia. We smiled bleakly. A man we knew, Carlo the Cop, said he thought, wrongly as it turned out, that we could reach Amphissa by following some eight or nine miles of the local irrigation canal. We said we'd try it, and they drank to our success.

It is twenty years since I first began to visit Delphi at fairly regular intervals. It follows that I'm familiar with the labyrinth of small squares, back lanes and narrow streets, one above the other, joined by flights of steep steps. We sat over a supper table in the gathering dark, looked at our maps and wondered whether we could rely on Carlo's advice. Who knew where the canal led to? No

155

Greek would admit to ignorance about his immediate neighbourhood.

Apart from the murmur of voices, the sound of laughter and the scream of swifts the town grew strangely quiet for a popular tourist resort. As for the swifts, those most aerial of birds which actually copulate in mid-air, they whirled over our heads as they swooped to and from their nests under the roofs of the buildings around us. Nobody, I suggest, has bettered Gilbert White in his description of what they are up to. In one memorable passage he says: "They get together in the evening and dash round the steeples and churches, squeaking as they go in a very clamorous manner; these by nice observers are supposed to be the males, serenading their sitting hens; and not without reason since they seldom squeak till they come close to the walls or eaves and then those within utter at the same time a little inward note of complacency."

We took to our bed, early, and were up and about again before the two main streets which converge on the short slope down to the Sanctuary were jam-packed with what my Great-aunt Clarissa called in her most disapproving voice "those sharybangs", those mobile easy-chairs for tourists the length and breadth of Europe. As we'd been in each other's company since the walk began, we were content to go our own ways until nightfall.

By climbing up by way of the wine merchant's own vineyard ("Tears of Eurydice") I outflanked the convergence and reached the stadium on the hillside some two hundred metres above the busyness of the Sanctuary. There amidst a protective screen of conifers the only sound you are likely to hear is the pleasant thrush-like song of Orphean warblers in sombre capes and jet-black masks through which can be seen, with the help of binoculars, their staring white eyes. Altogether a handsome bird with a commanding voice. In company with hoopoes they tend to haunt cemeteries and parkland.

The Sanctuary — what a splendid word! Man in the presence of what he feels obliged to venerate. Over a period of perhaps a quarter of a million years it has meant different things, even to some of the earliest relatives of the human race. Neanderthal man, that slightly bow-legged, chinless fellow with prominent brow-ridges and a receding forehead, had a brain in size and possibly weight as large as our own. Careful burials with funerary offerings and hand-prints on the walls of their tombs provide the earliest surviving evidence for religious beliefs.

Their successors, the Magdalenians, the art-inspired cave-painters of south-western France and elsewhere, were adept in the use of pigments and carvings on bone and ivory. Among the Greeks and early Europeans, certain springs and groves were set apart from the profane world. Complex rituals followed. In the Christian church, the Sanctuary is the most sacred part of the building.

At Delphi in classical times, I learnt from Peter Levi, musical festivals were partly replaced by athletic competitions, the Pythian Games. Pausanias claims that some otherwise unidentifiable man called Eleuther won a Pythian victory simply by his sweet loud voice, since the song he sang was not his own. He also mentions that

Hesiod was disqualified for not knowing how to play the harp as he sang; and that Homer came to question the Oracle "but even if he knew how to play the harp it would have been useless because of the tragedy of his eyes". The League added flute-playing to the list of events, but took it out because it was an unlucky sound when Echembrotos, winner of a bronze tripod dedicated it to Herakles "singer of music and the poetry of death". Funeral songs were accompanied by flautists.

The Council of Judges debated the matter at some length and substituted horse-racing for the melancholic sound of reeds. Since this is being written on Derby Day there is a case to be made out for its continuous success through the centuries. Less can be said on ethical and aesthetic grounds for replacing the flute with all-in fighting with whatever weapons the combatants agreed to, also a race for men in armour which must have sounded rather like a folk-dance for Daleks.

Mentally blocking my ears against the siren call of yet another warbler, the Sardinian species (*Sylvia melanocephalus*) which dances in the air, singing like our British whitethroat, I mooched down through the huge theatre to where everybody seemed to be bored by what the guides were telling them. The crowds were thickest in the vicinity of the great temple of Apollo where, in the manner of the ancient processions, they obediently queued up as far back as the circular area, the *halos*, notable for a handsome Ionic capital and a curved seat, the *exedra* for the priests.

Only the podium and peristyle of the temple are complete although several columns have been replaced in their original position. The building runs along the mountainside, supported by a magnificent wall of polygonal masonry. Deep below in its foundations used to lie the sacred chasm where the priestess was said to have been turned on by drinking the waters of Cassotis, composition unknown, and inhaling stupor-inducing fumes from the Underworld.

To the Oracle all the various cities and states looked for guidance in war and matters of foreign policy, especially colonial expansion; not uncommonly, the lovelorn turned up with questions about affairs of the heart. Before the Pythia got down to the job of answering them, mostly in ambivalent *aenigmata*, the priests inspected the proffered booty and, if adequate, interpreted the priestesses' shrieks and wails which have been likened to those of women in sexual transports. Were they, to put it plainly, being screwed in the manner of temple *hetaerae*? Unlikely. They were usually far from young and Euripides in the *Ion* says that at one period at least, the prophetesses were guarded by continent priests to ward off the profane. As a writer with a smattering of geology I find it difficult to believe that what the Victorians called "mephitic vapour" could have emerged from pink and brown rock largely composed of inert metamorphic limestones and dolomites. Drugs may have induced the Oracle's condition. Theophrastus wrote about opium in the third century BC and also Scythian pot.

A long succession of oracles did well out of the local industry from about 750 BC, the questionable date of the founding of both Rome and Athens, until Theodosius shut down the licensed prophecy shops in AD 381, that is

159

shortly after the Legions were recalled from Britain and not long before Alaric and his lively lads struck south through the Balkans.

What at least we may be certain about is that the decline and fall of the prophetesses marked the transition of the Homeric world of inscrutable self-interest — aided by the intervention of the gods — to the beginnings of solid moral principles with the new learning, the so-called "Greek miracle", somewhere in between. The vaults below the temple are now empty but had the Oracle been at home that morning and could I have asked her but one question — and were there unambiguous truth in her oracular heart — she might well have answered that the change was brought about by the swing from symbolic to conceptual thought.

Voluble guides were at work inside the Sanctuary and outside the turnstiles near the Agora remodelled by the Romans; they stood on the wall above the Castalian Spring where motorists are enjoined not to wash their cars in water used in ancient times for ritual purification. They talked in front of the blinding white and wholly inappropriate façade of the modern museum which, although it houses priceless treasure, much resembles a maternity hospital in Abu Dhabi.

I mingled, quietly, with outsiders in groups of Elks, Shriners and Daughters of Freedom engaged in a three-week crash course on European culture from the luxurious confines of a coach complete with bar, toilets and showers. They were getting the classical run-down from Reb Meyer, a strident New Yorker. As one of his flock put it, they "had picked him up in Thessaloniki just for the Greek stretch". Reb certainly knew his stuff and put it across in the corrosive Yinglish of the Lower East Side. He had been talking about the gods and the Homeric heroes, Perseus, Theseus, Odysseus and Herakles. "Jeez!" he said, "some guy that Herakles was. Excuse the expression, a real *gontzer macher*. David would have been glad to have him around.

"But d'ya suppose that sophisticated spielers like old Homer really believed that Zeus — who was known as the Gatherer of Clouds — knocked off just about everybody, from Danaë who was fooled when he appeared in a shower of gold? That he sometimes disguised himself as a bull or a swan when he felt randy? Who was he fooling? I ask you? Next to nobody! They was listening to a top-of-the-bill entertainer putting it across that it's a wise man who knows who his own father is and God help those who go around knocking off members of their own families." I began to warm to Reb.

"*Muthologica* means 'talking about things, the re-telling of old tales'. An egg becomes harder the more you boil it: that's why we Jewish boys put *bielers*, hard-boiled eggs, among the other goodies on the table at Passover. They are symbols of immortality.

"Ya don't think those tales hurt anyone, do ya? Well apart from one disaster ya couldn't be more on the ball. After we've had a bite and maybe a beer or two we're gonna drive about ten minutes to Arachova. And not far from that village we'll take a quick look at a place known to every dollar-grabbing shrink as the Crossroads. And what happened there, you ask me? I'll tell ya. Homer says that once upon a time the real old city of Thebes

161

was ruled by King Laius who for wife had a *shayner*, a beautiful girl called Jocasta. So pretty she was that this *shmuck* Laius asked the Oracle up there what he could do to protect her. It didn't really matter, he was told, because his number was up. He had been doomed to die anyhow and at the hands of his own son. And who was that? Surely you've heard of a guy called Oedipus?

"One night, not long after Oedipus was born, his dad stuck a knife through his feet. He bound them together and left the baby to the wolves and eagles on Mount Kithairon. *Oy veh!* Happily for him he was found by shepherds who took him to their king, a feller called Polybus of Corinth, who liked the look of the little chap and brought him up as his own son. He called him Oedipus which is Greek for Swollen Foot.

"Now we come to a bit of the story which is hard to swallow. Oedipus grew up to be a tough guy, good at games and apt to throw his weight around. Moody, too. Something bothered him. There were things that the folks at home wouldn't talk about. So what does this *shlemiel* do? He also goes and has a costly session with that Oracle. It didn't improve things when he was told it was his fate to kill his dad and have an incestuous affair with his momma.

"Thinking that Polybus was his dad he decided not to return to Corinth. Unhappy for him, on the way back from where you're standing right now he arrived at those Crossroads I was telling you about and met a chariot coming the other way. How was he to know it was driven by his *real* father, King Laius? There were arguments about who had the right of way. It ended in a scuffle.

Oedipus flung his javelin at Laius and knocked him cold. That might have ended the matter if Freud hadn't come to the fool conclusion that many if not most of us want to continue sleeping with our mothers and end up by hating our father. That's what Oedipus-Schmoedipus is all about. D'ya wanna sleep with your mamma and keep up the row with your papa? Don't let the head-shrinkers think they've got even half the answers. Over the last seventy years more people have been taken for a ride by Freud and his hangers-on than by Standard Oil."

Prologue to the Pindos

Because we hoped to see the emerging sun strike the eastern face of the Phaedriades, the cleft pillar of rock above the Castalian Spring, we set off early, far too early. Only the topmost turrets justified their name of the Shining Ones. In their shadows lay a jumble of monuments as untidy as a builder's yard: the Sphinx of the Naxians, the Stoa of the Athenians, the ruined treasuries of the Boeotians, the Thebans, Megarians and I forget what else. Yet that early hour carried its compensations: the light and the colours changed from minute to minute and, again right on cue, two immense birds of prey pitched off the topmost pinnacles and began to circle, slowly, in concert with a breeze which, heard from ground level, had about it the whispering rip of a scythe through grass.

There are two distinctly different opinions about the identity of those birds. There is first the classical one, which is that in a god-like gesture to determine the centre of the world known to his Olympian companions, Zeus — who considered the earth to be flat like a disc — released two eagles, one at the point of the sun's rising and the other at the point of the sun's setting. The birds met at Delphi over what became the *omphalos*, the huge stone navel of the earth. Below lay the sacred cave of Mother Earth's oracle, guarded by the monster, Python.

Even today the site is both overlaid and surrounded

by enormous beauty which ignores rather than defies exploitation since pilgrims, nowadays called tourists, have been tramping up to the shrine of Apollo and his successors for about 3,000 years. To anybody with a shred of imagination — if not spirituality — godhead seems inherent in the landscape.

The previous day I had heard — not for the first time — the story of the eagles from Reb Meyer who gave it a touch of authenticity by adding, "Folks around here will tell you the birds are the descendants of the original pair who pecked to pieces what was left of Aesop, author of the famous fables, who had been thrown off the cliff for poking fun at the local administration. They didn't realize he was just as much of a *meshuggener* as they was."

Madame Anastasia, our guide for the IUCN trip to Delphi which followed the Athens Conference*, had told us the same story. Already irritated by the fact that her audience was clearly more interested in purple-flowered campanulas, wild tulips, the Giant orchid (*Barlia*) and half a dozen other smaller rarities among the blocks of marble, than the history of the lovely Doric *tholos*, she incautiously mentioned the eagles.

Jan Dorst, one of the best ornithologists in Europe, glanced up at the birds without even raising his field-glasses. "Black vultures," he murmured quietly. She heard him. "Eagles!" she insisted, angrily. At this several professional biologists rallied to the support of their distinguished colleague. The delegate from the West German Republic muttered, "*Mönchsgeier*"; the

*See page 25.

165

director of the Paris Medical School called them *Vautours moine* whilst Harold J. Coolidge of the US Academy of Sciences, a pedantic fellow, gave their scientific name, *Aegypius monarchus*.

Outclassed by such a spread of expertise, our guide smiled wanly at the Mayor of Athens and his friend the Secretary-General for Tourism, and went on to speak rapidly, first in English, then in French, followed by German, about how between 1892 and 1904 the French parliament voted nearly a million francs to demolish the village on top of the site, rebuilt it further up the road and for years dug like moles into what became one of the greatest treasures of Greece.

Even from below Katie and I could see that the birds were unquestionably Black vultures: almost wholly sooty-coloured creatures with massive bills, stumpy necks, short tails and extremely broad and elongated wings, longer than any other vulture in Europe, over nine feet from tip to tip in some specimens.

With an occasional glance over our shoulders we watched them as we scrambled down into the gorge, searching for that elusive canal. They were circling, slowly, like an immense mobile. In the air they are impressive but at close quarters, as I had seen them on the carcases of sheep in the Pyrenees, they look morose if not downright ugly. They half-flap their wings, squeak, and stamp their feet in a grotesque dance to scare off rivals. In company with birds of prey throughout the whole world, their numbers are declining. The last we saw of Anastasia's eagles that morning was over Mount Kirphis up which is scribbled the zigzag of a mule track leading to places where you could well believe only the gods, the local shepherds and vultures feel at home.

It had taken us ten days of abundant sweat to get from Athens to Delphi via Thebes and Kirra on the Gulf of Corinth. That morning we paused on the rim of the gorge between the Phaedriades and Mount Kirphis not at all sure about how to reach the biggest olive market and capital of the region, the town of Amphissa, without bruising our feet on the first busy twelve-mile length of the mountain road to Lamia.

At Amphissa we hoped to be rid of roads for at least a week. All maps we'd consulted, all enquiries we had made indicated that Amphissa stood not too far above a network of tracks through two more impressive ranges, the Giona and Vardoussia, the prologue to the Pindos, the range that reared northwards to the Vlach highlands of Albania. We were following a route plotted by Lord Hunt in charge of a company of lively lads. Meanwhile, a minor setback: where in the name of all the marvellous, the multitudinous water gods of central Greece was that damned canal?

Water is the life-blood of the upland regions and the natives dispose of it as stingily as widows with meagre but regular pensions. To judge from the lie of the land on the steep slopes below Amphissa, the vast groves of olives are dependent on the up-welling of springs, and the water has to be shared out from communal aqueducts. On the face of it an admirable arrangement, but in that underground retreat near the bus station, Carlo the Cop had hinted darkly at a local Mafia run by the chieftains of two or three cooperatives who controlled wholesale prices and, if nothing worse, threatened to divert the water supplies of those incautious enough even to think of stepping out of line.

From our uneasy track which showed every sign of disintegrating into a riot of scrub we stared down an undulatory slope looking for a mere glimpse of that canal, a task made doubly difficult by localized irrigation ditches and shallow pools which winked like watery eyes under the unrelenting light. Because we were both thirsty and tired we made for a ramshackle farmstead surrounded by an impressive palisade of cactus, a place bigger than it looked at first glance.

Behind the back door were terraces of fruit trees: plums, apricots, quinces, almonds, and carobs or locust beans used mainly for fodder on stony ground. Perched up in the trees, cheerfully shouting at each other, were a dozen or more long-skirted women, young and old, spraying, pruning or maybe gathering fruit.

Could we come in? They laughed, screeched a welcome and waved their arms.

Inching through a wood-block gap in the cactus we were set upon by several mongrels who, by bounding about or lying on their backs, clearly wanted nothing more than to be scratched.

Apart from the cheerful dilapidation of the propped-up front door the place might have been a small villa on the Costa Brava with a vine-sheltered veranda and a tremendous view down to the sea. Two middle-aged men and an oldster fondling his worry-beads waved us to their benches in the shade. When they learnt we came from *Megali Brettania* a bushy-haired man with bright red eyebrows somewhere between Squirrel Nutkin and an Arctic lynx asked us in a nice mixture of Greek, simple English and sign-language if we'd care to take a little wine, or perhaps *soom milch*. He called out to his wife.

During the few minutes it took that cheerful soul to walk over with wine, barley bread and olives, we exchanged glances with our old feeling of bewilderment. Katie had asked how far it was to the canal. "Two hundred metres," said our host. "It is near the bridge, just below that tree over there; you can't see it from here."

"And does the canal lead to Amphissa?"

He answered her by closing his eyes and tilting his head backwards, slowly.

"How do we get to Amphissa?"

He pointed to a ribbon of road far up the hill, the one we had left two hours ago.

"Where does the canal lead to?"

He pointed to a road below us, the one up from Itea, then with a digging motion of his hand he made it clear that it disappeared underground.

"How far from there to Amphissa?" asked Katie.

He pursed his lips, shrugged and said about seven kilometres. He turned to me and smiled.

"No matter," she said. "We'll walk through the olives as we did on the way up."

After warm goodbyes all round our host said, "May good fortune be with you this day." And it turned out like that.

Hospitality shrinks mileage. The water of the canal —

fit to drink — was thickly populated by small minnows which scattered in a flurry as if a handful of gravel had been thrown in when arrowing kingfishers stopped dead in mid-air and hovered. We counted near a dozen before we struck the torment of the highway.

Nose-to-tailers indulged in promiscuous tootology when held up by small donkey-drawn carts. Holding her reins in one hand a dark-eyed girl with provocative breasts stood bare-footed on a hillock of small onions. With her left hand she finger-gestured the noisiest of her tormentors. Her black headscarf, we noticed, had been wrapped over her nose. A Muslim? Or was it to dampen the smell of bruised onions and dung? The donkey's backside had been draped in a bulging diaper to catch the valuable droppings. We endured, in fact rather enjoyed the spectacle, not least because in various places we could slip down maintenance tracks into the silence of the yards on both sides of the road.

We chose an archway of willows over a ditch the better to wander down that natural herbaceous border of purple and yellow irises, flowering rush, Love-in-a-mist and that most memorable of Mediterranean flowers, the Crown anemone, thought by some to be the lily of the field which surpassed Solomon in all his glory.

When Linnaeus visited England for the first time in 1735 he is said to have dropped down on his knees and lifted up his arms at the sight of acres and acres of gorse on the cliffs of Dover. In his day the plant was an absolute rarity in Sweden. We felt much the same when more Camberwell Beauties swooped over us.

This purple-brown butterfly with a yellowish fringe

to its wings is known as the Half Mourner in its native Scandinavia. Very few reach Britain but as a youth I saw one on the cliffs at Scarborough and duly reported it to the local natural history society, where I don't think the resident lepidopterists altogether believed a lad of twelve. When three or four were captured the following week and traced back to timber boats from Stockholm in the harbour, the *Yorkshire Post* picked up the story and misspelt my name, so that some people still think the butterfly was first seen there by the man who got to the top of Everest.

What with the Half Mourners and other locally common butterflies, including one with black blotches and red spots on its hind wings, the Eastern Festoon (*Zerynthia*), and a true mourner in almost black, the Great Sooty Satyr, I put down my sack, pranced after them and felt young again.

Olive yards are inhabited by a group of warblers which have no common name except the scientific one, *Hippolais*, and the habit of singing as if they were canaries crossed with nightingales. Plato's most famous pupil, Aristotle noticed this and said they were much beset by cuckoos. In this he was wrong, but the tutor of Alexander the Great could well be excused for slipping up on a small point of ornithological ethology. Those olive-green skulkers soar up and down the avian scale like prima donnas.

All in all it took us nearly six hours of pleasurable dawdling to reach the handsome township of Amphissa, known to the Turks as Salona and as late as the seventeenth century believed to be the site of ancient Delphi.

Sunday afternoon in the town square. Next to nobody about. Nothing open, not even a tavern. So we dozed leaning back on our rucksacks in the shade of a plane tree outside the locked-up temptations of an extremely well-stocked pastry shop.

Sleepy mutterings about what to do next were noisily interrupted by two truckloads of soldiers driven fast with police on motorbikes ahead and behind them, their sirens *ee-awing* incessantly.

To stretch my legs I stood up and sauntered into the next street to see if the tavern was still locked up. It was. On the way back to Katie a cop stepped out of a doorway and with no affability asked to see my passport.

That vague uneasiness at a policeman's direct questions is like being asked unexpectedly to drop your pants in front of a doctor. I smiled bleakly, wished him good-day, said *Engländer*, pointed towards the square and went through the motions of pulling on a pack.

He flicked through the pages. He seemed satisfied, said thank you in English, and touched his cap. Katie came along and took over.

Was there a camping-site in Amphissa?

He shook his head. "Closed," he said. "Where you go next?"

Thinking it better to name a big town rather than a venture into the outback, I said, "Lamia, perhaps tomorrow." Saying that there would be a bus going there in an hour, he gave us a full salute and a smile.

Although "wild camping" is officially forbidden in Greece we settled for an out-of-the-way patch with a water tap, near the town limits. With only the outer fly up and beds down, Katie was reading Pausanias. I mooched about among the olive trees, champing at the bit, yearning for company. At seven o'clock I walked back to the square, promising to bring something fresher than dehydrated chicken risotto for supper.

Somnolent Amphissa had woken up. People were talking and laughing in groups; chairs and tables had sprung up close to shuttered places which we'd never suspected were cafés and small restaurants. Couples hand in hand were beginning to stroll round the square for that endearing Greek custom, the evening perambulation, the *volta*.

Several cars were parked against the sidewalk. Among them was a misty-blue Mercedes. Surprised, delighted, I peered into it. Empty.

Disappointed, I strolled towards the well-stocked pastry shop now bright with lights and busy. M. Théophane, that trim bearded fellow who had reminded me of Svengali, was sitting outside over a coffee and looking at me.

He sighed. "Kyr' Ioanni," he began. "I have been sitting here for nearly an hour and beginning to get a little cold. *Allons-y*, let us go upstairs."

He steered me through the cascades of sugared fruits, *baklava*, those things that look like sticky Shredded Wheat, *mille feuilles, petit fours*, small fingers of almond cake, and *louhoumis* which we call Turkish Delight.

Upstairs in a small but finely appointed room he

173

motioned me towards a cushion on an ornamental chair of cedarwood. Except where niches sheltered a wealth of antique vases almost the whole room, that is the walls and the parquet floor, were covered with Turkish rugs embellished with diamond shapes, zigzags and quasi-botanical forms in a harmony of colours. "*Quinzième siècle*, from Ushak near Smyrna in Asia Minor," he murmured.

"Comfortable, *n'est-ce pas*? Before I left for Ascona and she came here, for many years Madame Konstania and I were neighbours in Famagusta — a woman of taste, eh?"

"How on earth did you know we should be here today?"

Théophane smiled. "I had business in Thessaloniki but drove down to Delphi today. I went to *la gendarmerie* to ask if you had arrived, and your friend M. Carlo Akhilleas told me you had just left."

"Was your business at Vergina?"

His smile faded. For a moment I saw irritation, a touch of hostility in his eyes.

"*Moi, je ne suis pas un vautour, une goule, m'sieur*. The site, I know is perhaps the finest discovery of the century. Who could have imagined that Philippe of Macedon was buried in the northern shadow of Mount Olympos except my good friend Professor Manolis Andronicus? Him I have known for many years. And now he has struck — how you call it? The jackpot. The one-eyed skull, the shattered bones, *les couronnes d'or*, the jewellery! Believe me, Kyr' Ioanni, I had no commerce, no contact with Manolis nor anybody associated with him. Some of them are *moins honnêtes* than others. I trade among traders. It is my ability to distinguish between them. Also the provenance of what they have to sell and whether or not *les objets* are what they say they are."

Perhaps to ease the tension he lifted up a decanter of Metaxas and raised his eyebrows. I nodded. "Now tell me, *m'sieur*, how long had you in Thebes?"

"Two days," I said.

He affected to look indignant. "*Eh bien*, if I had come to your country, to one of your famous cities, say York or Edinburgher and admitted I was there *deux jours* only, what would you have said?"

"But we intend to walk over 500 miles. How can we stay anywhere for more than a day or two? For people of our age there are limits to exertion."

"A wise man will not dispute with a man in a hurry," he said.

"Your proposition is disputed. The person who relies on proverbs doesn't realize there are two sides to a question, he knows only the roundness of answers."

"*Pardon, m'sieur*, but you have been *piégé* by your own aphorism. *D'après* Montaigne, a proverb is the literate child of common experience — *mais* it is good to play with words; I have few opportunities in this country. *En France* it is different. We have many disputants, and all our writers are important. I know little about the situation in your own country, but I have discovered myself that in Australia one is obliged to explain what a writer is. But to serious matters. Where do you go now?"

"Have you a map?" I asked.

He zipped open his briefcase and spread out a *carte routière*, 1:400,000 on the table.

"I haven't seen the sheet before," I told him. Ours were about half that scale and they were wildly inaccurate — purposively, in our opinion. Who did the Greeks think they were deceiving? What nation did they fear the most? Théophane repeated what he had told me before: "*Tout le monde.*"

With my finger I traced our line of march. It seemed we must walk some eight or nine miles up the main road towards Lamia and then fork to the north-west along a faintly dotted track, first to Kaloscopi then to Pira.

He shook his head. He had never heard of the places. "*Pays sauvage,*" he said. My turn to sigh.

"After that, Mavrolithari," I said.

At that he beamed expansively. "The place of black stones the size of golf balls. Volcanic. *Pas loin*, there is a famous temple to *Hercule*." He and an archaeologist had looked for it without success. "Did Pausanius mention it?"

"I don't know, but if it is so wild how did you get there?"

"In the Giona mountains, about twenty kilometres to the west from here, there is a direct road to it. It comes up from Evritani on the Gulf. Where will you go after the place of the black stones?"

"All we know is what's on the dotted line: Daphni, Anatoli, Marmara and Platanos, up to Timfristos."

"Have you any idea of what you will find there?"

I shook my head.

"One of the highest ranges in Central Greece, about 2,500 metres, I think. *Écoutez*, there is a road over the lower slopes and", he added mischievously, "*un autobus* about once a day. But no doubt you will walk. *Pour moi*, the only exercise I indulge in nowadays is backgammon. *Et après le* Timfristos?"

"To Trikala from Karpenissi by way of the Agrapha."

"Agrapha!" He bowed his head and put his hands over his eyes in mock horror. "Do you know what the word means? *La place sans nom*. No roads. They say one still finds wolves and bears in those deep ravines. During the German Occupation people fled there in their thousands. At the time of the Civil War it was dominated by ELAS. Trikala, now, *ça c'est autre chose*. Highly civilized. The Paris of Thessaly. *Dites-moi*, will Madame accompany you in this masochistic exercise?"

I nodded.

"Tell her with my compliments that she defies Nietzsche, who said marriage is a bribe to make a housekeeper think she is a householder. *Comme institution*, he thought it belonged more to the *domaine de la comédie* than philosophy. *Cela ne fait rien*. With the worries you are obliged to endure *en route*, perhaps it is that *amor vincit insomnia*."

He glanced at his watch. "*Mon dieu!* I have a rendezvous in Delphi in almost half one hour. *Dites-moi*, how long do you think you will want to reach Trikala?"

"With any luck about two weeks, perhaps a little more."

"*Bon!* We must have another talk together. I

recommend the Hotel Divani. About the time of your arrival I will leave a note there in your name, with my telephone number. Perhaps you will take another drink? *Non? Donc*, I must go. *Bonne chance*. As Gide always concluded his farewells: 'I give you my hand.'"

He squeezed mine, lightly stroking my palm with his forefinger as he said goodbye. We went downstairs and he drove off. A first-rate male impersonator.

I got back over an hour late. Katie is uncommonly patient but I'm pretty sure if it hadn't been for two or three pestiferous curs I should have been in the doghouse myself. I heard the clamour within 200 yards of where we'd put the tent up. Not the deep-throated barking and baying of guard dogs, but the yap and yelp of lesser breeds within the law.

With the exception of the outer fly, literally her last refuge, Katie had packed up. She said she'd been sitting on our rucksacks since soon after I'd set off for the square.

"I tried to shout to you," she said, "but you had gone and as for that damned fudge of yours, the dogs loved it and came back for more."

"But why didn't you chuck something at them?"

"You try," she said.

I turned round. The dogs were invisible in the dusk, but seemed to be closer, from the noise they made, to small mongrels than mastiffs. Two came quite near, growling peevishly. They looked like terriers. I slung a substantial piece of rock in their direction and they promptly bolted. Hero returned to beleaguered spouse and wasn't over-encouraged by her reaction. "They'll be back in five minutes," she said. "Do you want to put up with this all night? What's for supper?"

I told her that thanks to the intervention of the mayor, the chief of police and the neighbour of an old friend of mine I had arranged for a meal for two in the best restaurant in town. We occasionally go in for this sort of thing; it masks the platitudes of domesticity.

"What you really mean", she said, "is that for the last two hours you've been knocking back ouzo in that awful-looking tavern."

I kept up the mild deception until we'd nearly finished the aubergine purée followed by *barbounia*, which is grilled red mullet, before I told her whom I'd really met.

"What! That old poofter from Thebes?"

"You are referring", I said, "to Monsieur Théophane, a distinguished antiquarian, who not only sends you his compliments but has given us some valuable information about what we're in for. I have arranged to meet him again in Trikala."

"That's fine, but where are we going to spend the night?"

In fact on the second or maybe the third loop on the steep highway out of Amphissa on the way to Lamia, we encountered deserted roadworks. By torchlight we inspected and without qualification settled for a deserted workmen's hut where we slept like curled up dormice from near midnight until six in the morning.

Within minutes of stifling yawns and breaking wind in

our uninhibited way — though not, of course, without a muttered, "I beg your pardon" — we had but one thought and that was to put on jackets and nether garments before the road gang turned up. We needn't have hurried. Nobody arrived and we had the best of reasons for lingering outside the hut for nearly an hour.

In nearly half a century of cross-country walking I have on many occasions cursed roads, but at the very start of that brief but uphill bout with the Lamia highway we were presented with shelter and a wholly unexpected free breakfast within sight of artwork which, had it been carried off to the Thames embankment, the trustees of the Tate Gallery might well have been tempted to buy.

We had spent the night on that rare thing in the Greek countryside, an area of soft, flat and stone-free ground, the product of road-making on a steep hillside. For many yards both above and below an acute bend in a series of loops, engineers had blasted out hundreds of tons of hard rock, leaving untouched — except for in-filling — an almost vertical face opposite the workmen's hut.

This had provided political slogan-daubers with almost limitless opportunities for graffiti, another palimpsest of forty years of Greek history in blue and red lettering. The latest, the brightest ones reflected the political war-cries of the Communists, KKE and PASOK, the followers of Mr Papandreou, but below them in diminishing shades of colour and intelligibility we decoded and laboriously translated *Shit to the Bulgarians, Demokratia* and *Coalition*. Below them all, in letters so high and so incisive that the rock must have been cut to retain the ghost of the original paint, we read: *Those not*

Royalist are Communist, Down with Bevin and, in English, *Welkom to our Callant Allies*, a touching salutation.

To enjoy the last few feet of that political masterpiece we stood on the very lip of the loop. To our mild consternation an open truck, driven as fast as Greek truckers drive, raced up the hill towards us. It contained brimful baskets of fish. We flattened ourselves against the rock face. It swung round the bend with no apparent diminution in speed and, centrifugal force being what it is, flung a handful or two of sardines at our very feet.

Poseidon be praised! If not manna from heaven, we felt thrice blessed with a sea-fresh breakfast from Itea.

A small problem: we had left all our expendable gear, including a rather bulky aluminium frying-pan, with friends in Delphi. Usurping Katie's role as *maîtresse de cuisine* I insisted that *Sardina pilchardus*, one of the smallest and most toothsome relatives of the noble herring, should be treated as native custom demanded, that is to be grilled quickly, barbecue-fashion.

We needed a coarse sieve. There were several *in situ*. We borrowed one. We needed a small but reasonably air-tight oven. The Swiss Family Hillaby manufactured one from flat rocks lined with slates and bits of corrugated iron. Then screwing up a few pages of the *Herald Trib*, we pushed them into the base of our little stove and set fire to them. As soon as the sardines on the sieve caught the flames they dripped oil, which would have kept that fire alight for quite a long time. They were done to a turn in a matter of minutes.

When we got unutterably fed up with dehydrated

foods we put that fortuitous trick to good use on several occasions. The difficulty was to find a sieve; otherwise Greece abounds in the elements of oven-making especially among the carboniferous shales.

Days that begin well often carry a sort of talisman of sustained good fortune, and it went that way with us. After establishing our country of origin, destination, names and ages, cheerful gangs of workmen further up the highway showed uncommon interest in the health of Bobby Charlton, Madame T'atcher and Kyr' Scargill.

How much did our boots cost? Could they try on our rucksacks? Had we friends in Lamia? "By God, no!" said I and got a reproachful look from Katie. At one point they cheered so loudly at our approach that their mates on the loop above echoed the salutation although they couldn't have had an inkling about who we were. Our helpful friends introduced us to wayside springs whose water tingled our palates.

They pointed out distant peaks with incomprehensible and somewhat awesome names, since from compass bearings it looked as if we should be obliged to breach that wall; yet all this was done simply to make us feel at home. We liked those good-natured fellows and wished only that we understood more of what they were doing their best to explain.

Twice during that morning police cars hurtled past us with lights flashing and sirens screaming, and it wasn't until we met a couple of Irishmen, lads from County Fermanagh who'd jumped their ship in the Piraeus, that we heard about what was going on. Translated through accents as thick as their arms, it seemed that a Greek political prisoner, an ex-ELAS Communist bottled up on the infamous island of Makronisos, had escaped for no better reason than to shoot his brother who had brought about a family feud by joining what one of them called "the other side". Presumably he meant the politically mixed-up Security Battalions who were no less guilty of atrocities than the worst elements of ELAS. The story was that in a wood near his brother's home the fugitive had hidden himself for two days before shooting him through the coat, so he could tell him "a t'ing or two" before finishing him off. Without a trace of emotion, the Irishman said: "The police t'ink the murtherous bastard is still there, waiting to take a potshot at other members of the family who were on his brother's side."

"Where is this village?"

He didn't know. They were strangers. At night the trucks came to take them back to Lamia. Nor did they know where Makronisos was. His other gangers had been children at the time of the Civil War. We learnt later that the Greek Alcatraz lay off the south-eastern tip of Attica.

On the precipice below yet another loop we looked down on a vast quarry with men at work with cranes, bulldozers and other mechanical gear shovelling clay-like material into a procession of trucks. We had seen several of these operations since that day when we said goodbye to the hospitable Lieutenant Perouse on the dockside at Paralia. Most of them were under the control of the Société Anonyme des Mines Bauxites de Parnasse.

In Greece enormous deposits of hydrated oxide

of aluminium known as bauxite have a low-grade aluminium content and, lacking cheap electric power, Greece has next to no aluminium industry. Poor-quality bauxite is used in the manufacture of cement and refractories. M. Perouse had told us that SAMBP held proved resources of about fifty million tons.

The predecessor of the Lamia highway and its extension north was originally built by Britain in 1916 to avoid using sea transport to Macedonia when shipping was subject to enemy submarine attack, and there above that quarry we came to a full stop for a mildly dramatic quarter of an hour.

In large red letters a board propped up by trestles proclaimed: ΚΙΝΔΥΝΟΣ. Katie spelt it out, slowly: *Kappa Iota Nu Delta Upsilon Nu Omicron Sigma!* "Danger," she said. "Perhaps a landslide. Maybe this is where we start some real climbing."

The drivers of two trucks and a private car ahead of us were waiting impatiently. A cheerful little fellow in fluorescent orange-coloured overalls spoke to them one after another in an explanatory torrent of Greek. He came up to us. Katie heard him out politely before she wished him good day and regretted that, alas, she didn't understand a word.

Then began another fine example of Greek sign-language. The fellow was a born mime. In far less time than it takes to describe his act he began by closing his eyes, lowering his head and putting his right hand over his heart. We were receiving the profound regrets of *M. le Président* of Société Anonyme et cetera for the delay. Then he stood straight up and stabbed the air with his forefinger. A small crisis had arisen. Slow downward jabs with his finger in the direction of the quarry made it quite clear that that's where the danger lay. To underline his point he screwed his face up like a man who had incautiously bitten into an unripe plum. He put his hands over his ears and said *"Boom!"*

"The damn fool means they're going to fire a shot," I said, crossly. "Ask him how long we're going to hang about and tell him to get on with it."

After a brief question, Katie said: "Ten minutes, he hopes."

To the consternation of the little chap we leaned over the railings, the better to enjoy the spectacle. It happens that because of a day spent in the archetypal marble quarries of Europe, the Carrara series in Tuscany, during an ill-fated walk from Nice to Florence, I know a fair amount about what in a melodious Italian phrase means ripple-blasting. Six minutes to go.

A skilful quarry man who wants to detach a relatively small piece of rock from its massive matrix takes his hammer and chisel and makes a fine incision into the grain of the face. Five minutes to go.

This done, he picks up his mallet and drives a big wet wedge into the parent rock just below the point where he knows that, if he is successful, it will drop on to cushions of sand and then he hits it hard. Four minutes to go.

Much can be done on the grand scale with explosives. Small pockets of dynamite are fused and coupled up along the equivalent of that chisel-cut line. The important thing is not to blast out what might injure the face and the immediate product. Three minutes to go.

In Carrara this is enormously important. Marble is extremely valuable stuff. There are about 600 quarries throughout the Apuan Alps, worked in the times of classical Rome but abandoned after the fall of the Western Empire. Next to nothing more was heard about them until the growth of Pisan architecture and sculpture during the twelfth and thirteenth centuries. Today, once the huge blocks of marble are detached by ripple-blasting they are snared by a web of moving wires on wheels which put you in mind of Gulliver bound down with ropes by swarms of Lilliputians. The moving wires provide power for the hand drills and chisels of the master masons. Two minutes to go.

For bauxite delicacy doesn't matter. The object is to blast out as much as possible with a line of shots to determine the dimensions of the downfall and ensure that it drops near the waiting trucks. One minute to go.

The engineers scrambled into the back of one big truck which was promptly driven off. A hooter howled. Spurts of grey smoke sprang from the vertical face at intervals of about twenty yards, to the accompaniment of thumps no louder than from rolled-up carpets thrown from the roof of a house. And then an almighty explosion as from a battery of twenty-five pounders fired simultaneously, as the super-charge tore into the guts of the Jurassic limestone. We felt it underfoot but apart from the noise and a cloud of dust a prodigious quantity of rock fell to the floor of the quarry gently, like a coat that had slipped off a coat-hanger. As we trailed after the traffic ahead we saw that a police car had joined the queue behind us and it drove past howling.

For eight miles beyond the signpost to Kaloscopi we ran the dusty gauntlet of trucks carrying bauxite on a narrow dirt road from another quarry to the north-west. We did our best to scramble out of the way. We tied vests round our necks so that at the approach of yet another vehicle they could be pulled over our sweaty hair and sore eyes, but it didn't do much except increase our discomfort from the heat.

We had no difficulty whatever in finding the quarry which was even bigger than the one we had left. The problem was how to get out of it. The dirt road, the trucks' escape route, emerged from a death-white arena some two or three hundred yards in diameter, ringed by Cyclopean terraces too high to be climbed. It was curiously white-striped-with-reddish rock. Perhaps bauxite may be fairly compared with Joseph's coat. We never found out what it was. Clearly the immediate workings had been abandoned. Nobody about. No industrial gear. We felt like two ants on an enormous soup plate.

Ahead of us we heard a curious clinking noise punctuated by intervals of silence. It might have been a bird, perhaps a Greek Nuthatch. To avoid the ferocious light we clung to the shadow below the north wall of the quarry. We rounded a corner to find a bare-chested fellow on a terrace some fifty feet from the ground chipping away at what looked like a stone coffin. He waved to us and I waved back and bawled: *"Parakalo, pou ine Kaloscopi?"*

He made a downward chopping motion gesture with his right hand. We were bidden to keep straight on. His hand then jerked to the left and then pointed upwards.

"Efharisto!" I shouted and the echo shouted it back.

It all came out that way. Around the corner the terraces had been sliced to cut a series of steps, hundreds of them. Half-way up we were obliged to rest for a few minutes and then more up and up, until we came out into a wood on the very edge of the quarry where a knee-high signpost pointed to Kaloscopi, the place with the good view. Eight kilometres.

> O blessed shade and green'ry,
> Not e'en i' the courts of Shiraz Khan
> Could there be more gladness-granting,
> More enchanting blithesome place.*

In the classical Greece of long ago there was — and in my mental list of spiritual friends there still is — a great goddess, leader of the nymphs who usually accompany her. She is called Artemis, "Lady of the Wild Things". She haunts the mountains, the forests and even small woodlands where there are tree-cults with springs and rivers. She protects women in childbirth and she watches over little children, especially curious strays. Girls used to bring offerings to her before marriage. The homage is different in different parts of Greece but essentially it always goes back to those characteristics mentioned.

Her habitual appearance has been sung about by Homer and in the great literature of Attica. She is the virgin twin sister of Apollo. Of course the supreme goddess who haunts wild places must be a hunting goddess. Artemis was much more than that but the

*Christopher Tower, *Oultre Jourdain*, Weidenfeld & Nicolson, 1980.

Homeric knights had no relationship to the free life of nature except in the sport of hunting, so she is usually portrayed with a bow and arrows.

Conservationists say we must save forests because people enjoy them. St Francis, God's jester, thought we should save them for squirrels, not for men. Surely St Francis worshipped a God who was the God of both squirrels *and* men? The unknown author of the Benedicite, that canticle or song of praise put into the mouths of Shadrach, Meshach and Abednego as they stood in that fiery hell at the command of King Nebuchadnezzar, was much of the same opinion. The Benedicite may have more of a future than a past.

After being hounded on the roads by trucks we felt under the spell of Artemis in that superb woodland. We both heard and saw one of her familiars, a squirrel, the red species with its long bushy tail curled so far over its back, like a question mark, that the tip extended above its whiskery ears. It saw us and scampered up an Aleppo pine, making a reproachful chattering noise. From the safety of an upper branch it turned round and stared at us and I could have sworn that the handsome little creature winked.

We heard orioles, the warble of unseen warblers, the laughter of the Great green woodpecker and, more ominously, within minutes of taking to a meagre road within sight of Kaloscopi, a hamlet on a small hill, we heard yet again the unmistakable bark of a high-speed rifle.

High noon at Kaloscopi

An undistinguished place midway between mediocrity and downright seediness. A police car and what looked like an armoured van were parked in the shade of a plane between two taverns facing each other. A sergeant of police, his constable and a Civil Guard were talking to groups of locals and making notes. The sergeant looked up; he acknowledged my somewhat contrived salute and went on talking. Nobody else spoke to us.

Without ignoring the tremendous view, the privilege of the rather better-looking house on the far side of the square, we settled for its neighbour on the grounds that it didn't face the midday sun and we could see what was going on.

"Get the beer, enquire about food, but *don't* order anything until we've seen what they've got over there," said the ever-practical Katie.

I came back with the man of the house bearing two bottles on a battered tin tray. What with the dust and the heat of the morning it went down singing hymns. "He doesn't speak much English; the food's pretty trad, but he's got a fresh-looking moussaka and plenty of salad," I said. "I wonder what's going on?"

I finished the first two glasses, ordered some more and strolled over to the house opposite, glancing into the police car on the way. A rifle lay across the two front seats.

On the veranda, facing the vista, a short red-faced man in a naval jacket was talking to a chubby dark-haired woman in Italian, rapidly. A bull terrier at their feet half stood up and growled. *"Basta!* Georgio," he said to the dog, and greeted me in German. *"Buongiorno,"* I replied somewhat coldly.

I walked through the tavern. The food looked a bit dried up. Not much liking the look of Georgio, I returned to Katie via the back door shortly before the sergeant with a cigarette dangling from the corner of his mouth sauntered over.

"There might be some awkward questions about how we got here," I whispered. "Don't forget that we don't know much Greek. He'll probably speak to me. If I don't know what he's talking about I'll turn to you."

"Yes, but give me time — first try to find out how much English he knows," Katie replied.

Surreptitiously, perhaps *philotomo* in front of foreigners, the sergeant tidied himself up on the way over. He put on his cap, dropped his cigarette and trod on it and then gave us a crashing salute. Not to be outdone I stood up, army fashion. "Good day, officer," I said. I shook his hand and after a glance round assured him that Kaloscopi was indeed one of the most beautiful places we had visited. Did he speak English?

He didn't reply directly but smiled as he said, *"Parakalo,* pliss. Your passports."

Katie handed them over. He flicked through them perfunctorily, made a quick note and handed them back with a smile. He couldn't have been more cordial.

Where had we come from?

"From Amphissa," Katie said; "we are tourists from London." To my relief he didn't ask us where we were heading for. Apparently he wanted to know whether we had seen a small yellow car.

"No cars at all," she said, "only big trucks. What sort of car?"

An old Fiat. One door smashed. It had been painted white. Katie translated. We considered the matter, gravely and then both shook our heads.

The sergeant saluted. He took off his cap, shook my hand and hoped our journey would be a good one. Over Greek salad and warmish moussaka we decided he was as pleasant a cop as ever we'd met.

Katie yearned for what we'd eaten in Venice. I tried to cheer her up by observing that in Greece you get caught by the same old food whilst in Italy it's a case of the same old prices.

Katie sighed. Her feet were not at all good. More blisters, and she thought we might run out of talc and sticking-plaster. Madame had told her there was a small *maghazi* at the end of the street behind the tavern. "I'll go take a look. See you back here in not much more than half an hour. And no more retsina! We've a long way to go."

There wasn't much to see so I decided to take another look at the view through glasses. On the way I encountered Georgio who bounced down from the veranda, barking furiously. In a coarse phrase I bade him begone.

"He'll no fuck off if ye speak to him like *thaat*," said Naval Jacket in the slurred vowels and clipped consonants of Glasgow.

Andy McFarlane, Chief Engineer at the Andrea Doria shipyard in Genoa, asked me to join them. Since Katie had only said retsina, I accepted a small brandy gratefully. With an airy wave of his hand he introduced me to Maria, his chubby girl-friend. "The silly old cow can't speak much English, although I've been trying for years. Mind you, she understood that phrase of yours. I thought you were a Kraut or a Swede. Why didn't you speak out? What are you doing here?"

I told him, briefly. I didn't like the way the dog looked at me. "And you?" I asked.

"We've got a place on the Passo di Bocca with a view as good as this. Half an hour's drive north of Genoa. Had it for years. Bought it cheap. Now Maria's got a great-aunt in a bonny village called Pira about twenty kilometres from here. There's a delicate question of inheritance, if you get me. We have to keep an eye on it fairly regularly."

"So you intend to retire there?"

"Jesus Christ, no! I'd rather go back tae Glesga. Pira's a closed shop. They already resent us. They know what we're up to. Greek villagers are worse than the Wops in keeping foreigners out."

"But surely they'd trust a relative of Maria's?"

"Trust!" he almost shouted. "No Greek does *anything* without thinking what he can get out of it. It's self-interest right down the line."

I thought, momentarily, about why he kept visiting Maria's old aunt but didn't want to stem the flow.

"Greeks are a predatory people incapable of real friendship unless it's within their clan, their extended family. Whenever they extend effusive hospitality they're hoping for involvement. Tourists, a substantial part of the national economy, are key figures in this process so long as they don't hang around too long. Hope you've never told them you're an author who used to be a journalist? They'll be after your London address. As soon as a Greek gets an apartment, a small bank balance and credit, he's thinking about becoming a big-time property owner, a lawyer or a regional Deputy, even President. He's *never* satisfied with what he's got."

"Pira's on our route," I said. "Any difficulty about getting there?"

"A dirt road. It shakes the hell out of our old Citroën but in boots you'll be able to skip along. Go straight up through the village here for about five kilometres and then fork left. Now listen, laddie. We could spend another night with the old lady. Why not come along with us?"

The ritual refusal expressed as courteously as possible. "Thanks, but we're doing the whole jaunt on foot. We can cut corners off by following a track on our map."

"What map?"

Somewhat diffidently I pulled out our tattered copy of "Phokis Sheet 2". "Along this line," I said. He glanced at the sheet, folded it up and handed it back.

"Haven't you found that Greek maps are just plain goddamned inaccurate? They don't even mention small roads. A hangover from the military dictatorship. Where you heading for after Pira?"

"Mavrolithari," I said.

"The place of the black stones . . . yes, there's a track

of sorts there. We've been down it in a Land Rover. It's about twelve kilometres from Pira." He looked at the map. "Now let's see what's next . . . H'm . . . After that Daphni, Marmara, Platanos. At least five villages, some of them falling to bits. You'll probably meet only a few old men. But when you get to Platanos you'll be more than two-thirds of the way to Karpenissi, a big market town."

"*Brutto, brutto. Malagevole,*" murmured Maria.

"Shut up!" he said to her sharply. "She's saying it's rough going and she's right. Still, if you're determined to kill yourselves remember those names. No, just a second. I'll put a ring round where at least they ought to be on this map. Why on earth didn't you buy the latest Michelin? Those tyre merchants have a vested interest in roads, and at least they can distinguish between left and right and don't rely on clusters of dots to confuse the credulous."

"So you prefer your Italian neighbours?" I said.

"In our local village, yes. I've been there so long I'm near the top of the local pecking order. But not among the Genovese Mafia, who don't even trust each other. They drive flashy cars. They try to eat and drink with those who've got more power, more money than they have and they'll screw any wench in sight if it's not too much bother. I tell you, the Italians are a nation of artists. And with characteristic artistry they have managed to create a society that combines some of the least appealing aspects of socialism with nearly all the vices of the affluent society. I should know. I've lived there nearly half my life.

"For years they have suffered from a dreadful disease called *la dolce vita*. They invent marvellous words to cover up the vice, the suffering and the humiliation that lies under it all. And everybody knows it except the Italians. *Dolce vita*, my arse!"

I switched the subject to the cops and the interrogations. What was it all about? "Some guy's escaped from a local glasshouse. Seems originally it was a political affair but he's been behind barbed wire for so long that he's had nothing better to do than turn it into a family feud. Now he's intent on blowing the shit out of his brother who fought for the other side. There's Greek love and trust for you!"

"Isn't the brother around here somewhere?"

"Well, I think he used to be." He turned to Maria who'd been knitting as if we weren't there.

"She says Auntie told her the fellow got to hell out of it as soon as he heard that his brother had escaped. Now they're probably hunting each other. Beware of the Greeks when they're toting light artillery in the sacred name of politics."

"We've been told that he escaped from Makronisos."

"Never heard of it. I'll ask Maria." He spoke to her again in bursts of Italian. "She says Papandreou closed it down. The long-timers are somewhere up in the hills above Karpenissi."

I asked him if he'd heard the sound of the rifle shot. A slight pause before he said, "Sure I did and I know what the sergeant hit. It's in the back of his van over there. Georgio's been sniffing round it."

"One of the brothers?"

He laughed. "Not on your life. Just a wee staggie. The woods are full of 'em. You don't expect he'd come back empty-handed, do you? They're worth about 3,000 drachs in Lamia. If I could be sure of a haunch I'd gralloch it within half an hour." He looked at me. "It's best not to know too much around here."

I turned over that piece of advice mentally. Had I been politely told to mind my own business? How did he know what was inside the van? For the first time he seemed to be thinking of something to say. He began to look at my face, closely, like an interrogating policeman.

"Your mouth," he said. "It's sort of drawn up at the corners; it's too tight. Haven't you got a girl-friend?"

"She's out shopping," I said, "and it's about time I got back." His turn to look surprised, even slightly embarrassed.

"We didn't see you come in, and when you said 'we' I thought you were with a fella. That's good. Every man needs a woman in bed."

"I'm nearly seventy but can just about manage it twice a week."

He glanced towards Maria. "If I left it to her it would be every night. Wouldn't it, you silly old cow?"

She blinked. She looked puzzled. He glared at her. "I said you like a *good fuck*, don't you?"

She laughed until she showed every gold tooth in her head. *"Si, si. Molto bene. Tutta notte, tutta notte."*

He patted her hand. "Shc's not a bad lassie," he said.

"Thought you'd gone off with the town tart," said Katie,

who'd paid the bill and closed the rucksacks. "Now, do we stay around or take to the hills?"

"Depends entirely on your feet, me darling. How do they feel?"

"Lots better," she said. "The local shop's a shed next to her husband's garage. Meat only on Fridays. Bread every other day from eight until about half-past ten. A real kindly soul. God knows what she does for the rest of her time, sitting down there surrounded by sacks of flour, beans and a few old potatoes. I looked over her shelves. Couldn't find much beyond your favourite squid in tomato sauce, sardines, tea and a bit of rice."

"Nothing else?"

"Not unless we're in need of piles of detergents or *Peaudouce*, those disposable nappies."

"No medicaments?"

"Iodine, aperients, Beecham's pills and liver salts. I couldn't put across sticking-plaster or talc in Greek, so I slipped off my slippers and pointed to the dressings and went through the motions of sprinkling them with flour. She went upstairs and came back with just what I wanted. As she wouldn't take anything for them I felt obliged to pay little enough for what's going to be your favourite standby. Tinned squid."

"More weight?"

"Now what on earth *could* I do when, with a muttered blessing, she fumbled in a drawer, took out this little thing, and, without a word slipped it into my pocket."

A small plastic cross. I recalled what ex-Lieutenant Commander Andy McFarlane had said about what lay behind Greek friendliness and trust.

"Now, what's next?" said Katie.

"I'm all for pushing on for a few miles, maybe no further than the first reasonable place we come to for a dream home for the night. Let's try and have at least a couple of comfortable days. Apparently there's wooded country at the top of the hill. I've become a self-appointed authority on the district. That chap in a naval jacket wasn't an Italian, he's a pretty ferocious Scottish engineer. His girl-friend's got a relative in the next village, Pira. Wish you'd heard him. He trots out corrosive opinions on just about everything, but he's marked place-names I couldn't find on our map, which he thinks was printed during the Civil War. It seems that when we get to a village called Platanos we'll be more than two-thirds of the way to what seems a reasonable town, Karpenissi."

Seen from above, Kaloscopi seemed far more fertile and prosperous than from the track beyond the quarry we had no wish to remember. Plenty of water, terraced holdings and a fine field of golden grain, perhaps barley, over which jackdaws flew in the way that inspired Van Gogh for his last picture, the one before he killed himself.

The banks of the hill were star-dappled with white flax, *vinca* the periwinkle, and asters which was appropriate since their name in English means "a star".

The junction at the top appeared as Andy predicted: left to Pira, right to Lamia. We struck left into an alpine landscape of immense rocks and pines, Aleppo, Cephalonian and, an old friend, a fine specimen of the Scottish species (*P. silvestris*), blue needles and rusty red at the cross trees. It might have been a long beleaguered consul from Edinburgh, waiting for news of the Jacobites.

In far less time than we could have hoped for we came across what we had sought at sundown for near a fortnight, that rare thing in the wilds of central Greece, a truly comfortable haven for the night. There it stood, a plateau of reasonably soft ground, sufficient at least to hammer in the tent pegs without much effort.

Trees stood above a freshet of unclouded water. We could see enough dead wood for a small fire. We had a vista at our front door and the whole property stood just out of sight of a dust road. In his much-quoted "Night among the Pines" in the Cevennes, R. L. Stevenson, supported, physically, by his "diminutive she-ass Modestine", cannot have been better accommodated than we were an hour or two after the tensions of Kaloscopi.

Before we put the tent up, through field-glasses far below us I could just make out a line, maybe a dozen armed men in unidentifiable uniforms making their way up slowly through rough ground, like beaters on a grouse moor. I passed the glasses to Katie. "What do you make of that?" I asked.

"Well, if your friend Andy's story is to be believed they take stag-shooting seriously around here. You're sure he isn't an informer?"

"A damned clever one if he is. As he seems to be against both Greeks and Italians, maybe he's a double agent. I just let him speak and I happen to know the village where they live. It's Montoggia in the Bocca di Leone. I walked through it on my Apennine jaunt."

Then to our duties: mine to bring water and firewood, hers to do whatever industrious women do when left alone at home. The streamlet, about half a span in width, tinkled tunefully. A pity, I thought, to pollute its clarity with a wash pool, so I diverted a minute tributary into a reed-lined depression with a conduit hacked out with my skinning knife. Great to replay in old age the games of our youth.

Among the Aleppo pines were pillars of rock preaching in silent sounds to lesser brethren at their feet. The old bark of fallen trees was (to me) attractively riddled by recognizable bark beetles whose larvae had left behind strange hieroglyphs on the smooth wood below. Were they writing letters to mankind? I collected twigs for kindling and substantial pieces of wood for a modest fire in a protective hearth of rocks.

As Katie began to simmer a packetful of macaroni bought in the shop, to which she added the squid and tomato sauce, we heard the distant sound of a rifle shot, not below us but so far away to the north-west that I fancy we caught only the twice-repeated echo. It happened again, followed by what I took to be the faint chatter of a sub-machine gun. "How far away do you think that is?" she asked.

I didn't know, maybe four or five miles. Things seemed to be happening all around.

The macaroni and squid *à la mode de Kaloscopi* began to bubble. Katie spooned it on to plates and garnished it with crumbled feta cheese and wild thyme locally picked.

After an interval for polite belches and a nip of Metaxas with coffee, Katie rustled about arranging the bedding and I shoved the last resinous log on the glowing embers. I settled down, looking at the flickering light reflected from the walls of the half-open tent. Nothing I can think of, certainly not television, can stir up a traveller's memories more vividly than the light of an open fire.

That tent of ours with its front open to disclose its articulated ribs reminded me not of the night of the tepees of Chipewyans nor the igloos of the Sea Indians. In my mind's eye I went back to the Little People of the Belgian Congo. Our hemispherical headquarters there was about six feet in diameter with a framework of bent saplings on which the pygmies of Epulu had laid the shiny green leaves of the Mongongo trees used like overlapping shingles. More permanent huts were dirt cheap: they simply plastered the exterior with a skin of mud which promptly dried in the sun.

Given that limited floor space, a hut usually sheltered two clan-linked couples with maybe two or three children each. Seldom more. The responsibilities of fatherhood, taken very seriously, meant that the meat-providers had to spend valuable time pit-falling or netting deer, wild boar, small forest elephants and dangerous buffalo instead of indulging in what they loved most, that is the ceremonials of birth, circumcision, marriage, death and whatever their elders, the wise ones, dreamed up when, deprived of the joys of the chase, they felt like a night out with its prospects of free meat, home-made liquor and home-grown pot.

At the expense of Parcs Nationaux du Congo Belge I spent several months in the Congo, now Zaire. My guide through the Ituri forest and subsequently over the Ruwenzori, the Mountains of the Moon, was the late Jean de Heinzelan de Braucourt, a young Belgian aristocrat, a geologist and mountain-climber who preferred skipping about like a chamois, chipping away at rocks, to ritualized life in his family's elegant mansions. His excuse for taking me to Epulu was to find out, on behalf of PNCB, how many specimens of that rare forest giraffe, the okapi, with their velvet skins and short necks were being fall-trapped and eaten by the Little People instead of being delivered up for forest rights to the Belgians, who sold them to zoos. Devious are the ways of conservation.

More important than what I gleaned as a zoological correspondent were glimpses of the near-indescribable happiness of the Little People who among themselves spoke in a click language, Ki-Bira. Jean knew enough of the common language of The River, Ki-'ngwanna — which could be transmitted by drums — to pass on messages from village to village, and what they thought about life (*kicheko*), literally happiness and, without a shred of irony or envy, their attitude towards the *watu hakika*, the Real People, meaning everybody who didn't share their customs and philosophy.

I never discovered who were the gods of *kicheko* but everybody knew and feared the devil, *Bolozi*, the Evil

Eye, overlord of all dark mysteries. He was omnipotent. During illness he was even more powerful than *dawa*, the medicaments of the Real People.

His name was attached to all fearful things that dwelt in the Great Forest. Man-killing leopards were *Bolozi*; Army ants, probably the most formidable insects in Africa, were *Bolozi sifu*. They advance through the night in columns of uncountable millions. They have no permanent nests. They never settle down. Like the Huns and the Tartars they sally forth on one raid after another. They have been known to kill and devour a tethered horse. Surely they were the little soldiers of *Bolozi*.

"What do they do about them?" I asked de Heinzelan.

"They can't do anything," he said. "They get up and go. Their huts are not permanent. They live as close as they can to where the living is easy." We were staying at the time close to Camp Putnam where Anne Eisner Putnam spent eight years living among the Little People. This is what she said about them:

> I looked at the men, strong, happy and unspoiled by the complexities of civilization. Then I looked at the women, so functionally female in their nakedness, so obviously pleased by their lot. There was no hypertension, no ulcer-breeding unrest here in the Ituri Forest. There was fire and there was meat and cover and love and laughter. They wanted nothing else.

Around midnight, or perhaps earlier, since we took to our warm cocoon before the little owls began their monotonous *pee-oo* at two-second intervals (timed), I awoke under the impression — as I so often did — that they knew what had upset my deep dreams of nothing in particular. With much anxious fiddling with two zips I stepped out naked into a warm bath of air, armed only with a small but powerful torch. I swung the beam round in a semi-circle to find the nearest trees reflected momentarily showers of sparks as if a pinch of iron filings had been dropped into the flame of a candle. The pines were drinking luminous drops of dew. Then back to bed and an even deeper sleep until dawn.

In the moisture and the coolness, the lingering relics of the night, I yawned my way through the trees, across the dirt road where, clad only in underpants, I hopped through the cold wet and prickly herbage to the pool channelled from the streamlet. Brimful.

A few minutes sufficed for a sponge-down and a brisk towelling from head to foot. Ashamed of the slightly soapy state of the water in which Katie intended to wash her hair, I dislodged the dam, temporarily, enabling the water to whoosh down into the swampy reedbed below. To my dismay an unseen colony of little frogs resented the pollution with a chorus of chirps, yelps, peeps, burps and sustained trills. A dozen or more leapt to safety, not into the parent streamlet but on to the broad leaves of waterside plants. Some clung to the twigs of willows.

With difficulty I managed to capture one little bright green elf about an inch and a half in length. I held it lightly between finger and thumb, intrigued to see that the end of its arms and feet were knobbly adhesive pads. I had captured one of the *Hylidae*, the family of tree frogs, the finest amphibious singers in Europe. It leapt away, but not before the little fellow had urinated into the palm of my hand.

Coming down the dirt road towards the village we had left the previous afternoon I came across as strange a trio as ever you might have encountered in the mountains of Tibet: a very old man with all the dignity of his circular wrinkles, seated on a donkey, the very model of Modestine, the colour of a mouse, with a proud bearing, conscious, one felt, of the green ribbons around the base of her hairy ears. In his right hand the old man held a switch of twigs, which he brought down almost mechanically on Modestine's flanks in the way the old men lightly flick over their worry-beads in the shifting shade of a tavern during the afternoon sun.

At the end of a soft rope tied to the pommel he led an old cream-coloured draught ox with the huge brown eyes of Hera. A well-looked-after animal. When the rope tightened as it stopped to nibble something to its fancy he reined in without turning round. Apart from raising his switch in salutation he scarcely noticed me. An elderly white-bearded man in underpants was just part of the landscape, like a surprised hare or a glimpse of a deer.

In *The Palatine Anthology** it is recorded that: "Alkon did not lead his hard-working ox to the butcher's knife for he remembered with reverence his past toil. And now

*Tenth-century manuscripts deposited in Heidelberg University Library.

wandering at large through the deep meadow grass, he lows out his happiness at freedom from the plough."

According to the translator Forrest Reid: "Among the Greeks this scruple prevails. In Athens there was even a formal law forbidding a farmer to kill or allow to be killed a beast who had worked for him." Katie, less romantically inclined, thought the beast was probably on its way to a butcher's knife in Kaloscopi.

A steep descent led us to Pira. The village of waterfalls announces itself in three languages; accommodation, food and wine stores. One of us wondered why we couldn't have found a similar place at nightfall.

"Anything wrong with last night's pitch?" asked Katie.

I am intolerant of that sort of argument which didn't end there. Should we or should we not have a look at the place? It was, I agreed, not on our route. No, we couldn't have just a word with Maria's aunt! We didn't even know her name, and who would want to meet two complete strangers at eight o'clock in the morning?

If we were to keep our schedule we had, I reckoned, about seven or eight hours, allowing for a bit of food and a siesta on the way. Why did we have to keep to a schedule? Because we didn't want to arrive in Macedonia in time for Christmas.

It took us about half an hour to find out that the short cut of somebody's imagination led to a main road *above* the village; more time, incalculable, to wind through a maze of little houses with prosperous plantations watered by as many fountains and pools as you are likely to encounter in Versailles. Nothing needs to be said about disagreements over finding our way back to the notice-board. *Così fan tutte*.

Gradually the abundance of water, orchards, cultivated fields and a fine stand of trees began to disappear until with a progressive sense of desolation we were venturing an almost barren track hacked out of the side of a cliff. Had it not been for recent tyre marks we might have thought we had strayed on to a footway that led nowhere.

In places the serpentine path had been crevassed by flash floods which had left behind a scree of rocks and stones in the gulf below. What couldn't be imagined was how the gaps could have been shored up without dumping many tons of material. Surely it would have been more practical to have blasted into the right-hand wall of the cliff?

Katie walked ahead around a bend in the road whilst I paused to shake out a bit of grit from one of my boots. I hurried after her to find her cautiously looking down a subsidiary track. She motioned me to the inner side of the cliff. The police van stood some forty or fifty feet below. Through glasses I could make out the wreck of a yellow-coloured car lying on its side nearby. The sergeant was taking photographs of a half-open bullet-ridden door.

Whirlwinds and
water-nymphs

A pleasure always to find a priest with a glass of liquor in his hand. In this way he seems better equipped to grapple with the Devil than men of God armed only with cups of herb tea and biscuits. In the tavern at Mavrolithari we watched an old *papas* arrive on a donkey with the dignity of Our Saviour on his way to Jerusalem. Clearly he had much to say to his fellow topers, who addressed him affectionately as *Papouli*. Unfortunately he spoke too rapidly for us to make out what was most on his mind. With a nod and a smile to the company all round we took to the ale bench outside.

The village looked much smaller, much poorer, certainly less ostentatious than Pira except in one geological particular: Mavrolithari advertised itself. From the moment we switched off that arid track and climbed towards good timber on a hill and heard the sound of cicadas, the keynote of a botanically rich soil, we saw the small black stones, some highly polished by glacial action — obsidian perhaps or diorite, forms of volcanic lava. I may be wrong. We subsequently lost our specimens. Enough that we had arrived at what M. Théophane and the McFarlane of Renfrewshire had told us about: the Place of Black Stones.

After about half an hour on our own, a well-dressed

couple strolled across the square towards us; she short and Italianate, he tall and languid. Katie recalled them passing us in a caravan on our way up the hill. In fluent English Dora introduced herself and then her husband, Theo, a pleasant unparticular man, taciturn even when answering questions in Greek.

By contrast the Adorable Dora — as we referred to her afterwards — was rarely without something to say, an exuberant brimful-of-life person. Within minutes we learnt that "himself" was an architect in Thebes where she taught English and French and "some little time as a lecture person in University of Athens. I own small house here," she said, correcting herself by adding, "I mean *we* own it but only come for long weekends and school holiday times."

Theo stood up and said, "*Signomi*," before walking away. "He has a customer here. What do you call it? A client for holiday home? He is specialist in *reconstruction*. What is that in idiomatic English?"

"Doing old places up so you can't see it from the front. Disguised modernization. It's what we call 'putting in all mod cons', meaning all modern conveniences: indoor bathroom, lavatory and kitchen appliances. Sometimes a carefully concealed garage."

She smiled, repeated "all mod cons" and wrote it down before asking who could stop English people doing what they wanted to with what they owned.

"Local bye-laws," I said. "A complicated matter. They are different from place to place. *Byrlaw* is a very old word, perhaps Saxon. It means 'according to local custom'."

Unexpectedly she asked, "Why do you walk so far?"

The perennial question. The perennial answer. "Because I can't imagine anything more exhilarating. When I'm in top gear or even slightly above it, it's almost indescribable, you might compare it with that gear called overdrive in a powerful car. I'm scarcely conscious that my arms and legs are working together. I keep up momentum by leaning forward very slightly."

"Even with those huge things on your back?"

"Well, yes. That could be called a sore point. Without them there'd be no stopping us. But they mean almost complete independence. We don't worry too much about the weather or reaching somewhere to spend the night."

"And how about you?" she asked, looking at Katie.

"I love it. I think I was born to be a tramp, or maybe a donkey."

"Don't you get bored with nobody to talk to except each other?"

"I don't think so," said Katie. "He tends to go on a bit about his beloved beetles, frogs, diorites and things, but I spent fifteen years in Ceylon where nobody was interested in geology and natural history unless it had to do with growing high-grade tea. We both find things here which we have never seen before."

Dora said she was much in the same position. In Thebes her husband spent most of his time at home in front of a drawing-board, planning alterations to old broken-down houses and buying building materials for his workmen. But, as she put it, "I'm more interested in the sort of cement that holds people together, especially in a place like this. By buying and selling we can always go and live somewhere else. We've already had three places."

"But what do you do when he's talking to his clients?" asked Katie.

"I know the people who live here permanently and I like to know what they really do. They seem to like us if only because we do some work for them when our builders are around, and I bring them odd things from the town that they can't buy locally. There are only about twenty families. In the 1940s there must have been a hundred or more."

"Was the village occupied by the Germans?"

"Yes. They burnt the place down and the local people disappeared into those mountains you can see over there, the Vardoussia. Only one old house remained. Theo rebuilt it."

"What do the villagers do in the winter?"

"They have a *maghazi*, a baker, the man who runs this place, a Civil Guard, two or three old Greeks who have come back here on a pension after years in America, a few odd-job people who act as caretakers for holiday homes such as ours, and a shepherd and his crippled son who look after almost everybody's sheep and goats. The old man knows them all by name, usually very rude names. He tries to make sure that the Vlachs don't drive in and steal their grazing by night. You know who the Vlachs are?"

I nodded and left it at that. Near two o'clock and we had miles to go before dusk.

"There's one thing we'd very much like to know," I

said. "What do these old shepherds think about when they're up in the hills, alone, presumably for most of the year? We've seen a dozen or more, some of them two or three miles from the nearest village. When we've completely lost our bearings we've relied on them."

Dora's face lit up. "That's what I've wondered for a long time," she said. "Nobody in Athens seems interested, certainly not the anthropologists. Maybe one day I'll write a small thesis about it myself. What I'm much sure about is that they are people with great 'sensitivities'; men all time in communication with nature. They can hear, they can see and even smell things a long way beyond what we can, like the sounds of small animals, even field mice, the talking to each other of birds, the marks they leave on the ground, the smell and the calls of jackals. They move about so that their sheep and goats don't eat everything down to the bare rocks. People here tell me that some of them chew the sticky stuff, the resin of wild cannabis and I think perhaps that makes them lose their sense of time except for the position of the sun. My theory is that the old shepherds have instincts that go back to people perhaps earlier than the Hellenes, those who worshipped Mother Earth."

"And surely Artemis, Lady of the Wild Things?"

"Yes, that's her! Where did you come across her in Greece?"

"We felt that in spirit she wasn't very far away in the woods at the top of that enormous quarry on the way to Kaloscopi."

"Surely the leader of the nymphs has never been honoured in your country?"

"Perhaps under a different name. Only fragments of our oral tradition survived long enough to be written down in the Roman alphabet by scholars such as Tacitus. Certainly not by Christians trying to lead people away from the old gods."

I told her that we had found that shepherds sensed our presence when, looking at them through glasses, I felt almost certain that they couldn't see us. Dora thought their dogs knew that strangers were in the vicinity.

At that point Theo came back with a jug of wine and *mezedes*. It was somewhat embarrassing to learn that Dora assumed we would come back to their place, the one he had rebuilt. She expected that we would stay with them for a day or two. They'd so much to show us. We said . . .

Before we left I asked her about the wreck of the yellow car and whether they knew the story behind it. She looked surprised. They'd only arrived an hour ago. Surely, I suggested, they would know in the tavern? Theo went back to ask. While he was away Dora asked us where we proposed to stop for the night. Daphni, we told her — what sort of place was it? Could we get a bed there?

"A strange little place. Primitive," she said, "falling to pieces. We've only looked on what's left of the village from the road above, the one that comes up from the Gulf. It's not going to be easy if you stick to your dirt road. Don't wander down little tracks among trees; in the open you can see where you are going. You'll be climbing for most of the way. Are you *quite* sure you won't come back with us? On the top road we could run you there tomorrow in about half an hour. Why waste a whole afternoon over twelve kilometres?"

Theo came back smiling and shaking his head. The situation, as Dora explained it, was that the *papas* had seen the car and made enquiries. "Priests", she said, "get to know just about everything; it's their business and most of them are supposed to be politically neutral. They are like weather-vanes, they swing with the wind. As for this business of a political feud, it's nonsense. The kid was a bank robber. He and his brother were far too young to have known anything about the Civil War. The priest thinks the man in prison escaped to track down his brother who'd made off with most of the money."

"But we were told the political story twice, the last time by a man we think was pretty close to the police."

"Yes, and where do you suppose it all started?" She nodded towards the tavern. "Probably in a place like that. You can't imagine what it's like in a small village where, because the oldsters haven't anything better to talk about, they sit around facing each other, each one knowing exactly where his companion used to stand. And their fathers before them. They are old soldiers, still fighting the war."

"But why should the police get into the act on what looks like a political ticket?"

"Dead men often save the courts a lot of time and the police a lot of trouble. Isn't it called balancing the books? All Greeks are politicians at heart — and don't forget Greece was the birthplace of mythology."

During walks through Europe and elsewhere I have

often had the impression that I am a strolling player, privileged to look briefly into the acts, the minor dramas of others, pushing off before I get the hang of what it is all about.

As we struggled up one hill after another, climbing, always climbing until it seemed we were at the same altitude as some of the snow-capped peaks around us, we were obliged to stop, regain our breath and wonder what else had happened between Kaloscopi and Mavrolithari. Much of it seemed inconsistent if not improbable. Who had been shot? Was he the driver of the yellow car?

Dora certainly gave us comforting advice about that arduous trudge to Daphni: always keep high at junctions, she said. We kept high, ignoring what in the States are called "tote roads for loggers", enticing tracks leading down to plantations of spruce and cypress with the regularity of corduroy. We were reminded forcefully of the Euclidean predilections of the British Forestry Commission.

In addition to the calls of cicadas, the belch of frogs and the sight of untidy old trees the odds in favour of encountering a concealed village are progressively doubled by increasing numbers of wayside shrines like birdcages on stilts, each with a burning wick in an oil-filled Pepsi-Cola bottle or a discarded jar still bearing a tattered label. The light flickers on a faded illustration of the Virgin with miniature bunches of still-fresh flowers at her feet, offered, one supposes, in the name of the recent dead.

Around a sharp bend in the track Daphni appeared as if, centuries ago, a once-prosperous hamlet had tumbled down a sunset-facing slope of abandoned terraces. No barking dogs, no blather of goats, no huckling of hens; nobody about except an old granny in black sitting on a doorstep with a Persian cat in her lap, knitting. She didn't look up when we greeted her. She was blind, but at the word "taverna" she pointed limply to a huddle of buildings with a breakneck of stone steps to the upper floor.

I mounted them and knocked. The knocks echoed as if from an empty barn. Somebody called from the back. It wasn't easy to reach the back but whoever it was called again. A quadrangle of dilapidated buildings seemed to be clutching each other as if in shared grief. Impossible to guess their age. The hinges and scrolled metalwork of shutters on the ground floor had rusted and all but fallen down in wafers of speckled gold. Above them what had been windows in pairs were gaping holes, like eye-sockets in a row of skulls.

At the back stood a done-up building with a smack of Turkish-Greece about it, surely not much more than a century old, facing a wilderness of prickly grazing on an up-slope.

A young fellow, meaning fortyish, in jeans and jersey topped by a black beret, gave the impression of being brought back to life unexpectedly. He yawned prodigiously. In Greek Katie asked him if he could provide us with a small room and a bed for the night. At first he didn't seem at all keen on the prospect.

"*Mais c'est un mauvais moment.*" A few seconds' pause before he added, "*Alors! Peut-être je ferai des préparatifs.* You now have drink?" In an endearing mixture of French flavoured with English, "Muzzi" (Mustapha) Androcles had everything to offer the hungry and thirsty if they were addicted largely to mutton stew and ouzo. It came out later that he was born in Cairo, before his parents came home to Lamia just before events in November 1973 when Greek army tanks and security forces crushed a non-violent demonstration at the Polytechnic in Athens. It was the Junta's mindless action over what later became a far more widely publicized eponym for self-styled leaders armed only with guns: the Hellenic equivalent of Tiananmen Square.

Muzzi led us upstairs into what was clearly the sleepy aftermath of a Bacchanal which had started the previous night. Two or three of a company of maybe seven or eight were leaning back, snoozing, mouths open, on wall benches behind tables bearing empty glasses. Others were playing a lethargic game of cards. Two, I seem to remember, were re-enacting the final goal of a national football match with their fingers dribbling a ball of screwed-up silver paper. Amiable disputes and much head-shaking about who had first tripped up somebody on the other side. Nobody, fortunately, seemed aware that strangers had arrived. Clearly a good time had been had by all.

Katie quietly asked our host where the toilet was and he pointed down into the yard where even half a dozen bantams appeared to be asleep. Time: seven o'clock. Would we eat with them in about an hour? Good! He put down two glasses, a quarter of ouzo and a jug of wine and went out. He came back with a bunch of keys, a brush and, I couldn't imagine why, an impressive felling axe.

Katie told me afterwards that the lavatory bowl was filled with dead leaves. She thought it best to scoop them out together with a lizard or two and a small salamander before she sat down, wondering, unimaginatively, what the company used.

From upstairs came the noise of a tremendous crash followed by much brushing before Muzzi returned to say our quarters were ready. On the way there he apologized for the state of the door, saying he couldn't find the right key. He had only been there for a week, looking after the place for his uncle and had been obliged to bust the lock open. A practical man.

The place looked makeshift but serviceable: a wire-framed bedstead and no linen, since we had told him we carried sleeping-bags. The permanently open windows were framed by swallows' nests and looked on to the courtyard. Katie asked if we could have some water and he brought up two full canisters about half the size of dustbins.

After late supper in an almost empty bar we returned in the dark to find the floor wet. One canister was leaking incontinently. Only one thing to be done. To the consternation of the bantams I pitched the rest of the water out of the window. The birds squawked as if they'd been kicked, and flew off like misguided missiles. Maybe I saved their lives.

Towards midnight Katie nudged me and put her fingers across her lips. From below a most curious noise: muffled yelping as of puppies scrambling to get at their mother's teats, interspersed by a high-pitched whine. Foxes? Badgers? I couldn't make it out. I snapped on the small torch we keep at the ready. The beam lit up two reddish animals bigger than foxes, smaller than wolves. Jackals! One half-turned and bared its teeth before they both slipped away.

Though they are not among my familiars I had seen the Golden dogs (*Canis aureus*) on several occasions, especially in Khartoum after dark where packs emerge from the sewers and hunt down and eat anything edible by jackal standards.

I recall nothing else of that night, except that for hours on end swallows twitter in their sleep.

As crows fly in Evritani, the *nomos* we'd entered the previous night, we were about forty miles from Karpenissi, but we walked twice that distance in the four days it took us to get there. The first one, 17 May, opened with a dawn that wasn't so much rosy-fingered as riotous. The wind rose and cohorts of clouds were at odds with each other.

Far to the south the volcano-like peaks of the Vardoussia stood out as nipples against a ceiling of high cirrus, whilst from the down-slope to the north we saw puffs of low cumulus at intervals, like cannon smoke in a Victorian print of a battle-scene.

I never trust clouds moving in opposite directions in the mountains and when Katie asked what I thought we were in for I said rain with such conviction that I had to cheer her up by adding that unchanging weather is as dull as dining with a vegetarian.

In fact it didn't rain until we were almost within sight of Karpenissi and by then our only thoughts were upon reaching food and shelter before dusk.

We plodded along a wooded ridge at about 3,000 feet. Dora had told us that the down-slope marks the edge of the flood plain drained by the river Sperkios which flows due east from the Timfristos range above Karpenissi, then through Lamia to the Maliakos Gulf. The river is ten times older in the folklore of mythology than ever the Thames or the Tiber and the fertile plain is reputed to be the home of the river gods.

To get the hang of the ancestry of these gods we must accept what has been passed down from Homer and Hesiod. They sprang from the conjugation of Gaea or Ge, the personification of the earth, and Oceanus, the god of the waters which surrounded the earth. Dora could relate most of these improbabilities as easily as a child recalls much-loved fairy tales.

"Who believes in the nymphs nowadays?" I had asked Dora.

"More people than you think," she said. "Ask them. You'll be walking high above the Sperkios for several days. All the little streams you come to flow down to the parent river. The shepherds have their own names for them, although they're much alike. There's *Aspropotamus*, the white river or *Rematia*, the ravine, or the torrent of the old river, *Paleopotamus*. If they know of a spring or a secret supply of water they'll probably keep the name to themselves. When you were a boy didn't you have favourite places, somewhere where you found things that you thought only you knew about?"

221

* * *

Long after Amstel time we were still on that narrow
peninsula with good timber on both sides and a ridge
just ahead, at right angles to our track, but not a drop of
water in sight for two travellers whose thirst matched
that of Tantalus. Far from dropping rain, the high cirrus
had disappeared but for no reason that could be accounted
for a truly prodigious wind sprang up. At first I took it to
be the Bora, that north wind that disrupted the Persian
fleet at Salamis, an event which started a commemorative
cult among the Athenians. But it was too warm. Distant
landscapes shimmered in a heat-haze like a badly tuned
TV picture. Unable to recall the name of the god of
the south wind, I mentally composed a prayer to Zeus,
Gatherer of Clouds, in the hope that he would take his
rumbustious strays off somewhere else.

Could that prayer have been answered, obliquely?
We rounded a slight bend where the wind seemed to be
giving us a shove up our backsides instead of coming at
us sideways as it had done earlier.

In earlier walks I have come up against several famous
winds. The *ka-utcha* is known to the Athabascan red-men
as the killer, the famine-bringer who drives the caribou
south, right out of their territory. On the flood plains of
the Nile you will meet the *haboob* and the *khamsin* so
called because it blows for fifty days. Further south on
the High Ruwenzori I climbed up into the fury of the
masungu, the one who beckons and cannot be gainsaid.
In Europe I have been pushed backwards by the *sirocco*,
and the *föhn* of the southern Alps which afflicts the
temperamental, the Swiss say, with a particularly painful

form of migraine. But all these were lateral winds coming from a known source. Never before had I experienced a wind that seemed to rise from the ground below.

It came from convection currents. Warm air is less dense than cold. We were trudging along a high causeway, and whatever the winds on the warm plains below were called they were rising to meet us in gusty squalls.

I had a premonition. Nothing paranormal. Just as a dog's nose twitches before he knows why, I sensed something ahead. Through a screen of trees on the far side of a sharp bend we looked down on a sorry collection of ancient buildings surrounded by cascades of musical water. How in the name of the blessed saints, not to mention the local gods and goddesses, the family Spirides and their few neighbours managed to survive in their shacks on stilts through the blast of winter is something we could scarcely imagine.

We had not only arrived there in the compassionate season of mid-May, but on a day of very special providence. From among the swaddlings of thick protective sheets of green canvas the men were unroping a large, metal, slightly rusted object about the size of the engine of a small car. Here indeed was the nearest they had ever been to *deus ex machina*, and their own machine too: an old electric generator.

Whether or not it was a communal cost-sharing enterprise for fuel we never discovered. What was certain from the centre of activity, a very small taverna-cum-*maghazi*, was that the fairy godmother was Aunt Eugenia, from what she called *Kairdiff* in

South Wales. She appeared to be a relative of Kyria Koula, wife of the man of the house, and, temporarily at least, that kindly but stern-faced woman ran the place.

To us she spoke Welshified English with hesitancies and recourse to Greek words and gestures. Everyone else was addressed in rapid authoritative Greek. No questions about how or why we had got there. We were bidden to sit down. She extended her hand palm downwards and rapidly patted that invisible dog. Then she went on re-ordering the establishment, giving us time to look around. Their problem: the disposition of an old box-like television set in a fretted wooden frame which could never have been used and an equally ancient refrigerator, its enamelled door crazed and yellowed.

They tried to shove the fridge under the shelves of packets of biscuits and tins of chopped-up octopus, squid and sardines. Nothing else. Why not? We wondered what monopolist supplied the stuff, with its guaranteed shelf-life. We had run into his wares from Corfu to Cyprus and bought them only when there was nothing else. The fridge couldn't be accommodated without shifting the usual piles of boxes of detergents and disposable nappies. Result: impasse. Aunt Eugenia left the inert hardware to admiring neighbours and turned to us. Food? Anything they could offer, we said. Without a glance at the shelves she motioned us to the back of the house where from the top of a wood-fired stove she spooned out some tasty chicken with vegetables. This done she wished us good luck and went off somewhere else. We never saw her again.

Outside in the yard below the wind was giving a

pretty fair imitation of a wind machine. The gusts had redoubled in strength, making conversation impossible with Katie who trudged close behind. We regained the ridge, striving to keep to the thickest avenues of sturdy pines. Without that intermittent shelter it would have been stupid to venture further.

As path-finder I tried to give the impression I had the whole affair under control, to memorize all our twists, turns and selected junctions so that we could, if necessary, retreat back to our friends awaiting almighty power from the generator. We certainly couldn't put our tent up on that tormented ridge, but I had the feeling that we might come across a loggers' hut or perhaps enough stacked timber to build a lean-to. As we were on the long axis of a formation that closely resembled a draughtsman's T-square I wondered what we should have to contend with on that high bare ridge due ahead.

Struggles against winds that come against you head on and hard can be overcome by leaning forward and lifting your feet up in the manner of a circus horse. For a mile or more this can be exhilarating, like walking in the fantasy of a dream or a space-fiction world without gravity, the essence of that fluid movement brought to theatrical perfection by Marcel Marceau.

This wind had no set pattern, no accustomed form. We were knocked about by an opponent who made up the rules as he swept towards us. An uppercut, but not a meaningful blow. A subtle feint. By the time we had counteracted one gust by leaning towards it a smart left from somewhere else all but knocked us over.

This was no nymph, no ward of the Mistress of the Wild

Things. We were up against a malignant demon, protean in his different guises. With trepidation we approached the lateral ridge. Anti-climax. Far from climbing up on that local Table Mountain our wayward path slipped aside, down into an unseen ravine where on a road of sorts we were protected by cliffs of limestone hung about by garlands of red and white valerian. Within a quarter of a mile the wind gradually whimpered away until it became no more than the stertorous breathing of the sea heard from afar.

The ravine opened out into quiet and fertile country where, after our blustery bouts, we came to the conclusion that the story of Aeolus who, together with his six sons and six daughters, had tried to bottle up the four great winds was not a wholly improbable myth.

In Marmara, small rickety windmills clattering like plastic toys profited that day from only light breezes. Goats with bloated udders were wandering among the new sprouts of vineyards. Nobody about except an angry middle-aged laundress who, pounding away at soiled clothes in a huge barrel of water with a paddle, was curiously abusive when we tried to ask her not only where the taverna was, but how to get into the village.

We walked through two narrow passageways only to find ourselves in the same cul-de-sac. We went back to the laundress where Katie repeated her questions in the kindest of voices and I resorted to sign-language by pulling a wry face, patting my parched lips and sawing my stomach in half. What she said we couldn't make out since she picked up her paddle again and whirled it round her head. I wonder which of us looked the most stupid?

On our second run we discovered that the village on that steep hillside was layered, with one long row of houses above another, three rows in all with a tavern and a shop in an isolated square. The four serious drinkers there were almost silent as if awaiting fatal news, but the landlord brought in the fellow from next door, an ironmonger and smith who spoke some English.

We drank Amstel and he ordered us *souvlaki* from the open-air stall outside. From the smith we learnt that the previous village, the one with the generator, was Paleohori, the old place, a name we encountered several times each week, and the streams around it were "the Shining Ones", presumably more daughters of old Father Sperkios.

Further gossip was interrupted by a loud crash outside. A spirited donkey at the end of a trailing tether seemed wholly unable to stand on more than two legs at the same time. Called Pépé or Pipi, she had recently been shod and seemed to be trying to kick off her heavy shoes by plunging movements which brought sparks from the cobbled square. I tried to stand on the rope and was pulled off my feet to the amusement of a dozen or more people who had mysteriously appeared. The owner tried to throw a halter over her ears and they were last seen belting up the hillside.

Donkeys, in my view, have a hard time of it. They are beaten throughout their lives and at their death from exhaustion their skins are stretched across drums for celebrations and martial endeavour.

At the edge of dusk we settled beside a conversational stream, another tributary of the river below. If the citizenry of Marmara don't remember the white-haired couple who walked down and told them scarcely believable tales about where they had been, they will surely recall, we think, Pépé or Pipi who had the better of them all that afternoon.

The affairs of the butcher bird and the kind-hearted cop who misled us beyond measure began at half-past four in the morning when we could well have done with at least another hour or two of sleep. I woke up, as I so often did, at the sound of noises I couldn't make out. A bird, for sure, but what sort of bird? From somewhere only a few feet above our heads came a completely unmusical succession of broken, discordant sounds accompanied by a sustained high-pitched nasal whine like that of an indignant bumble-bee trapped in a matchbox.

Had an owl, I wondered, caught a huge stag beetle, or a magpie a field vole? Those are noises I have known since childhood, but this was unfamiliar, neither owls nor magpies. The awful racket continued for perhaps a quarter of an hour when, unable to ignore it further, I crept out into a clammy dawn.

An ashen grey and black creature rose like a sinister ghost from the topmost point of the bare branches of a stricken conifer. It hovered for several seconds like a kestrel in search of field mice before it gave a high-pitched yelp and floated off into the mist: the Great Grey shrike, largest of the European butcher birds, which from its watchful stance, sometimes maintained for half an hour or more, is precisely described by its scientific name, *Lanius excubitor*, the butcher's sentinel or watchman.

Although the bird had temporarily disappeared from sight I could still hear that high-pitched nasal whine, and traced it to a festoon of rusted barbed-wire on the spikes of which were impaled a seemingly dead grasshopper or two, a decapitated dormouse, a curiously blue bee and a large beetle, *Acanthocinus*, with antennae more than twice the length of its body. Both insects were moving feebly and squeaking, an unpleasant sight and sound even to an entomologist. The barbed-wire was the butcher bird's larder.

Katie, clad only in her smalls, had finished paddling about in the stream and wanted to know what I thought about a breakfast of pilchards and potato crisps. I thought better not tell her about what was on the shrike's plate until we had finished our own. Before we were ready to pack up the sentinel bird flew back in a series of glides with extended wings and settled on a distant tree, where it behaved as noisily as before. We were hurrying. We were both tired and in need of re-creation.

At Amstel time we heard a church bell ringing at intervals somewhere down in the valley below, although there wasn't a tree to hide a building. Was it an omen? Up on high we were alone among the trees. I've known this from two long walks made years ago. It may have been an omen. I hold with De Quincey that not to be at least a little superstitious is to lack generosity of mind.

The ironmonger of Marmara had told us that some twelve kilometres beyond the fast stream, the one he called "the noisy water", we should find ourselves at the foot of a steep track on the way to Nikolitsi where he recalled a small tavern. There he thought they would remember his name, Gorgio, son of Otho, yes, like famous king of long time ago. His grandmother had made nine children. They all had famous names: Venizelos, Konstantine and Botsaris, after the liberty-fighter who had killed "thousands of Turkish in time of your Lord Byron". Gorgio's father "thought it all much stupid. We were teached to work with our hands". With an imaginary hammer and chisel he demonstrated how for many years his brother had worked in a marble quarry.

We walked to Nikolitsi with considerable pleasure on a carpet of Greek cowslips called *Elatior*, a rarity in Britain — but where on earth was the tavern? Two or three dilapidated buildings hadn't been used for years. Should we stick to our comfortable track or climb up to what looked like an old barn?

No need for decisions. Within minutes a Land Rover bounced down towards us with a smartly dressed policeman at the wheel. He left it outside what was presumably the local lock-up. He went inside, made a brief phone call and came out all smiles.

Problems? There were no problems. The tavern was the barn-like building above. He had just left it. How far? Why, we could see how far. Perhaps 200 metres. I pointed upwards. Could we reach the top of the hill from behind the tavern? He looked puzzled. Katie translated slowly. Why, yes! Easy! Through the trees. How far? On that point he was a shade uncertain. A kilometre, perhaps two or three. We should have given serious heed to two important words, *missos* (perhaps) and *ipano* (straight up).

With some reluctance the young fellow behind the bar put down his tabloid with its enormous headlines. He regretted he had no food to spare but agreed to put ice into our warm lager. On one point at least he offered some solace, and that was that as far as he knew the track at the back of the establishment joined a little road behind the top of the hill.

This wasn't true and what neither he nor the cop appeared to know was that after about a hundred yards the so-called track, a loggers' loop road, defeated by a wooded cliff, turned round and, as we discovered too late, came back to where we'd set off. That is, the track came back. We didn't. We soldiered on and, after a performance rarely seen outside a cage of gibbons in a zoo got to the top, tired out, sweating to our underpants and exasperated.

Carrying the worst part of thirty pounds, I climbed not one but several trees on a stretch of near vertical cliff by using arm- and foot-holds with the alacrity and circumspection of a thoughtful sloth. Trees which grow in precarious places endeavour to stabilize themselves by aerial roots and adventitious shoots at the points where the leader, the main branch emerges from the ground. These are the rungs of arboreal ladders, clumps of temporary foot support which enabled me to haul up our rucksacks and hang them on to something else higher up so that the step-by-step process could be repeated, *ad fatigationem.*

through obstinacy, fortified by the misbelief that we should rejoin the track that didn't exist up there. Yet most bad things come to an end and we reached a hogback-like crest laudably bare on most of the down-slope but rather steep in places, where we were obliged to jog trot, that staggering run you can't avoid when you are carrying something too heavy.

We sat down under a tree for a bite and a pot of tea. Our relief at getting there without more than a few scratches was tempered by the uneasy feeling that the track ahead meandered back to Nikolitsi. The prospect was no more pleasing to the right where the track seemed determined on swinging round in a south-easterly bearing, that is wholly in the wrong direction. I went to spy out the land.

It was damned hot on that winding track. What could lie around the next corner? A lunarscape. Thin scrub. A few goats, some of them trying to climb up the ruins of trees. *The Waste Land*:

> . . . where the sun beats,
> And the dead tree gives no shelter, the cricket
>   no relief
> And the dry stone no sound of water.

Behind a slight depression about half a mile to the north of the track I made for a spire of smoke as slender as a cypress. The Zeiss brought into focus the source — a modest fire at the centre of several angular tents, a few people, two or three trucks, and beyond a herd of sheep or goats on some tolerable grazing, perhaps the remains of somebody's crop.

Their dogs sensed me. They barked. Accompanied by a man with a slight limp they moved in my direction. I waited until they were quite near and then lifted up my arm in friendly greeting. What with the fire, the womenfolk and the goatherds in the background, the scene could have been the opening of the second act of *Il Trovatore*, the one known best for the Anvil Chorus. *"Chi del gitano i giorno abbella?"*

Whether his days were ones of pleasure I shall never discover. It was a safe bet that they were not *gitani*, that is gypsies, a race with which the Vlachs are at odds in the manner of rival predators. The elderly fellow with his black cape and metal teeth was almost certainly on my side.

"Good day — *bunâ dzua*," I began and shook his arm with enthusiasm. *"Eshti Vlachos?"*

He was for sure, and grinned, showing all his gold and silverware. He spoke rapidly. By frowning, touching my lips and holding an imaginary pea between my forefinger and thumb I sought to put across the fact that I knew about as much *Vlachos* as he *zburask Angliski*. As for being lost, I opened my arms limply. I looked up at the sky and slowly shuffled round in a circle. He understood. *"Dukesku,"* he said. *"Tsi loku?"* What village did we want?

"Hori Platanos," I said.

More nods of comprehension. After pointing with his stick to an unusual hill to the north-west, he half crouched and peered deep down into a clump of daisies. There we should find a ravine and a torrent (ripple of fingers) and a *small* village (my gesture with the pea) and called as far as I could make out, "Curious and curiouser."

"*Graz,*" I said. "*Ashits,* yes. *Dukesku.*"

We embraced and in the best style of *opera buffa* yodelled, "*Adio, adio*" at intervals *da capo al fine*, until we were out of earshot.

What lay between Katie's shady nook and the Vlach's impression of a ravine and a noisy torrent is of no account except that we got there by turning off a track to the right which he had indicated by two fingers. Better by far his vigorous gestures than the cop's exuberant imagination.

But for two incidents we could have steered down that weird winding gorge in bath chairs without stopping. The first was an immense but harmless coiled snake like an outsize in Catherine wheels. Before it shimmered away Katie stopped, trembling slightly. She detests snakes of any kind, the outcome of her days as a young mother on Ceylon tea-plantations. She can't forget the day when the nanny allowed her first-born within arm's length of a family of baby cobras.

The second incident had to do with a mild argument about the name of the next village in Greek on a very old signpost. Katie decoded the letters aloud whilst I examined the map. "*Kappa, Omicron, Epsilon . . .*" she began.

"Curious and curiouser," I said.

She looked up surprised. There are times when she underestimates my linguistic abilities.

Near the foot of the gorge two cataracts coalesced and crashed over a twenty-foot drop into a tree-shaded pool, the resort, if ever we saw one, of the naiades. Off came boots, pants and vests and we took to their sanctuary for ten minutes of sporty splashing. I rolled about in the deeps, floated on my back, duck-dived head down, and decided the water tasted somewhat sour. Magnesium perhaps. Knowing the effect on the bowels of that purgative stuff I treated it cautiously. Katie in the whirling froth of the shallows thought her skin felt somewhat soapy. Curious and curiouser.

Back on the bank, we dried on a small shared towel, lit the burner and ate something tinned flavoured with wild herbs. "Tea tastes odd," said Katie, firmly putting down half a mug full. "Where did you draw the water?"

I nodded towards the shallows and, to confirm its clarity, I poured out about an eggcupful into a small transparent container. It looked a bit cloudy. "Flocculent," I said, loftily.

As I washed up the plates and cutlery I noticed that, after slowly whirling round and round, nearly all the foam eventually floated downstream but not all of it. In a back-water there was perhaps more foam than there should have been. Below that vortex the remains of an animal could just be made out, but only from its horns. I mentioned the matter to Katie, casually, a day or two later.

For two or three miles there was neither water to be seen anywhere nor a drop in our rolled-up plastic containers. My tongue felt as dry as a tram-driver's glove and Katie, salmon-pink about the arms and face, was perspiring profusely.

I heard a braying noise from afar and paused to ensure

it wasn't a raucous crow or a malcontented goat. No — our old friend, a donkey, that audible emblem of a Greek village! As we had so often done before we tracked it down to a village in a hollow, the legacy of fugitive people. Perhaps something more subtle than the love-potion lay behind Titania's affection for that famous beast.

A half-cousin of the horse, the domesticated breed was uncommon in England until Gloriana came to the throne. Donkeys fascinated Darwin, and far from being stupid they have what a friend of mine who has kept a pair for years describes as quaint intelligence and strong affections. A Greek we met in Thebes who had for long been expatriated told us he almost cried for his native village when he saw one pulling a cart in Kansas City.

The tethered beast which beguiled us down to Curious and Curiouser deserved more than her two plump thistles with prickly leaves for a salad, and nibbled Katie's arm to have her ears pulled. To our dismay, as in Marmara, on our first foray up and down Main Street — perhaps a dozen unusually neat houses with fruit and vegetable gardens — the she-donkey appeared to be the only inhabitant, notwithstanding our uninhibited door-knocking and hallooing.

Had not the family Kyllini rushed down two flights of stone steps as if the upper floor were on fire at the first house we had come to on the way in, the one near the donkey, we might have helped ourselves from the hand-pumped well behind their gate, but it wasn't necessary. We were overwhelmed by irrepressible hospitality.

Our water-containers were filled to distension. In their large, comfortable living-room we were pushed, repeat pushed, into their best chairs by the affable mistress of the house, daughter of old, toothless and ever-smiling granny who on a chain next to her bosom fished out a small gold-framed photograph of her late departed in a military shako, class of 1940. He looked as if he were fairly old even then.

Madame reappeared with a pewter plate of goodies. Although far from hungry we selected two with calculated discrimination and even before I had swallowed mine she shoved another one, a bun dripping with honey, into my mouth. Never before had I been forcibly fed.

In came the master of the house, a young bearded fellow with a gentle face, who carried an earthenware pitcher of milk and a newly honed felling axe. We had heard him at it in the back garden. He bade me try its edge which I did with my forefinger, nodding and making out that I could shave with it. At this he went out and returned with a huge scythe over his shoulder, walking slowly, theatrically, as if the spectre of death.

This much tickled the whole family except granny who, not to be outdone, struggled to her feet and from among the relics and family likenesses on the mantelpiece under the crucifix took down a red-sealed glass bottle and shook the pebble-like contents vigorously. They were her gallstones, extracted, we were given to understand, about five years ago.

The master poured out the milk but only for us. An interesting drink, very slightly sugary and less cheesy than that of a cow. He watched me anxiously as I smacked my lips before going to the window and pointing out his donkey. I wanted to know the animal's name and ventured on *noma*. Puzzled looks. Katie — whom I'd introduced — pointed at the creature and said, *"Pos se léne?"* Laughter all round.

My turn to get into the act. "Modestine?" I asked. "Zoe? Poppaea?" At each suggestion they shouted, *"Ohi!"* Clearly they were building up to something. "Delphine? Elena?" I shrugged, closed my eyes and raised my chin.

In a chorus they all shouted, *"Katerina!"*

The marvel is that we got away in just over an hour.

Under an atlas of stars that night we drank wine in the company of nightingales and cicadas. Rather sweet, distinctly alcoholic, Malvasia which Nico Kyllini had pressed upon us, saying it came from his native Crete.

In London about a year later I was ferreting through an anthology by Richard Stoneman for some elusive line about early travellers in Greece recommended to us by Our Man in Athens. In it I came across this intriguing paragraph from Robert Byron's *Europe in the Looking Glass* (London, 1926):

We ordered a bottle of syrupy brown wine named Malvasia, first manufactured at Monemvasia in Sparta. This wine, which we had also tasted at Ferrara, was the original Malmsey, exported to our notoriously drunken island, in which the Duke of

Clarence, whose bones now hang in a glass case on the walls of the crypt of Tewkesbury Abbey, met his unfortunate end. It is a strange coincidence that not only did the wine of Malmsey have its birthplace in Greece but also the Dukedom of Clarence. One of the oldest titles of the English monarchy takes its name from a small town on the west coast of the Peloponnese . . . As the dinner progressed, enough Malmsey to have drowned a hundred Dukes of Clarence seemed to disappear. The small town is Kyllini, now called Glarentza.

If it's a true account, an extended record of travel on foot should reflect the changing moods of the narrator as surely as a cardiogram the movements of his heart. Of the two remaining days it took us to reach Karpenissi, where we expected to be up against different problems, in wild terrain we stumbled badly in the path-finding sense of the word. In brief, through misinformation which should have been double-checked at the start we failed to cross the capricious River Sperkios at the nearest available bridge and were obliged to walk downstream and up again in an arduous loop of fifteen miles.

We were assured by an oil-merchant in Platanos that we could wade across the stream in a dozen or more places. All a matter of asking local fishermen where it could be done, he said and, as in the case of another local person, the cheerful cop at Nikolitsi, we took his word for it.

By lunchtime we were on the track to Pitsi which for those foolhardy enough to retread our trail for themselves

239

lies at the very heart of the matter. In the tradition of young Lochinvar whose steed was the best, dust-polluted Pitsi should be renamed the Sperkios Leap.

Huge bulldozers were grubbing up cartloads of what looked like asbestos. White-faced and parched from the dust, we turned our backs on Pitsi and walked on. A dire decision. But, as we thought at the time what did it matter? We could see an unexpectedly small stream which in places could have been jumped across.

An hour passed and then another which brought us to Levkas and a mildly riotous wedding celebration in the village square. The groom and the bride went through ritual gestures of reluctance then were carried off, physically, on the shoulders of kinsfolk and may God bless their union. As for ourselves we needed solace beyond the drink so freely offered. A taxi-driver, a local man who volunteered to drive us anywhere we wanted to go, was authoritative, sympathetic but discouraging. He assured us that the stream below was the creamy-coloured Aspropotamus, a small tributary of the parent stream which looped north at the bridge eight kilometres below Pitsi of accursed memory. As for wading across the Sperkios, there had been storms over the Timfristos range and — as we should discover at the bridge far downstream — at no place was it less than about two metres deep in mid-current.

That sultry night — and it doesn't matter where it was — we saw only a few stars towards dawn. The next day we arrived in Karpenissi in torrential rain and wet to the skin.

Karpenissi

The last hundred yards of that unseemly baptism were watched with mild amusement by groups of students under the vast canopy of the Edelweiss, the leading *kafenio* in town. We scuttled towards it.

Karpenissi, pop. 5,000, is described in Michelin as "majestically situated in a high alpine valley surrounded by snow-topped mountains and ski slopes". The town itself, a higgledy-piggledy collection of busy little shops, bars and middle-grade hotels, commands the approach to the High Pindos and stands high in Greek estimation for its resounding victory in the days of Botsaris and Byron.

Katie promptly made for the women's quarters to tidy up, leaving me steaming gently in the company of two listless blondes from Sweden. They were there, they told me, to study silviculture at the local forestry college, the biggest in central Greece. I said I knew something about conifers and had once lectured at their home university. Their suggestion that we might meet again after supper became less enthusiastic, I felt, when I told them that my wife and I had just trudged in from a day-long scramble over Timfristos.

Without much enthusiasm I listened to the girls' gossip about college life and the lack of anything to do at night in a small market town. When Katie returned she enlisted the girls' help with what she calls the laundry lists, that is accommodation, shops, restaurants and the like.

We were joined by a young Swedish tutor, an expert on the classification of soils. This brought me back to what we were most in need of: large-scale maps. But I knew that it was as diplomatic to talk about them openly in Greece as about the sterling–rouble exchange rate in the centre of Moscow.

We learnt that for timber production and experimental purposes the college either owned or had been granted the right to use a large tract of forest, formerly a royal hunting-ground some ten or fifteen miles away. We should be wise not to go near it, our informant told us. It had been used as a large political prison and, for all he knew, the situation hadn't changed.

Between Karpenissi and that wholly unknown terrain, the range of Mount Olympos which harboured a military training-station and an airfield, our major obstacles were the Agrapha mountains ahead topped by a village and a rather mysterious place, Vlahogiania, the haunt of the Vlachs, some twenty-five miles east of Trikala.

According to the Royal Geographic Society in London there were neither rural roads nor marked tracks to either of these places; nor had we been allowed to take photo-copies of their detailed maps. Agrapha means the place without a name or more accurately "unrecorded for taxation purposes", a toponymic dating from centuries of Turkish occupation when it was unsafe for a foreigner to venture up to a place five hours from the nearest road.

"How did you get here?" asked the tutor.

"Painfully," I said. "Mostly our own fault. Acting on local advice we clung to a spur of the Vardoussia although we all but got blown off the ridge above a place called Anatoli. Things went well until we reached Pitsi where, not knowing about the new by-pass, we took some fool's advice that we could wade across the Sperkios. Perhaps we could have if we'd been on stilts but the river was in full flood and it cost us a day via the bridge east of Vitoli where we spent the night. Then Timfristos. Have you any idea how many loops there are in that little road up to the village?"

He shook his head.

"We counted about twenty before we discovered there were as many or more on the down-slope to Agios Nikolaos where I would have stopped in an old barn as it began to piss down but, fortunately I suppose, before we unpacked our gear I found that the hovel crawled with more scorpions than I've seen before."

"What were your reactions?"

"As a naturalist they intrigued me, the first I'd ever seen in Europe. In Kenya I was once stung on my thumb. Damned painful. If I'd been alone in that hut at the foot of Timfristos I think I'd have stopped for at least long enough to have collected a specimen or two, but as things were Katie was tired and she doesn't much like the sight of the creatures, so off we trudged, here, through about twelve kilometres of suburban slums."

He smiled sympathetically. "I tell my class that if they want to learn about soils they should taste them for acidity and get the feel of them under their feet."

"Soils, yes, but ferro-concrete, no. We're tackling no more roads."

"Where are you off to next?"

"According to the little we were told by the tourist board in Athens it's the Agraphiotis river with a tributary that rises under the village of Agrapha."

This came near to the truth. Shelley held that basic truth is imageless though Saint-Exupéry considered that truths as he saw them might clash without contradicting each other.

Katie reckoned it about time that we found an hotel. Benta, one of the students, said she knew the management of a comfortable one nearby and offered to take her there whilst I stayed with the tutor, who gave the impression he was solidly on our side. Katie said if she liked the place she'd book in, take a bath and change, and I could join her — but I hadn't to be too long, she added.

Speaking slowly as if he'd been turning over the ins and outs of the matter, Palinurus the Pilot, as I shall call him, repeated the word "Agraphiotis". "For the last two or three days we've been hit by some very strong easterlies," he said. "Flash floods have cut the track in several places."

"What do you suggest we do?"

"To start with, you'd be advised not to tell anyone you've been talking to me about getting through the hills. They don't encourage it around here. The Agraphiotis, I know, is the shortest route but at this time of the year when the snow is melting it's much the most difficult. Make for the Tavropos river at Megdova bridge and see what conditions are like when you get there. If the bridge hasn't been damaged, as it was last year, follow the little road to Hrisso and Agios Dimitrios. You're carrying a small tent? Good! Then you needn't rely on anyone for accommodation.

"If I were you I'd climb up to the ridge where there are few trees and not much scrub, even for goats. Nobody takes sheep up there any more, not even the Vlachs, but on the high tops there are small tracks, hundreds of them, which have been used for centuries. What's important is that something more than general directions should be clear in your mind. Watch your compass. The little village you must ask about is Marathos. It lies deep down in a valley to the north-west. You will have to climb out of it and then from the very top you will see Agrapha village."

"And beyond that?"

"I don't know," he said. "I've never been there but you'll find many people over the age of sixty in this town who were taken up into the mountains as children during the German Occupation. When they're not engaged in local feuds Greeks will go to extraordinary lengths to help each other. They say you can put your Greek in a jug, boil off a dozen barbarian strains and the essential Greekness will be left at the bottom, like salt evaporated from sea-water. Mind you, I wouldn't say as much for their flashy multi-millionaires nor the modern descendants of the old families like Tsaldaris and Venizelos who are always at each others' throats in what they call the *politikos kosmos*.

"Listen! If you really want to see the boss at the forestry school, phone his secretary at this number and ask for an appointment. If you get one, be careful what you say. He's more than somewhat devious. *Don't* say you've had a word with me." He paused. "Your wife, I see, is coming back with my friend Benta."

He promptly switched the conversation to the growth rate and peculiarities of various kinds of pines (*Pinus*) which, as he pronounced the word to rhyme with Venus, sounded mildly Rabelaisian. He rose to go. "I'll see you later," he said. "Remember! Be careful what you say at the school."

I went back with Katie.

"It's called the Elvetia," she said. "A quiet sort of family place, also used by the leading traders in town as an unofficial Chamber of Commerce. I think we've struck gold. There's half a dozen of them in there now. They couldn't be more friendly. One of them called George — can't remember his other name — is a warm-hearted person, a tailor and draper. Take your rucksack up to our room and change that filthy shirt. Come down as soon as you can, as George has got something he strongly recommends for my feet. I'll tell you about it later. There's a lot of goodwill in this place."

George Papadopoulos, a name about as common in Greece as Paddy Doyle in Dublin and Dai Jones in South Wales, offered me a coffee and, turning to his friends, merely said, "This is Mister John, Madame's husband." No formalities. A short man with spectacles and a moustache, he looked the very essence of ordinariness, but he gave us one of our two keys to Karpenissi.

"So this is your first visit here?"

"Yes, but I heard about it before we left London."

"Really! What are we famous for?"

"Marcos Botsaris," I said.

Delighted looks all round. The master tailor smiled. "His statue is in the market place. Tell me more when you come to the shop tomorrow. Madame has my card." He shook hands with us and the company filed out.

Katie looked at me. "Crafty husband," she said. "What do you know about Botsaris?"

"Quite a lot," I said. Perhaps as much as he does. "I've done my homework."

"Uncharitable thought: you only spent five minutes with him. His daughter is studying history and English. He was in Australia for fifteen years and went to night school to learn the language. The old man with him, the one with the grizzled beard, is a pharmacist, and the wife of the one with the bad scar is a hairdresser. George has given us the address of two restaurants where he says we have only to mention his name."

We ate that evening in the place next door, underground and as cool as a church crypt, and pooled what we'd been able to find out about the forestry school.

Katie's theory was that the student, Benta was very fond of and might even be the mistress of the temporary director.

"That complicates things," I suggested. "The lecturer's also very fond of Benta and I've given him my card to pass on to a secretary with a view to meeting this man. I'm going to phone tomorrow. I wonder if by 'secretary' he really meant Benta? Hope you didn't tell her I write for a living: that won't go down well with civil servants."

*　*　*

We saw George Papadopoulos at his best in the morning when, from behind metre-ruled counters backed by bolts of cloth and made-up suits he could lay his hands on shirts, chemises, fine fabrics and fents for two or three customers at the same time; a man, one had the impression, fully in charge of an environment of his own making. The picture of all-round competence was enlarged considerably that night when we, guests in a house as well organized as his work-place, saw him go down into the wine-cellar to milk an affectionate nanny goat.

By that time we felt that the events of the day were running in our favour. The soles of Katie's feet were still painful but Grizzlebeard, an apothecary of the old school, could find no evidence of sepsis and agreed with George that, under layers of lint and gauze, a light touch of pure olive oil, the best in Evritania, would do more for her abraded skin than dabbling about with antibiotics — although we might carry some as a form of insurance. He and George also agreed that cotton socks were better for her feet than the woollen ones of the type I had clung to since childhood.

The man at the school put me through to an extension number where somebody, certainly not Benta, read from what seemed a prepared statement. It said that the acting director hoped to be able to speak to the distinguished Englishman at half-past eleven the next morning. Yes pliss? Unsure about that qualification I asked if I could visit him at any time that day.

A three-second pause before the message was repeated as if on an "Ansaphone". Perhaps it was. "Thank you," I said. "Yes pliss. Yes pliss, *ne parakalo, efharisto. Yiasas,*" adding, "Cheerio," on behalf of all distinguished Englishmen.

I put the call through from a *periptero*, one of those social lighthouses on street corners for the sale of anything from newspapers, magazines and stamps down to chocolate, soft drinks, toothpaste and diarrhoea pills. To discourage their use as a public library the daily papers profusely displayed outside are hung up latitudinally, but to no avail. The locals queue up to scan them at risk of ricking their necks.

The one we used regularly was run by another adopted Chicagoan who, whenever we appeared, even on the opposite side of the street, popped his head out of the dark recess and bawled, "Hiya, folks! What's cookin'?" This together with our association with Grizzlebeard and Scarface who ran a sophisticated wine and pastry shop, and above all with George the tailor made us feel as if we'd been granted honorary citizenship. But there were hermetic undertones to this sociability. Only the affluent traders joined in with a sprinkling of lawyers and agents in a subterranean resort of their own. The group Katie introduced me to in a back room of the Elvetia would no more mix with the students and travellers in the Edelweiss, where we had met Benta and Palinurus, than they would be seen among the alcoholics at tables inside and outside two or three taverns almost next door to each other.

My regard for trees dates from childhood when I

escaped to a lair among the branches of an old lime in our garden in Leeds. Long afterwards, with my younger brother Joe, an historian with a home in the Forest of Dean, I was threatened with libel when I wrote about some of Britain's arboreal slums. As a professional critic I visited government forestry stations in several countries but never one more depressing in appearance nor unhelpful on the part of the management than that place on the road into the Greek mountains.

The acting director and his secretary had gone out for the day and nobody knew where. Could they find out who was in charge of the place? Apparently not since they shunted me into a back room until, fed up with being ignored, I walked out and looked round on my own. Next to nobody about, certainly nobody who knew English until, accidentally, I walked into the library to find Palinurus the Pilot at work on a pile of examination papers. He looked up, surprised.

"Why did you come today? He's gone down to Athens. I could have told you that."

"He invited me to be here at half-past eleven. At least the person I took to be his secretary did."

"And what did she say?"

"She didn't say anything except repeat what sounded like a dictated message. I thought she didn't know much English and didn't understand my suggestion."

"Yes, that's always useful when you're faced with an awkward question." He drummed with his fingers and then picked up the phone and spoke to someone whom from the tone of his voice I took to be a colleague.

He put the phone down and sighed. "I was going to

suggest you came round tomorrow but a friend of mine here says the old bastard has left word that he may be away tomorrow as well. I don't believe him because he sometimes lies when it would be in his own interest to tell the truth. Chronic deception is a progressive disorder. Well, my friend, I'm afraid you've been swept off. No! That's not good English. I mean brushed off. Stood up. Tell me, what did you *really* want to see him about?"

"I wanted to look at your maps. Ours are almost useless."

He lifted up both arms and then pointed to a cabinet of long narrow shelves. "But they're all here. Why on earth didn't you ask me?"

"I didn't know who you were. We've been brushed off so many times by Greek officials I thought I'd try an oblique approach, that of forestry."

"*He's* not a bloody forester, he's a small-time politician. That's our problem or, rather, the problem of the Greek forestry service. The elections are coming up. Do you suppose that even PASOK dares risk losing votes by reducing subsidies to those who scrape a living by keeping uncontrolled sheep and goats, the foresters' worst enemies? Now, what can I show you? I've got to be away in about half an hour. More politics. I'm trying to brief a man who I hope will get the top job here, a Greek who was trained at your place at Rothamsted. But what does it mean to me? By then I hope to be back in Stockholm."

The maps were 1:50,000 which I took to be two centimetres to the kilometre. They showed alleged water-courses and springs dampened or dried up long ago. They were old maps surveyed by the UK Ministry of Defence in 1972. Under the supervision of the Pilot I made copious notes and a quick breakdown of the Greek soil situation based on the work of one of his fellow countrymen. Palinurus suggested we should take a drink together that night. I said he'd already played his part as the Button-moulder. He laughed. "No," he said, "I have no casting ladle. This is the market-place of the Balkans, not Scandinavia."

Between half-past one and five o'clock Karpenissi closes up like a bed of oysters at low tide. The resting time, the Hellenic siesta. Shutters have clattered down, their owners resting on their verandas at home. Watchdogs sleep in the shade. An old tomcat with frayed ears, too tired seriously to stalk its favourite playthings, bright splotched butterflies on the pots of flowers, watched them flicker from one nectary to another. The tip of his tail still twitched. No predator is ever really asleep, and his back feet opened and closed like a parrot's claws when it's washing. His toothy jaws opened and closed in a soundless miaou.

All this I saw when, leaving Katie asleep at the Elvetia, I made my way up the street, past the apothecary's place and the hairdresser's shop to an uncompromising statue of Marcos Botsaris which smacked of official Russian portraiture in the days of Stalin.

Marcos Botsaris was a Vlach. We had learnt this from Nacu Zdru, on that day when the *Flying Tortoise* was smashed to pieces. He led the Greek Resistance forces against the Turks during one of their attacks on Missolonghi. "Allah! Allah!" they shouted as they rushed forward and planted ladders to climb on the trenches, but the Greeks' musket-shots and sabre-strokes made them fall "as thick as frogs". The town with its low defence wall finally fell to the Turks. Ibrahim Pasha, who led the victorious army, boasted that his men collected 3,000 heads and that ten barrels of salted human ears were sent to Constantinople for the Sultan's delectation.

The sequel to that story was told to me by Loula, the attractive teenage daughter of our friend, George the town tailor. She said Botsaris escaped and that when Byron arrived in Greece in 1823 he brought a letter given to him in London by Ignatius, the Orthodox bishop, with the request that it should be handed to Botsaris. Presumably it commended Byron's intelligence, his organizing abilities, his wealth and European reputation for backing the Greek struggle for independence. Unsure of the whereabout of Botsaris, Byron, then in Cephalonia, sent it by messenger to Missolonghi, adding a note about how much he yearned to meet the famous fighter. But Botsaris had left when the messenger arrived.

How he managed to trace him to Karpenissi, "that Khyber Pass of the Pindos" doesn't seem to be known but he did receive the letter and was "much flattered by the commendations of the champion of revolt". He had much on his mind. The Greeks were disunited. Botsaris had been through the grinding mill of oppression. He was born at Suli in Albania, and his father Kitzaris had been murdered by that suave, enormously rich puppet-master, Ali Pasha who had confided to a concubine with a good memory that he could double-cross the Devil.

This Botsaris knew. How best then to double-cross

a double-crosser? He joined the hugely patriotic Greek society, the Hetairia Philike. Together with other Suliots he made common cause with Ali against the Ottomans and with the instincts of a good aggressive general sensed strong support around Karpenissi. Under his leadership a mere 300 Suliots won an outstanding victory against more than ten times that number of Albanians paid with Turkish gold. But Botsaris died in the battle on 9 August 1823. Among the great ifs of history is what might have been achieved had he and Byron met earlier, when Byron was bouncing in bed with the Countess Teresa Guiccioli and Botsaris complaining about the inadequate earthworks of Missolonghi.

The pop-up man in the *periptero* took some time to tell me a mildly obscene story I'd heard years ago, before he confided that my "Swedish friend" was in a little place on the opposite side of the street. Palinurus and I had a few drinks there. "It seems he's just had a helluva row with Benta," I told Katie who, kneeling on the bedroom floor, was examining the seams and buttons of our jackets and pants with the zealotry of an old-clothes dealer. We intended to pull out early the next day.

"We'd been talking about all sorts of matters from Botsaris to wolves and bears before I happened to ask, perhaps incautiously, how Benta was. He didn't answer for a moment or two and then said he'd never in his life been closer to smacking a woman's face, hard. Apparently about an hour after I'd left the forestry school the ambitious bastard, as he called him, came back in one of their Land Rovers. Benta got out first. Far from going down to Athens they'd been out for an afternoon spin to where, with any luck, we'll be tomorrow — Megdova bridge over the river Tavropos which, incidentally he thinks has been poisoned."

"And then what?"

"He first asked Benta why she hadn't been about her work and then, when she waffled, whether she thought being screwed by the boss might advance her diploma for forestry. I'm compressing this, of course but he was rather excited. You can imagine the confrontation."

"Has Palinurus spoken to the boss?"

"Yes, he told him he thought it unwise to ignore an appointment with a man who might have got him a job in England! Perhaps, unintentionally, I've bust up a beautiful romance, but if so Palinurus doesn't hold it against me. He's convinced Benta's a go-getter who could go a long way with a man in the same league."

"What's this about bears and wolves?"

"Bears, to quote him, are 'very rare except in bad weather on the Albanian border'. He heard there used to be one near Arvanitovlach, now Kedrona — I've got the details on the recorder. It's a village in Macedonia where Nacu Zdru comes from. The old creature turned up regularly in winter and the villagers loved it. They left their garbage outside at night. Then some Austrian arrived with a high-speed rifle and shot it. I wonder if it could be our friend on the train, the man who got on in Venice? Palinurus says he was lucky they didn't shoot him. He got out quick.

"He doesn't think wolves are particularly rare but natives — who get a bounty for knocking them off — exaggerate their numbers. He thinks it should be paid

255

only if they can produce the whole corpse. He says if we ever get into a claimant's territory we should try to examine so-called wolf-kills to see if the bodies are badly torn or were born dead. Wolves kill lambs by seizing the belly flesh or the hams; dogs that go wild grab the ears. And wolf and dog tracks are quite different. Wolves' hind legs normally swing in the same line as their forefeet: as he puts it, 'They single foot like foxes do.' But he doesn't know anyone else in his Department who cares a damn about them apart from the opportunity they afford for a few days out in the mountains."

The Place Without a Name

To master what mileage we could before the sky became a burning-glass we turned our backs on Karpenissi at cock crow. On a gritty road I switched to loose thoughts on what the cocks were crowing about. If the theory is valid that intelligence among animals, including birds and man, can be correlated with brain size compared with body weight, the so-called galliform birds which include turkeys, pheasants and domestic poultry are a nut-brained lot but likeable in eccentric manners and edibility.

We've often said, Katie and I, that if ever we get that place in the Howardian hills we'll have a dog or two and a flock of free-ranging fowls, preferably bantams, but they must be persuaded to spend the early hours out of earshot of our bedroom.

At some 4,000 feet that morning the cries of the Karpenissi flocks became fainter, but from isolated holdings around us the soloists seemed to be in intermittent touch with rivals far away.

One outstanding Caruso among cockerels, lording it about among his drab harem on a mound of garbage, selected a vantage point, shook his blood-red comb and golden hackles and, after some throat-clearing, vented a slightly cracked top C. Then, the effort over, he appeared to be listening. Back came a call and then another. The repetitions were so marked in their phrasing that they might have been echoes. But were they? We heard several more. Could it be that the dialects of cockdom were being thrown across the length and breadth of Evritania? Perhaps even further to where there are different accents in Phokis and Thessaly?

I was reminded that many years ago my friend, the late Alan Civil that superb horn-player, told me that he and his family, also professional players, were on holiday in Switzerland where, on some platform, a few native tourist-trappers got up in feathered hats and lederhosen were demonstrating their virtuosity with one of those immense alpenhorns used originally, it is said, to summon cattle for feeding. They offered a small prize to anyone who could produce a coherent sound on the instrument. Its echo, they said, could be heard from many miles away.

From the curiously regular time-intervals and his knowledge of acoustics, Alan felt reasonably certain they were in league with players in a distant valley on a strictly timed basis. Seconds before the crucial blow he managed to delay the performance on a technicality, to the point where the echo was heard first. To the delight of a small crowd, Alan's daughter, their youngest, played the elements of a popular tune in harmonics which is all these musical dinosaurs are capable of.

Things seemed to be going far too well for complacency. The corner we cut off diagonally gained us an unexpected bonus in terms of altitude. To the tune of "Old Macdonald had a Farm" we versified extempore farewells to the peaks and ski slopes of old Timfristos which, seen far away to the east, looked contemptible. We advanced, cautiously, *allentamento*. Rough country ahead from which no cocks crew.

Shortly before midday we were within a few hundred yards of two shacks surrounded by pubic-hair-like bushes on the crest of an almost wholly bare mound. Not a tree in sight. A situation to be dealt with, *presto*. We were hot, tired and thirsty. The first shack stood under a palisade of scaffolding, the hallmark of a Greek lodging-house on the way up. An old man whom we took to be a roadsweeper was still sweeping up the same patch he had been when we first saw him ten minutes earlier. There seemed to be no reason for this: the patch appeared no different from what we'd been walking on since we'd trudged out of the aromatic conifers. Neither gruff nor affable, this ill-dressed fellow would have looked better with a shave the previous week. Ritual greetings were reciprocated. Then my standard follow-up in hilly country: rarely, I said, mendaciously, had I seen a finer view. This pleased him hugely. He nodded, vigorously. But where, I asked, smacking my lips, could we get a drop of water?

He looked surprised, and pointed authoritatively at the shack almost next door which could be charitably described as a tavern of sorts. Unqualified thanks on our side. We waved farewells and left him to his rhythmic brushwork. The door was locked. After repeated bangs a wholesome-looking young girl appeared with a very small suckling noisily engaged in finishing its lunch.

Food? Yes but *ligos*, only a little until her good cousin

arrived. As for drink, they had plenty. She waved towards four or five bottles and the refrigerator.

A flashy car pulled up outside. The driver, as vulgarly dressed as the flags and stickers on his vehicle, immediately began to shout at the nondescript sweeper-up who shouted back and shook his brush in mock-aggression. They were obviously acquainted, but on what terms? Difficult to tell among argumentative Greeks. The driver strode in laughing, pausing only to shout something over his shoulder.

We learnt that all three were related. The newcomer held the honoured rank of godfather (*koumbaros*) to the baby which he squeezed, clumsily, until it cried. No matter: it would be rich one day he told us, twice within five minutes. He owned property locally and abroad. He had recently returned from South Africa where he paid niggers to work for him for gardammed next to nothing. Different from his five years in Arkansas where they had gotten uppity. Did we know Hollywood? Great place. His boasted close association with Tom Mix and Marilyn Monroe made it clear that we were dealing with a highly imaginative traveller.

Before the sweeper-up, his cousin, joined us and he modified his extravagances, we learnt "that the poor bastard's chief fault was that he'd always worked for someone else". That way he wouldn't get nowhere. Now he was working for *him*, and he smacked his chest. He owned the house in embryo, the bar and another one in Athens.

"But what's he sweeping up for?" I asked.

"Waiting for a load of sand and lime. He's been waiting

for days. He's got a concrete-mixer at the back. All he's done is oil it. That's what I'm here for, just to get him off his ass. Some guys are coming up here tomorrow and I want two floors on that joint by the fall."

We ate there. We ought to have stayed there for at least another hour or two but in trying to bang the table he shared with the compulsive sweeper-up, the friend of Tom Mix nearly fell over. He had already drunk too much. We walked out into the ferocious heat.

A bad afternoon, that. The road just beyond the tavern dipped sharply, not in a series of loops but in one downward plunge which we could follow with our eyes until it disappeared into the haze. We carried, we thought, all we required: salt tablets and a litre of water that sploshed about in my pack with an annoying *ploonk ploonk plop* in time with our walking. With Katie in front to set the pace we trudged along, some twenty-five yards apart.

Since there was nothing of interest to look at — scrub vegetation with next to no bird life — I couldn't take my mind off that diabolical heat. I tried to recall what I had done in the deserts of North Kenya when even my almost nude native Turkana were obliged to wear plaited crowns and epaulettes of palm leaves. As for diversion, there came back the memory of when, for want of something better to do, I had tried to work out the time of the day from the length of my shadow but had become irritated because I couldn't cope with simple geometry.

At nine o'clock in the morning my shadow was almost exactly equal to my own height. At ten o'clock it was a little longer than half my height, and at precisely midday — within two degrees of the equator — I had no visible shadow unless I stood with my legs apart or jumped into the air. Mezek, my young cook and personal servant who had previously been employed there by Wilfred Thesiger, watched these antics with ill-concealed amusement. Why had I felt in better trim then than now? Simple answer: I was younger, fitter and carrying only a 30.06 on a sling.

We trudged on: *ploonk ploonk plop.*

We were suffering from hyperthermia, which is basically the release of nitrogen into the blood tissues. I had learnt this before I left for Lake Rudolf from Peter Preston, fellow clubman and former head of a RN research establishment at Portsmouth. He had been in charge of affairs in Malta when word came through that a team of Japs had bought an oil-diving concession in deep water off the coast of Libya. Wanted immediately were gear and instructions about how to treat the "bends", their local consul said. A caisson and cylinders of compressed air were shipped off at once. They were handled incompetently.

When word came through, weeks later, that two men had died in the chamber, the British team in Malta assumed that the divers had been treated too late. At news of yet another death soon afterwards, an expert flew to Bizerta. His radio report was notably brief, Navy-style. He glanced at the blood-red corpse. He felt the cylinders. They were hot. They had been left uncovered in the sun. The victims had been boiled to death.

This incident is on medical record. Others are of

questionable verity. When Charles Sturt, the British explorer took one of the first parties of white men into a desert of South Australia in the summer of 1845, he reported it so hot that the screws on their wooden boxes fell out, their hair stopped growing, and one full but badly stoppered barrel of water, hauled on a cart by Aborigines, was reduced to a few pints in twelve hours. Except for one incident in yet another filthy hut we had nothing to match this, but we felt downright uncomfortable and occasionally dizzy.

The going was downhill. No shade from either rocks or trees. No signposts. Because we didn't know the distance to the next hamlet we rationed our water. The friend of Tom Mix had told us that the river was about ten kilometres away, a gross understatement. We had already been on our feet for several hours.

From a typically curt statement by the late Humphrey Bogart ("You'll fry") when he predicted that a girlfriend of his would wind up on the hot seat for murder, we still refer to that hovel as "Bogy's place".

About the size and condition of an abandoned bus shelter, the floor fouled with droppings from goats, shepherds and recent travellers. With an armful of twigs still called broom we swept up enough space to put down our rucksacks, and leaned up against them. Katie lit the butane stove to make tea with the rest of our water whilst I fumbled in an outside pocket of my pack into which I'd incautiously dropped two pens. My fingers came out bright blue. The biros had blown their balls out.

* * *

Salvation ahead. A mile or two below that sordid shelter we saw a rich pasture refreshed by a stream that wove in and out of the shade of trees and a cliff of soft grey dolorite. Small cataracts talked in a variety of tongues. An ideal caravanserai, we thought. *Carpe diem*. Should we call it a day? Had there been a single tin or packet in our meagre stores which we didn't dislike deeply we should have stopped there. Outcome: compromise. Katie bathed whilst I explored the stream. An hour later we ambled down through avenues of acacias, planes, and pink-flowered *Cercis* to Megdova bridge which spans the river Tavropos.

A friendly place. A lotus land. We were neither ignored nor interrogated. Women nodded and smiled. Their menfolk outside taverns stroked their worry beads. We settled for a camp-site that couldn't be seen from the road; a comfortable corner on a carpet of pine needles in the shadow of a ruined chapel.

The evening was marked by two incidents, one of them heart-touching in its simplicity and the other downright macabre. An old man who looked as though he were merely out for his evening stroll among the riverside willows walked towards us. In one hand he grasped a tall stick with a carved head of the kind used by shepherds, and in the other two long-stemmed roses. We greeted him and he replied cordially. He walked round our zipped-open tent with mild curiosity. He didn't peer into anything. He paused for a moment before handing us each a rose, the first, almost ceremonially, for Katie.

She talked to him for a few moments — where did the road lead to? How far was the next village? Apart from his sociability it seemed clear that he'd come to tell us that the river water wasn't drinkable. He pointed towards it, moistened his lips and shook his head. We showed him our container, filled at the village tap. "May your night be a good one," he said, and walked back as sedately as he arrived.

Our first sight of the Tavropos had been from the bridge, a metal one surely modernized from a military construction, which forced the water into the narrows where it ran fast and deep flecked by streaks of yellowish foam, the detritus of the recent floods. We walked back along it and struck upstream where, as we neared our camp-site, we heard the clamour of sea-birds as on an urban garbage dump or in the wake of a harbour-bound fishing boat. That evening I made for where the sound seemed to be coming from.

A fearful sight. During the spring floods the Tavropos had carved out a basin about a hundred yards in diameter, marked by bone-white islands and substantial holdings of more trees and scrub. Among them dribbled streamlets which coalesced in deeper channels lower down.

At my appearance a vortex of scavenging birds took to the air screaming and croaking — crows, gulls, fork-tailed kites, ospreys and a few buzzards, some of them carrying the whole bodies of fish. The islets were tenanted by rats and other animals impossible to identify in the fading light, possibly catfish which had come ashore for the stranded spoil.

If anybody knew what had really happened to the river they weren't prepared to say much in the adjacent hamlet of Parkio, where in the tavern restaurant we ate that night.

Katie left early with a friendly local woman, leaving me to gossip with a bus driver who spoke English. No, he wasn't a local, he said. His mate would pick him up there in the morning. Unable to tell him anything about the fate of Spurs and the Arsenal, I did rather better on the amenities of Coventry where his youngest brother drove a truck. I asked him bluntly what had happened to the river.

"Poison," he said, cryptically. "A lot of it."

"Pesticides?"

As he didn't understand the word I whirled my finger around and buzzed like a helicopter. He knew what I was getting at.

No, it wasn't that. The police had been talking to a man in a village not far away.

"What was the poison?" I asked. He shook his head.

Did the local people know?

If so, he said, quietly, they wouldn't say anything.

The full moon had about it the colour of a corpse. The jagged silhouette of the chapel looked sinister, but before we turned in I noticed that we were almost surrounded by an old ditch in which grew those handsome plants of our native hedgerows, the mulleins, with their woolly foliage and butter-yellow flowers which "sheweth like to a wax candle or taper cunningly wrought".* In both Britain and abroad the folk names of these plants range from Our Virgin's Candle to Snakebane. "If a man beareth with him just one twig of the powerful wort he will

*Henry Lyte.

266

not be strucke with any awe of wilde beaste or the horned one." Hermes is reputed to have given mullein to Odysseus before he encountered Circe, and after that he "dreaded none of her evil works".

During the night, turning uneasily at the shriek of a bird, I discovered that the mullein, also known as Velvet Dock, wasn't proof against marauding ants from the pine needles under our sleeping-bags, which we were using as a mattress.

When the first light made the downy mulleins glow like incandescent fire we were ready for the road, but abandoned it for a serpentine track which we found ran alongside the river where:

> . . . the very deep did rot, O Christ
> That ever this should be!
> Yea, slimy things did crawl . . .*

Upon that slimy lea. We never discovered how or why the river had been poisoned.

We knew that a famous stream close to our moorland cottage had been virtually sterilized when a local farmer flushed the remains of half a gallon of DDT into his lavatory. Eels in their thousands were seen trying to climb out of the water.

The new village of Viniani is indistinguishable from any other recently built out of concrete blocks, except for a sadly impressive civil war memorial and a locked-up *periptero*, the paper shop which must have been sheer hell

---

*"The Rime of the Ancient Mariner", S. T. Coleridge.

between ten in the morning and five in the evening.

Some jolly, well-dressed schoolchildren were waiting for the bus. They tried out their English homework on us. We said we loved them all, and waved as they boarded. We trudged on towards Agrapha, uphill nearly the whole way.

That grim monument in the square at Viniani, like others, scores of them throughout the length of the country, is a testament to the Greeks' predilection for slaughtering each other. The repetitions of surnames in groups on those memorials showed that whole families — particularly the youngsters — must have been wiped out within a bracket of two or three years. It's possible that the slaughter itself may not have been quite so dreadful as the wholesale and nationwide distortion of values for which such wars are directly responsible. I am borrowing freely from *The Flight of Ikaros* by the late Kevin Andrews* who, as a much travelled archaeologist, fell in love with the country and became a naturalized Greek citizen.

He was there ostensibly to study medieval fortresses but his life changed when he went walkabout and became the godfather of the young, the charming and violent Andoni Kostandi from the village of Agrapha, who had forgotten how many people he had killed and when bored and ill in hospital, as he so often was, admitted to his *koumbaros* that he yearned to go out and kill someone else. This is how the author described him to a fisherman he met in Kalamata:

*Penguin Travel Library, 1984.

As we sat over our coffee I said, "One thing I have learned on my travels recently is that very few people have any inner life at all. I am thinking of a friend of mine — the most completely likeable person I have ever met. As I know him, he's good through and through. Apart from terrific courage, he's the best husband and the kindest father: a person who hates to cause embarrassment or unhappiness or even disappointment to anyone he's fond of, yet he has slaughtered so many people that he's lost count of the number. I even hesitate to say how many. Anyhow the number doesn't matter. And he's not even anxious."

"How do you know?"

"Because he's proud of it!"

"How do you know?"

"Because he has no other standard."

"He won't always be proud of it."

"And how do you know?" I asked.

"Because you can't always stay with the outer forms of things — things like honour, power, revenge. Some day he'll come to a crossroad, a moment of crisis, of judgement. Everyone meets it sooner or later. And then he won't be able to escape himself. That's when his life may begin."

At Amstel time in yet another village without a name we leaned back and admired the view, which might have been Bournemouth before Branksome Chine was doomed to popularity. The mountains were out of sight. Before we tackled them we made a number of resolutions. First, no more mad-dog stuff under the midday sun unless trees were as plentiful as in that nicely disordered grove of Oriental spruce. This giant is not as exotic as its name sounds. An admirable tree, a native of the Caucasian mountains, its strength lies in its neatness. It has short needles that sit tidily on its twigs, a model of arboreal grooming. Had we that manor house on the Howardian Hills and the means to keep it up, we decided we'd plant *P. orientalis* around the back of the heather garden.

We also agreed that it was downright stupidity to try and walk for more than two hours, say six miles given reasonably easy going, without at least half a litre of water to spare. Last resolution: we needed at least one good meal each day. No more trying to sweat things out from dawn to dusk on tea and tinned stuff. Dehydration and rubbery squid had reduced our bowel movements to much straining for meagre reward. We paid and left.

By contrast with the barren country we had seen in the past few days, our upland trail now led us through diversified landscape. Some of the abandoned terraces of vines and other fruit trees were coming back to life. This puzzled us. Before we left Karpenissi, Palinurus had told me that Greece had lost more than ninety per cent of her original soil. He had learned this, he said, from Karl Fries, his father's tutor at Nordiska Museet and Skansen in Stockholm. Fries had worked out erosion rates from the richest soils of other Balkan countries, which have always been less densely populated than Greece and then extrapolated backwards.

"How far back?"

"To prehistoric times. In the *Critias*, which was written about 2,500 years ago, Plato deplored the fate of Arcadia.

The process was well under way even in those days. He said it was sad to see the old soil which had broken away from the high lands, sliding away ceaselessly and disappearing into the dark sea. By comparison with what used to be there, Plato said 'They were looking at the skeleton of a sick man. Their soft fertile earth had wasted away.'"

To judge from the height of the trees, about eighty feet, and their close-knit uniformity, the hallmark of a man-made plantation, some foresters who perhaps fought under the flag of Venizelos, the man who made Crete a part of greater Greece, had planted that most adaptable of the great family of conifers, the Macedonian pine, whose dark, well-furnished spires shaded where we walked that afternoon. This Balkan tree is supremely adaptable. Given a little encouragement it can grow in almost any soil, including those with a touch of lime.

Up we went, contouring, not worrying over much where we were heading for as long as it was a few points west by north. The Macedonian pine was interrupted by a carbonized waste of timber laid low by fire. "Impossible to control," Palinurus had said, "until mankind can control lightning." Then a glade. A pocket of Arcadia had come back to life. Bright yellow broom, *Genista*, "young Harry's nosegay", with some umbelliferous plant like cow parsley at its feet and thyme, too, inching up, anxious for a look at the burning sun.

Butterflies were in love with the place. Blues, Clouded yellows and among them the Tiger swallowtail, most beautiful of the European race flickered over the ground. "Here", said Katie with the determination of a woman

271

who'd found a tea-room during a wearisome shopping day, "we are going to stop."

With probing tongues like watchsprings, butterflies are delicate feeders. Some groups, however, have an indelicate regard — by human standards — for urea, excrement and putrescent carrion, which is used by collectors to tempt the Purple Emperor down from the tops of trees in old forests. Putting to work a trick picked up from a game warden in the tropics, I took off my sweaty shirt and waved it about gently. Mild response.

A little encouraged, I rubbed my hands under my armpits and held them up as if in an invocation. To my huge delight and Katie's surprise a swallowtail whirled up into the air, sweeping in wild curves, soaring in splendid circles until, gliding with extended wings, it settled on my slightly moist fingers. Of such are the simple pleasures of itinerant naturalists.

That warden had told me how one morning his headman came to tell him that a young girl had been found dead in a nearby forest glade. She had been raped and strangled. She lay on her back with one arm behind her head. Her posture, the warden said, was so peaceful that for a moment he thought she had fallen asleep. What surprised him most was the sight of her eyes, for below the lids two large blue butterflies had settled and were slowly opening and closing their wings.

Time we were off. In that fine profusion of forestry the trail led us up to a platform some five or six feet wide near the upper limits of the conifers. There we ambled along with neither prevention nor peril, except a five-hundred-foot drop on the sinister side.

Hours passed. The sun sets precociously in high places. The walking rhythm established earlier had became almost monotonic, and we felt as if we were on a comfortable up-going elevator on which the scenery on one side, the right, seemed to be forever higher and higher. Glimpses of bleak hills through the thinning trees afforded no comfort and there was no sound of water. By seven o'clock or it could have been eight, we were in need of somewhere to put at least our mattress down. But the trail was insistent, like a single rail-track. There was nowhere else to go.

It began to grow dark. I left Katie in a stony embayment and scuttled ahead. Two short blasts on my whistle meant that at least I'd found a refuge of sorts.

Around a sharp bend the trail narrowed as it swung round a sheer drop of some hundreds of feet. Nothing for it but to scramble up the bank above. I took off my rucksack. Hard going on what on Dartmoor is called clitter, that is banks of loose shale. Pausing for breath I looked around. The whole defile to the left was spanned by four power-lines, supported on our side by an immense pylon standing four-square on a grassy platform about a hundred yards ahead. I made for it. Satisfactory, I thought; that is, if I could rejoin the track below without much effort and together we could both scramble up. I whistled, she answered, and we spent the night there, comfortably.

Not long before dawn I awoke to the distant sound of

a melodic howl. In degrees of probability a dog on the loose, I reckoned, or a jackal or, less likely, that eerie but most glorious of mammalian calls of the wild, the rising and falling glissandos of a wolf. Katie stirred and we both leaned forward listening.

Minutes passed. Another call, further away by far and from a different quarter. I decided we should try to take a compass fix on where the sound seemed to be coming from, but we heard no more for a time, and drifted back to sleep.

During that trip to Uranium City* on the border of North Saskatchewan I had heard a great deal about wolves from trappers who hated their guts. They tore the precious ermine, mink and silver fox out of their claw traps, but the men admitted that for their sledge-teams there couldn't be better leaders than a cross between a husky bitch and a wolf.

I had seen wolves from the air when flying over mile-long herds of caribou migrating north towards the snow line to escape the skeeters and No-see-ums. Those wolves, though supreme predators, ran alongside the herds in twos and threes like Cossacks shadowing Napoleon's retreating army. Without the wolves to keep them on the move and tightly packed, the caribou — relatively brainless ungulates — tend to "yard", as the Scottish call that movement among Red deer: they stop and moon about where the living is easy. In the case of the caribou dependent on a moss, technically a lichen,

*See pages 141–2.

they will stop on their return trip in the fall until the snow closes round them and they are done for.

I decided to make recordings of wolf calls, and asked a trapper how to get close enough to a pack without a parabolic reflector around the microphone. Easy, said that fruity-voiced Québecois; come with us next week when we peg out our husky bitches on heat. Their erotic cries will bring them eager lovers from many miles around. It came out that way. A spectacular performance.

The scene: a clearing among Jack pine scrub above Lake Athabasca. The time: near midnight with the sky ablaze with the shimmering blue, green and purple light of the aurora borealis. Everything we touched produced a shower of sparks in that log cabin. I worried about the tubes, the thermionic valves in that heavy recorder. I turned it on for a test run. The playback sounded as if I were speaking within earshot of the Niagara Falls. We insulated the thing in a nest of blankets. Reception? Tolerable.

Five or six huskies were staked out at intervals of about fifty yards. Even before the pegs were hammered down they announced their sexual condition by copious urination and heart-throbbing calls.

In complete silence, like a commando operation or a spoonful of mercury splashed on corrugated cardboard, the wolves slipped through the trees, a pack of maybe a dozen animals.

They assembled around their leader, the king dog. He tiptoed forward toward the nearest excited bitch, but stopped on his haunches to announce his seigneurial rights with a howl that began slowly and rose and fell within an octave. Apart from much vigorous tail-wagging the pack was quiet and still.

As far as I can recall the scene — I carried both a stopwatch and field glasses in addition to a notebook and tape-recorder — he covered that bitch in two minutes sixteen seconds. This done, he rolled aside, licked himself, stood up and howled again, this time more softly and in a different key.

At this, what must have been one of the best lupine choral societies around Lake Athabasca responded with a group howl before, with remarkable orderliness, they set about pleasuring their chosen partners. Those low in the pecking order hung about obediently, as if in an exclusive bordello.

That concerto between the king dog and his pack became the overture and leitmotif of a series of radio programmes called "Men of the North" for what was then the BBC Light Programme, the popular rival to the austerities of the Third.

Some years later Dilys Breese, doyenne of the Corporation's Natural History Unit, phoned to ask if I would care to come down to Bristol and comment "live" on the language of wolves, accompanied by somebody who, as she put it, politely, "understood music". I knew the best man in the business, that maestro of the French horn Alan Civil. We went down to Bristol together and not knowing what he was in for he stole the show.

Before we arrived BBC technicians had edited representative recordings accompanied by spectrographs, that is electronic charts in terms of pitch, frequency and time in split seconds.

The programme opened with that superb howl by the king dog; the producer described briefly what it was all about, handed one of the sonograms to Alan and asked if it meant anything to him. Not knowing that it was upside-down, he scanned it and shook his head, saying he was not surprised as he'd played first performances by Birtwistle and Stockhausen. Could he hear some more?

There were times when I thought that Dilys, a pro to her fingertips, looked a bit anxious when the unscripted half an hour bore some resemblance to the "Goon Show". We had agreed, she and I, that I shouldn't dwell over-much on the biometrics of canine copulation. Alan only mentioned the word "mounting" twice, and sang the rest.

He pointed out that the howls of the king dog, the virtuoso, contained "at least five harmonics either a little above or a little below an octave". He thought it interesting that although most if not all the wolves started *pianissimo*, only the pack leader had the ability to rise to a *messa di voce*, apparently on one breath, before sliding down a bit incoherently to where he had started "within the tonic". This threw us completely.

He explained that by *messa* he didn't mean a "sung mass" nor even a *mezza*, a half-voice; the virtuoso could hold or, as Alan put it, "place" his voice in a *crescendo e diminuendo* on one long sustained note, something popular in the palmy days of Italian *bel canto* in the eighteenth century. Could that be where the wolves had originally picked it up?

Very unlikely, I thought, but a darned sight more interesting and, I suspect, intellectually more productive than dreary biochemical analyses of canine urine on wolves' well known pissing-points at the foot of trees. To illustrate his point Alan asked for the soloist's best piece to be replayed at half speed, where he analysed the modes, quietly, and then added his own voice harmonically, so that we were given an impression of how the king dog carried — as it were — half a dozen calling-cards which had to be acknowledged by his underdogs. Trappers around Athabasca had assured me that wolves very rarely fight amongst themselves. Dominance has been ritualized by their musical howls.

A blood-red dawn. Katie had poured the tea out. I had begun to shake the dew off the outer fly when a noise that resembled someone tearing a sheet of old calico ended in a double explosion as if both barrels of a shotgun had been fired almost simultaneously. Situated as we were at the foot of the highest lightning conductor in the Pindos, we had to get out quick. On the scree down to the track we again heard that howl which rose and fell within an octave. It came from somewhere on the floor of the valley invisible to us. The howls were repeated, twice. Perhaps the animals were as concerned about the gathering storm as we were.

No rain at first, but the wind rose and among a forest of conifers it had as many voices as the sea. Gusts of increasing violence carried greyish-white dust. It partly obscured the sun which appeared and disappeared like a lemon behind a tumultuous wrack of clouds. The dust was loess, a geologist's term for sun-dried earth and sand which may have been carried for many hundreds of miles. Unlike the case of the *meltemi*, this is not the ground-up floor of the Balkans. The chances are high that, originally, it blew down from central Asia.

On the track to Marathos, the last habitation before the village of Agrapha, we were bustled, buffeted and then towards midday drenched to the skin by rain that came at us in stair-rods.

Looking back on the affair I think we rather enjoyed our sense of invincibility. No matter that we were soaked through and through; our much battered rucksacks, we knew, were porous but all spare clothing, our maps, passports, cash, credit cards and the like were doubly insulated in plastic bags within the cocoon of the tent.

Emotions are curiously inexplicable affairs. At the very height of that storm, when we were mostly preoccupied with keeping below the tree-line, Katie told me, afterwards, that she had been thinking about one particular tea-estate with a lot of exposed rock, at Menikdiwela in Ceylon, when with two small youngsters in the nursery she became aware that during a violent display of lightning, blue flashes were coming from the power-points.

At the siege of Sebastopol, Tolstoy jumped out of the trenches and ran towards the bastion under heavy fire from the enemy. He was horribly afraid of rats and had just seen one.

My own thoughts that day went back to the Congo, the Mother of Rivers where in an antiquated stern-wheeler we were carrying two precious pairs of okapi between Bumba and Stanleyville, now Kisangani. On the first day out we ran into an apocalyptic storm. For twenty hours we were showered with lightning that wiped out the difference between dusk and dawn. It could have been a coronation fireworks display.

On the bridge the handsome Kabala tribesman held the mahogany wheel between his fingers and thumbs. In his eyes, in the delicacy of his touch one could see what Joseph Conrad so admired. On either side a fellow tribesman operated searchlights, trying to pick up reflectors on islands in that continental drain which, thereabouts, is some ten miles wide. Showers of lightning reduced huge forest trees to blood-red pillars of charcoal.

The ship, the *Lieutenant Lippens*, was shoving two barges ahead. The storm had blown the generator in the galley but somehow they had managed to get the refrigerators going with auxiliary gear. Captain Jean-Paul Marin occupied a cabin just aft of the bridge, whilst five of us, myself and a Methodist missionary with his unhappy-looking wife and two howling children, shared the rest of the space on the top deck. About 800 blacks swarmed in the bowels of the boat. They sang, they drank and kicked up a hell of a cheerful noise.

Jean-Paul had more than his share of worries. He had run headlong into a bank of problems, personal and professional. By far the worst was that someone in the Company had told his wife 'way back in Brussels that he shared his cabin on the *Lippens* with a beautiful black bird, a young Kabala girl with breasts like chocolate ice-cream cones. This I knew, since she had come aboard the previous day, her name long forgotten but unquestionably an eyeful.

Mme Marin had gone to OTRACO,* Jean-Paul's employers, and demanded to be flown to the Congo to sort things out. He had heard this by radio but was partly excommunicated by chronic static. He couldn't reply and had a pretty shrewd idea she would be waiting for him at Stanleyville. He was already a day and a half late on course. We had run into enormous banks of water weed, *Eichornia*, the so-called Devil's lilac, some of it two or three hundred yards wide. This meant reduction to half speed, sometimes running astern, and churning up the river into soapy froth before the helmsman managed to forge ahead through narrow weed-free channels.

That night I quit our antiquated ship at Yangambi in the company of the Captain's consort; me for a three-day journey by Land Rover to the foot of the Ruwenzori, the Mountains of the Moon and she, presumably, back to her father. At moon-rise, next to no sound on the great river except for the "talking" two-toned drums of the Lokeli tribesmen, the Congolese equivalent of the Morse code. For me, at least, the storm was over. I never discovered what happened to Jean-Paul.

Seen through the weeping trees a small mosaic of roofs appeared and disappeared far below us, like a glimpse of Lilliput. We heard a roaring noise as of escaping steam from a ruptured boiler. It came from an invisible cascade about half a mile away. Later we saw where quicksilver

Office d'Exploitation des Transports Coloniaux, Voies Fluviales.

streamlets poured over a cliff to float down behind the topmost screen of conifers.

Marathos has been rebuilt out of a huddle of ancient, perhaps seventeenth-century houses on the scree of a landslide. The inhabitants, about five or six families, are no more deprived of water than a community on an offshoot of the Niagara Falls but, unlike fertile and equally well watered Pira where we saw the bullet-ridden car, the place looked as if it were falling apart, dependent only on small crops of vegetables and herds of goats.

I knocked on the open door of the first ramshackle house we came to. Inside a middle-aged man with a long sad face like a horse sat at a table taking an ancient alarm clock, an Ingersoll, to pieces with the aid of a tin-opener and a small screwdriver. Without a shred of curiosity he looked up, said *"Yass"* in a faraway voice and went on with his tinkering. Somewhat put off by almost total disregard, I asked if there was a tavern in the village. He sighed and pointed down the cobbled passage which served as a main street, and we heard the sound of uproarious laughter.

Instant hospitality. A small card school broke up. Chairs were pushed towards us. Impossible at first to guess who the landlord was. The company helped themselves and tossed the reckoning on the top of a barrel. The usual questions: where had we left our car? Did we want a drink, food? The feeling of apprehension which had beset us since we caught our first glimpse of the village flooded away in the house of "Kaiser" Kapodistrio, native of Aetolia, the ancient region north of where Byron died. A good, a very whiskery fellow with handlebar moustaches and huge sidechops. In addition to some English and German he spoke his native Greek slowly for our benefit.

Within half an hour we learnt that Kaiser ran not only the pub-cum-grocery store but was regarded as the headman of that cheerful little hamlet. He and his plump wife looked after us from the moment we walked in.

After lingering over the first meal we had eaten since we left the electric pylon in a hurry, I asked if they could put us up. At this he shrugged his shoulders, pulled a wry face and pointed upstairs. It came through in polyglot accompanied by gestures of mock discomfort that his father and mother-in-law had arrived and they had only two *schlafzimmer*.

Was there no other place?

He nodded slowly. "*Ja, ja. Jawohl*, a good man, a kind man but strange, *wunderlich*." He pointed up the narrow passage to the first house we'd called at, the man with a passion for pulling mechanical things to bits. He called to his plump wife who took us back to the house of Nico Notopolos, the melancholic fellow who seemed to live in a world of his own making. He floated ghost-like from room to room, showing us his curious treasures.

Above the ruins of the alarm clock on his work bench stood the tarnished components of a brass astrolabe, an instrument for measuring the altitude of stars. In one piece or even in bits it must have been worth a lot. On the walls of our bedroom were shelves of dusty, ancient, fretworked radio sets, Murphy, Mullard, Ferranti, Pye, Ekco, Cossor and others we couldn't make out. Nico bounced on our bed. *Kalos, kalos*, a very good bed, yes? As for the radio sets, especially the Pye with its price-tag (19 guineas) still stuck on to the veneered walnut, we told him, truthfully, we had never seen a finer collection.

As we left for the tavern at dusk he stood in the open doorway, shading his eyes against the sun, looking up at the immense defile. Without turning round he said: "Look! There she is. My wife." Through glasses we saw a woman driving a herd of goats down a track steeper than anything we had encountered that morning. She never faltered. She walked slowly but she walked straight down, shouting at the laggards. The morning's rain had given way to a glowing evening.

In the tavern Marcos, a customer who had just driven up with supplies from Karpenissi, said in almost word-perfect English: "A strange one, that; he lives too much inside his head and that's bad for anyone." He took another pull at a hand-rolled cigarette made from raw local tobacco, spat on the floor and repeated in Greek his opinion of the man who took things to pieces. The company nodded. They had heard it all before.

"But he's got a wife," I said. "We saw her coming down the track about half an hour ago. Doesn't she look after him?"

"Yes, but the question is who looks after her?"

I couldn't understand what Kaiser said which brought a laugh all round and I caught a glance from Katie that meant enough is enough.

We ate and drank there, laughed at bits of the conversation translated by Marcos, and we managed to get a quarter of an hour with him alone before going back to the bedroom of fifteen radio sets.

Though he had met Nico regularly for several years, seen his strange objects and had bought one of his bone flutes made from an eagle's wing, he said he didn't know what made him tick. Who could tell what went on in other people's minds? "The sad one", as he called him, believed in witches, demons and the spirits of the woods and the streams, particularly one we'd met before called the *daouti* who, from the stories about how this creature terrifies the shepherds and their flocks, I took to be Pan.

"Do you believe in these things?"

He half smiled and shrugged his shoulders. "*Mystika pragmata, kala pragmata?*" Secret things, perhaps good things: who knew?

"What does the village think about Nico?"

He leaned forward confidentially. "They are sorry for him, he was here before the *makaronades*, those Italian bastards. As most of the villagers are from outside and don't really know what went on in the old days, I think most of them respect him — at least they did before he married that goddamned Vlach."

"Do you really think she is one?"

"Course I do. Who else could walk down a hillside like that?"

The story was that when the village was bigger than Agrapha, he had met her when, like all the other lads, he took his turn at looking after the communal herds of goats. After his father's death he inherited the house and saw more of her. It came as a surprise to everyone to learn they were married. There was a small band of Vlachs above the village who took up their winter quarters around Trikala and Larissa when the snows began to fall in mid-October. The strangest part of the story was that Nico had hinted to someone that even when she went away he could keep in touch with her. Nobody knew how he managed it.

The village of Agrapha sits on a steep slope amidst a range of peaks a little more than 6,000 feet in altitude. It took us nearly ten hours to get there, probably our most difficult day, marred only by unsuccessful efforts to cut off the loops of tracks trodden by those who knew far more about short-cuts than we did. Viewed in the round, the dramatic moments of life are apt to fall singularly flat.

E. M. Forster has pointed out that life is full of false clues and signposts that head nowhere. He says that "often with infinite effort we nerve ourselves to a crisis which never comes. The most successful career must show a waste of strength that might have moved mountains and the most unsuccessful is not that of a man who is taken unprepared, but of him who has prepared and is never taken."

Strange that in isolated villages such as Marathos enquiries about how to get to the next place were usually answered in terms of the nearest road, even though we tried to explain it would probably be double the distance that we should have to walk if we could cling to paths. Was this, we wondered, concern for our safety or for some reason of their own? Kaiser knew quite a lot about the track over the top and, we thought rather begrudgingly, told us that if we got into trouble we could follow the waterfall to get up on to the bare plateau.

The day started well. We were weaving through good timber. A loud deep bark. A bright red roe-deer, a female with two wobbly fawns at foot, stared at us for a second or two with upturned muzzle and then plunged down through tiers of trees which had taken us at least half an hour's walking time. Katie mopped her forehead and wished that for that day at least she had been born a deer. My eyes were on a patch of slightly moist sun-dappled mud on which half a dozen butterflies were almost invisible until they rose in the air together, fluttering like a spotted handkerchief in a breeze. We saw that feeder on grasses, the Great Banded grayling in hot pursuit of a would-be mate. Again we watched the beautiful Apollon whose floppy flight makes it easy prey for collectors.

Most people with a slight interest in natural history seem satisfied if they merely know the name of a bird, a plant or an animal. Could there be, I wonder, some lingering element of word-magic here, some feeling that knowing the name gives one power over the creature specified, the sort of feeling that leads primitive people to conceal their personal names from all except their intimates? An enemy, learning their name, might be able to use that power for evil purpose. Unless the creature is a useless parasite or a predator the most difficult question of all to answer is: "What good does it do?" This presumably is a hangover from the anthropocentric universe of the Middle Ages when everything had a

287

purpose in relation to Man with a capital M. Today, against a background of countless galaxies, astronauts walking on the moon, geological time and hosts of wild creatures, there is still no answer to the function of, say, dragonflies, water-skaters and mayflies, except that they add marvels to days in the country.

The sun told us that it was somewhere between about ten and eleven o'clock and I didn't like the look of our progressively worsening nature reserve. The shady conifers were being invaded by acacias, the spurious blush of Judas trees, and more and more of that impenetrable scrub oak.

The track broke up into occasional branches. We clung to what looked the most trampled down. Where was Kaiser's waterfall? No cicadas, no butterflies nor songbirds for comfort, only skittery Crested larks on patches of sand.

At one point the track divided purposively. There was no way of choosing between them. Both to the left and the right we caught glimpses of the bare ravine. We put our packs down, took out our whistles and trudged off in opposite directions. I felt reasonably sure we should cling to a north-west, not a north-east bearing.

My path wavered uncertainly before it swung round a bend where due ahead I saw it had been cut by a waterfall, small but too precipitous to be waded across. Yet immediately above there stood an alternative track, almost a staircase with a series of steps about fifty yards in length. Thereafter it moved steeply but steadily from side to side to another bend from which could be seen a down-trodden path through a sparse wood. I reckoned we could climb from one level to another without much difficulty. The whistle had scarcely touched my lips when I heard a short toot from Katie. I went back to where we had left our packs. She had not even walked out of sight and beckoned excitedly and pointed when she saw me.

In a hidden depression of bare rock and loose shale below us we saw the nut-brown woman, old Nico's wife, driving her herd of goats directly up the dry bed of a stream. Her steps put me in mind of a sleep-walker. With her eyes apparently fixed on the ground she never hesitated except to throw a stone just below a group of strays. They bleated and scampered up in front of her in a ragged line, starting a small avalanche of stones. We needed a rest. We sat down and watched. No trained sheepdog in a trial could have bettered her. From past experience we sensed that she knew she was being watched but she never looked up.

Impossible to calculate her speed of ascent, but I guessed it equalled ours on our laborious zigzag upwards. In terms of altitude gained in feet per hour we were probably outclassed by three or more to one. A born mountaineer. Seemingly without effort on something close to a cliff, she could match in speed and agility a reasonably good walker on the side of a hill. A Vlach in her natural environment.

She switched to a diagonal traverse and we left her to it, going back for our packs and on to the waterfall where we drank, washed our feet and took to the upper track. A stumble here and there. A resolute pull up for Katie when both our loads were safely perched, and we were off again. On the wildlife front we were much on our own except for prickly stuff and dreary asphodel which rattled in the breeze. A rather large grass snake (*Natrix*), a harmless creature although it may reach a length of eight feet in the Balkans, uncoiled as if heavily oiled before it slid away. I looked round: there might be many more in cavities in the scrub. The species is remarkable for its polygamous habits. In the breeding season it collects up to a dozen females and as many as a thousand eggs can be found in rotting vegetation. A pair of ravens or a jackal could wipe them out in half an hour.

Above us, more difficult to make out even through glasses, we again saw the mysterious warden of goats, always referred to by the women of Marathos as Nicolaina, using the feminine form of her husband's name as one might say she-Tom or she-Carlos. Going in the same direction as we were, she was moving towards a small plateau of grazing at a height of probably four or five thousand feet. We both heard and saw the by-product of her relentless drive minutes before we caught a glimpse of her.

A boulder crashed down, leaped into the air and bounced off a projecting rock where it split into fragments that tinkled down like a kind of spray, considerably wide of our track but near enough to compel a sharp look-out.

We paused to watch. Anxious for a fresh bite amidst that barren waste, the goats scampered ahead stirring up small avalanches that progressively increased in force. They put up a variety of creatures from red-winged grasshoppers to a pair of mountain hares and a bare-necked vulture, the Griffon, which, hitherto unseen, arose from behind a rock like a genie from the earth's interior, circled the disturbance and flapped off, disconsolately, I should imagine. When the goats and their warden settled on that patch of coherent grazing all became quiet again.

What we couldn't make out was why Nicolaina had literally clambered up to a small and isolated pasture when, as we had seen on the forested trail to the place where Katie had first spotted her, she had outflanked shady glades more than fit for omnivorous goats. Could the explanation lie in Kaiser's marked reluctance to support our plan to scramble over the arduous but more direct track to Agrapha? Was that Arcadian haunt of roe-deer, perhaps wild boar and those ridiculously small doves we had heard a small communal hunting-ground? On what was their economy based? Almost certainly not entirely on sheep and goats, although old Nico and his agile wife may have been responsible for grazing the common stock of the village. Was that the way in which Nicolaina made some reparation for her irregular association with the local band of her fellow countrymen, the Vlachs, those Ishmaels regarded by some extremists as scarcely mammalian? This is odd because although most Greeks fear the countries around their northern border, as a nation they are singularly free from that distressing and almost universal complaint, xenophobia. That morning Nicolaina may have been on her way to rejoin them, temporarily. We had no direct evidence one way or the other except that she was heading for the barrens and not the next village. Speculation and curiosity about what we saw was what always kept us going.

On a narrow track still within sight of that talkative stream we were obliged to walk one behind the other, with me in the role of path-finder some forty yards ahead. Uncompanionable but necessary when there was the danger of starting more avalanches. When I reckoned we were within an hour of reaching what had been uppermost in my mind, the top of the ridge and what lay beyond it, we stopped for a rest and a drink where I asked Katie what she had been thinking about.

She paused for a moment and said the remarkably deep blue colour of the sky, emphasized on all horizons except the one immediately ahead by the ring of unmelted snow. She didn't recall it when she used to live at a similar altitude in Ceylon. The grotesque towers of jagged rock surprised her: why hadn't they been flattened and smoothed like most of the others? She admitted being scared by the shower of stones dislodged by the goats but not as much as by vertigo when she daren't look down to where the track narrowed around a sharp turn in the rock face. Did I think there would be more of them ahead?

At heart I didn't know since crests are not uncommonly false ones, but Kaiser, I told her, had assured me that when we got over the ridge we should be able to see the village of Agrapha.

Nicolaina and her flock were out of sight. As far as we could see we were the only human inhabitants of the central Pindos, that vast arena of marauding hordes, bloodshed, brigandage, foreign invasions, mass slaughter, the destruction of whole villages, internecine strife, treachery, family feuds and heroic resistance, all enacted within lunar landscapes. The mountains were strangely quiet. Could it be that with hindsight they were listening?

In asking Katie what was uppermost in her thoughts, I really wanted to know how long she felt capable of pressing on, of enduring long stretches under fierce sunlight with about thirty pounds on her back. Her feet, I knew, were blistered, certainly worse than they had been. Perhaps she read my thoughts. Among other matters she told me more about her feet. We were two of a kind. I had a pain like toothache at the base of the spine when cautiously I lifted up my pack as we started off in the morning, which sometimes never wholly disappeared during the rest of the day. Would it not be advisable to get down to the plain and come back in the autumn, I wondered. Or should we finish the whole venture then and there? Was it sheer age on my part? Perhaps. Even the Flying Dutchman came at last to port.

Dark thoughts were quietly recorded soon after we set off again. They were sparked off by a glimpse of yet another horizon far behind that gap in the immediate snow-line. Not a mirage. It didn't lie between our line of march and the sun, but whenever I looked it appeared to have risen by a few degrees. Two dome-shaped crests in colour somewhere between blue and violet, as if we were being peered at through the eyes of an old whore.

We could have done with a touch of the old stuff. We hadn't one. A song, then. With a throat that felt like warm cottonwool I croaked out: "Beer, boys, and bugger the Band of Hope" to a tune a quaver or two from the "Soldiers' Chorus" from *Faust*. Katie smiled wanly, so, taking the lead again, I got back to thinking about something to think about.

The ancient custom of transhumation, the taking of flocks up to the high pastures in the spring when the plains were as dry as sunbaked stubble and bringing them down before the snow started to fall, was the third stage in the evolution of man's activities — that is, before the coming of fertilizers. For millions of years bands of shaggy-looking fellows ate anything they could find from fruits and berries to carrion filched from agile predators, especially big cats, and what could be picked up on the seashore including flotsam such as dead seals and whales. Then came Man the Toolmaker, the artificer of weaponry, flint axes, spears of bone and yew wood, and metallic products culminating in the atomic bomb. Before they dabbled in intertribal slaughter on a big scale, the wisest hunters found they could fill their bellies most easily by cooperation. They could scarcely fail to notice that wolves were in the same line of business.

Wolves, the outright enemies of mankind? Far from it. From the abandoned young of those sagacious animals that, like themselves, hunted in packs under undisputed leadership and discipline, primitive man acquired the domesticated dog, that vital first step on the road to pastoralism. This took place some ten or eleven thousand years ago. Man had reared an obedient hunting companion with sharp teeth, a creature who could run much faster than he could. Goats and sheep were probably domesticated from their wild ancestors some two or three thousand years later and that nicely balanced partnership between man, dog, goats and sheep has persisted until the present day.

Paradise is somewhere in the Near East; Jerusalem is the centre of all countries and nations, and the world itself is a flat disc, surrounded by oceans of water; so the monks, the mapmakers of the Middle Ages, saw the world they lived in. Towards three o'clock on that afternoon blaze, our own horizons were slowly but enormously enlarged. We topped the crest and immediately opposite us, at our level but separated by an immensity of air, stood the village of Agrapha. It took us three hours to get there.

Tavropos, tortoises and Trikala

When at last we got to grips with a large-scale mountain-climbers' map it became clear that the dominant village of the Agrapha range is surrounded by peaks within circles of peaks all of which are close to — or rather more than — 7,000 feet in height. For centuries, probably millennia, invaders from the west or the north would have had to thread their way through the gorges and foothills of Mount Delidemi; those from the north would have had to cope with the sprawl around the sharp nose of Borlero and the saddle of Plaka whilst, as we discovered for ourselves, the southern approaches stand high above the Agraphiotis river. Like eagles from their eyries, the Agraphiotes could have seen enemies advancing across the void around the place called the Village Without a Name; more appropriately it might have been known as *Aproseetos*, the Inaccessible, isolated but not aloof.

Before we got there we recalled our friend George Papadopoulos from Karpenissi telling us that as a boy he and his family and friends had been whisked up into the range when invasion threatened their home town; he scarcely remembered it except with gratitude. Others had had much the same story to tell. Could it be that we had arrived at the Geneva of the Central Pindos, a constant refuge for people or nations at odds with each other, or another Marathos dependent primarily on a great gush of sparkling water?

Difficult to say, but what we were sure of by the nods and smiles of the people around the cafés and restaurants from the moment we walked down their narrow main street at right angles to a cultivated slope of Mount Koukourountsos was that they were on our side.

We were the first strangers they had seen that year. Were we mountaineers? It seemed easier to say yes.

An old man, Carlos with the map, who seemed to be in charge of the place offered us a drink and directed us to the house of a kindly soul who promptly adopted Katie. She insisted on kneeling down and washing her feet; she offered us a pleasant room and suggested a meal, an omelette with those Greek beans we enjoy so much.

As we sat on the veranda feeling at peace with the world we heard the sound of eggs being broken and the sizzle of boiling oil. Nearly twenty minutes passed. Wasn't it ready? Under the pretext of ordering another carafe of wine I wandered through to the kitchen, saw the big omelette on a plate and asked if I might take it back to our table. "Oh no," she said, "it's still hot. Hot food is bad for the stomach."

I forget how I managed to get round that one without seeming impolite, but it explained much that we'd had to put up with in Greek kitchens until we'd learnt the necessity of saying, "Hot, hot, please," — "*Zestos zestos, parakalo*," when we pointed to trays of food that had been kept lukewarm for hours.

Carlos strolled up to ask if we were satisfied with the

house, and stayed to catechize me gently, presumably on behalf of the village. The usual questions: where had we come from? How had we got to Agrapha on foot? Our age? Had I been in the army? This enabled me to ask about what had happened locally.

He was eighty, he told me. One of the few remaining natives. His contemporaries had either been killed, died or moved away. Those there today were mostly refugees from the Italians who had just stayed on. The Germans hadn't thought it worth while to send their armour into the thinly populated mountains but had bombed the village, twice. He chuckled when he said that on the second occasion there was nobody there. They had scattered. After the Occupation all the mountains of Greece were in the hands of one Resistance band or another. ELAS ruled Agrapha, and that was a bad, bad time. Members of families had hunted each other.

Against those terrible stories of half a century ago, the Agrapha of today had about it an air of serenity, a touch of Shangri-la. An ancient priest in full canonicals had a benign smile for everybody, an immoderate thirst and a flowing white beard which would have got him a job as Father Christmas in any Western store. Oldsters gossiped in the tavernas, clicking their worry beads. Worry was man's function: women hadn't the time. Those not scurrying about carrying things knitted furiously.

We stayed only a couple of nights. On a route he was familiar with Carlos showed us on his map how we could work our way round Borlero and Plaka, those twin domes which earlier I had likened to the eyes of a whore. He assured us that once up there it was downhill through forested country to Kastania and Lake Tavropos. Easy words for hard going on which I don't intend to dwell since it was largely a two-day repetition of that breath-taker up from Marathos, but downhill.

Tavropos. Now that was different. A ten-mile long, narrow, mostly artificial lake, presumably a reservoir fed by that river beside which we had walked on that hell-hot day, our first out of faraway Karpenissi. But that Megdova, or Tavropos, had flowed south, this one north. The two names, we learnt, were synonymous; one ancient, if not classical, the other modern. Gravity being what it is, somewhere along the flow line there must be a common source.

With a carrier bag of cold meat, bread, tomatoes and wine bought in Kastania we strolled round the ins and outs of the lake's shore-line, looking for the ideal camp-site. We found one under some alders reflected in the water. During the evening we heard some fearful shrieks which came, it amused us to imagine, from those hell-born birds the Stymphalides with their brazen beaks and iron claws, considered by Pausanias to prey on mankind. Among a host of other monsters they were killed by Herakles, most celebrated of the heroes of antiquity. They were, in fact, Loons or Great Northern divers which for many weeks had been my companions on the Appalachian Trail.

Within a couple of days of Trikala we managed to lose ourselves close to Mouzaki and slept in the open among bales of maize stubble, but were fortified by glimpses to the north-east of the great Plain of Thessaly. As we

299

inched round the edge of that steam bath we kept as high as we could. We found tortoises which, here in their native environment, can scuttle away on the tips of their claws. No wonder these heat-loving animals, captured generally in their hundreds of thousands in North Africa, Turkey and the Balkans for export as pets, rarely survive an English winter. Criminal destruction.

We lunched in a humble place where with apologies the lady of the house seated us near an unkempt priest who could be heard eating his daily free meal two or three tables in front of us. Before each mouthful he crossed himself as if swatting flies. He knocked things over and asked for another plateful. Our hostess flung down what she had been crocheting, a fine shawl in unbleached homespun wool, and stamped off. Katie asked if she might continue the intricate pattern. Instant friendship.

That night we found a grassy knoll as smooth as the Sussex Downs with a few flat-topped boulders on which we could lay out our gear. A shepherd approached. We greeted each other. I told him we were sleeping there. Just for one night. Was it in order? "*Endaxi*," he said. He accepted a cigarette with dignity adding two significant words, "*Adio, graz*," before walking down the hillside as surely as he had walked up. The words mean "thank you" and "goodbye" in Vlach. Thereafter all was quiet as we lay on the ground, our eyes impressed with the diamonds of the poor, which are the stars.

A curious awakening about five o'clock in the morning. *Clack, clack, clunk*, repeated as if temple blocks were being struck by a child. I rolled over to see a large tortoise attacking another one almost concealed under a boulder, with its head withdrawn. The aggressor was butting the edge of its shell with its own shield. It turned, saw me and ran away as fast as a rat, to be followed by the other tortoise. What were they up to? Two rivals fighting it out or a courtship pattern peculiar to a very ancient group of animals whose relatives on equatorial islands weigh up to half a ton? Quite simply I don't know.

The Plain of Thessaly, "mother of flocks and homeland of horses for Olympic charioteers". We had seen the statue of the most famous one in the museum at Delphi. He wears the expressionless expression of cab-drivers throughout the world. Here were horses in straw hats, donkeys in diapers, carts with solid eccentric wheels, cheerful peasants on ancient tricycles, and rows and rows of brightly painted beehives.

Trikala, tricolour. Fascinated by all we saw, from the white-washed walls of the old Turkish-style houses pleached with blue clematis and the bright red of ramblers, we made philological play with the name as we walked down to the trickling river. We recalled *Roumeli* by Mr Leigh Fermor, to whose sensitive ear the word "Dodecanese" seems a sea-song sung by twelve sponge-fishers, "Athens" a canticle of columns, "Thrace" the beat of a drum, "Hymettus" the hum of bees and "Trikala" the stork's beak rattling from a broken minaret.

We saw pairs of those symbols of fertility only in Pigi

301

and Parapotamus, two suburbs we should have forgotten but for our disgraceful conduct there.

In both places pretty young girls in their very best embroidered dresses slipped out of their homes carrying basket-work trays of all manner of dainties. Shyly they dropped a curtsey and offered them to us with a phrase we couldn't understand. Thinking they were for sale and having already eaten, we smiled, thanked them, said something simple, and hurried on. They looked wholly taken aback, saddened. We learnt later, I don't know where, that on behalf of the Mother of Jesus they were the gifts of virgins to strangers, in a ceremony which probably has something to do with the Gateway of the Virgin, the Porta Panagia, by which one enters the town. May the Mother Herself and those young girls forgive us. We wholly misinterpreted a heart-touching custom.

Above the trickling river, the Pinios, and close to the old quarter and the bus station, we made for the comfortable Hotel Divani, where, as he had said he would, M. Théophane had left a message. Would I please phone him after ten at night at Metsovo, some forty miles away in the mountains of Epirus? Katie sniffed. "As far as he knows we haven't arrived," she said. "Let's go take a bath and pretend to be civilized."

This is easy in Trikala, once famous for the oldest known sanctuary to Asclepius, the god of the medical art and recreation. To Homer he was not a divinity but simply "the blameless physician of deep knowledge".

On our side of the river, we were flanked by narrow streets of craftsmen's shops and tavernas with trays of aromatic vegetables and slowly turning roasts over beds of glowing charcoal.

On the other side, across a choice of brightly painted bridges and a public garden, are restaurants and glittering shops designed to empty the wallets of visitors.

Towards sundown the principal thoroughfare is closed to all wheeled traffic for the *volta*. This slow parade for lovers, would-be lovers and families with their young all done up in their best was as a royal performance for which we'd seen the rehearsal in Amphissa. Music was played but it was quiet music from several sources, mostly cafés and restaurants, and there was orderliness almost everywhere. Crowds, yes, but mostly in twos, threes or fours sauntering up and down, then round again, unwinding between everyday work and the ordinariness of life at home.

Note the word "almost". That night two Greeks, one less a considerable portion of one ear, were hauled off to the cooler for fighting with lethal cutlery outside the doors of our highly respectable lodgings. The night porter Basilides (Bassy for short), an energetic old man, had called the cops. Katie was ready for sleep so she told me not to be long, and under cover of getting some useful information Bassy and I shared one or two stiff ones.

The two combatants, youngsters by his standard (he admitted to being on the wrong side of eighty), were the grandsons of two political chieftains, Royalist and Communist (ELAS during the War of Independence), who had been threatening to kill each other since they had first handled rifles misguidedly supplied by the British in Cairo. The one deprived of part of his ear was the grandson of Velhouiotis who, as even I knew, under the *nom de guerre* of Ares had boasted, rightfully it seemed, that he had killed hundreds of men, potential allies who had disputed his right to run a private army in the mountainous Albanian border region. They had been cornered and killed in the Pindos by the Rightist forces, the Colonels. His head had been cut off and displayed on a lamp post in the square just below our bedroom window. Bassy had seen it. It proved such a popular attraction that it was taken down and pickled for exhibition in Lamia, where Velhouiotis came from, and in other centres of unrest.

"A bit late, weren't you?" said Katie the next morning.

"Yes, but I heard a lot more about the fight from the night porter. It's a feud, goes back to the Occupation and the War of Independence."

"But they must have been in prams at the time."

"Maybe, but their grandfathers were big-time Resistance leaders who fell out about what they were fighting for, and they're good at hating each other. Anyway, I have news for you: I got through to Théophane and he's going to take us for a joy-ride in the mountains. He's sending us his car."

"You mean *you* are. I've got an appointment with the best hairdresser in town at midday, and I want to do some shopping. He's your friend; you go off with him."

"I didn't say today. It's coming after breakfast tomorrow."

Some argument ensued. From the very start of the trip we'd agreed that whenever we stopped for two or three nights in a town such as Thebes or Delphi we should spend a day on our own. We had been in each other's company from dawn to dusk for days. Théophane had been quite explicit: he couldn't come to Trikala himself, he had business in Metsovo, a Vlach village, he said. He'd send his good young friend from Crete, Kalonaros, to pick me up.

"Madame might prove difficult," I had suggested. As if he'd read my thoughts he'd said, "Afford yourselves then a little vacation. There are excellent shops in Trikala. No, wait! Another idea. Perhaps she too would also like to go sightseeing. On the way here one goes through Kalambaka and Meteora with its columns of rock, the skyscrapers of nature. Kalo, as you must call him, will introduce her to a lady friend of mine there, and at whatever hour pleases her we will pick her up on the way back to the Divani. One word, though: Kalo has some difficulty in speaking, he has had an operation to the throat. You will come, then?"

"I told him I would phone him back after I'd spoken to you," I told Katie. "How do you feel about it?"

"Good idea," she said. "Théophane and I have not met each other. All I know about him is what you've told me. He's clearly not interested in meeting me, and I'm much of the same mind. How do you explain that?" Not wishing to go into the obvious, I suggested negative telepathy.

If it hadn't been for a procession of mule-drawn carts carrying vegetables on the long straight road to Kalambaka I had the impression that Kalonaros at the wheel of the Mercedes would have covered the twenty-five miles in less than half that number of minutes. An extremely good-looking man with hair in glistening ringlets. He was, I should guess, about forty years old and a very courteous driver, permitting himself only a gentle hoot as he purred past other vehicles in that air-conditioned mobile armchair. His limitations in speech were made up for by a wealth of gestures.

We saw the skyscrapers of nature long before we got among them. These extraordinary rocks have been likened to the decayed and irregular dentures of gigantic mammoths. Katie, confident in her new hairdo, had picked up the literature the previous day. The vertical monasteries have earned three stars from the Guide Michelin. Originally, that is during the sixteenth century, there were twenty-four of them. The monks were hauled up in rope webs like netted trout. Today only four are inhabited.

The days of jointed ladders pulled up in an emergency are no more, and the nets are now strictly limited to hauling up supplies. Occasional romantics who misguidedly hanker after the good old days when the traveller was pulled up uncomfortably squeezed into an outsize string bag are quickly cured of their rash desire by one look at the rusty windlass, especially if told the gruesome story that the rope was never changed until it broke.

Kalo circled the cobbled town before pulling up — as I had anticipated — at the door of an expensive restaurant. Madame was waiting to greet Katie, warmly. Kalo touched his watch and raised his eyebrows. What time should he return? Katie said quietly, "Thank M. Théophane warmly. Tell him I should have loved to have met him but must return to Trikala by taxi for another appointment. Perhaps another day . . ." Ahem. We were off again.

Next to no traffic beyond the town. At eighty or ninety miles an hour in that almost silent car, the sensation was of floating landscapes by Turner. Miniature villages appeared far below on the snow-topped landslides, Tringia, Kastania and Kerassea. With a map on my knees I followed their slow progression. Minutes passed and they slid away to be replaced by others, all much alike. How many, I wondered, were among the last resorts of the Vlachs? Field glasses showed that all the lower houses stood on stilts, and were reached from the floors of valleys by sinuous tracks.

We swung up the highest road pass in Greece, 1,690 metres, and passed a ski villa used in summer to house the snowploughs. Another loop, and then down the other side to the tourist-populated show town of Metsovo. All the way a splendid road, shown off by a splendid driver.

"Kyr' Ioanni," he greeted me, his hands on my shoulders. *"Nous sommes les oiseaux de passage, eh? Comment ça va?* How well you look! But too thin, perhaps. Is it that you do not eat well in the mountains?"

Disinclined to tell him about tinned squid, biscuits, fruit and coffee in remote villages, I sketched in our route briefly, mentioning the manhunt and the bullet-ridden car between Kaloscopi and Piri. The thought occurred to me that questions almost always came from this shrewd

307

collector of objects and ideas. What I wanted to know was what he had been up to and what was he doing in Metsovo?

Théophane airily waved the bullet-ridden car incident aside. "When Greeks are not engaged in national wars, and then only with enormous help from the big nations such as yours to get them out of troubles — mostly which they make for themselves, they are fighting each other on the political edges of old antagonisms. It is within their nature, as a small nation of large ambitions and, *au fond*, supreme opportunists."

"But you told me you came from Famagusta. Surely that is — or at least it used to be — part of Greater Greece?"

"Allow me to correct you, *mon ami*. I said that was where I was born, a different matter. It may be that I could have said that I am a Cretan Jew, or a part Vlach. Birth certificates are part of the *bataclan* of bureaucrats. The large family of my father came from a ghetto in Smyrna. Why is it, do you suppose, that I know so much about Anatolia and the Taurus mountains? But *qu'importe*? In *Enosis* I do not believe. Fundamentally, that is to say on the paternal side, I am of the race of Ottomans who blocked the advance of the Mongols in the thirteenth century."

He changed the subject. "*Dites-moi*, did you attain Mavrolithari, the place of the black stones? Is there any news of the Temple of *Hercule*?"

"No one knew. I think it's merely a village tradition. But what are you doing here?"

"I am trading, *naturellement*. It is in my blood. I love

beautiful *objets*, and here and in nearby Ioanina, the city of the Ali Pasha, there are for sale icons and ancient Turkish rugs."

"Who's selling them?"

"Rich Greeks, who because of the oil and the shipping difficulties have not much money in hand. I have a very important engagement in Ioanina this afternoon. Please to come with me. It will not be a long time."

The sinuous road through Metsovo wriggles down a steep hill. On both sides of the approach to the square are solid two-storey buildings with well spaced windows, and gardens at the back. They are, M. Théophane assured me, typical of several townships in Epirus.

We were sitting on a balcony. Down the road waddled old men in blue serge tunics, with long white woollen stockings and wooden shoes adorned with pom-poms.

"Do you know who they are?" he asked.

"Yes, Vlachs. We met one of their chiefs on the train from Venice to Thessaloniki. We've seen them up in the hills. I know a few words of their language." His turn to look surprised.

"What I didn't know", I admitted, "is that in this town at least they look so prosperous."

"Prosperous! These are only *les petits bourgeois* entertaining the tourists. They are paid to do it. However, there are Vlach millionaires. They are among the people from whom I am buying *objets d'art*. Come now! First a little lunch, then Ioanina. We have much to talk about."

If Kalonaros, our chauffeur from Trikala, may be

compared with the charioteers at Delphi, Théophane, seemingly so worldly wise, had something in common with Phaethon who was notable in mythology for atrocious driving. Like a badly trained stable lad trying to show off on a thoroughbred, he flung the Mercedes around hairpin bends at an appalling speed and usually on the wrong side of the road. When immediately ahead of us, sanguine motorists — rare among Greeks — refused to let us through, he hooted incessantly, and all the time he talked whilst I did my best to answer through clenched teeth.

Did I not know that the Vlach, Averof, was so rich that he had presented Greece with her only heavy cruiser, which was named after him? Answer: no. Had anyone told me that one of Greece's prime ministers, Ioan Koleti was also *un roumain*? Same answer. And so on until, to my heartfelt relief, he pointed far down to an immense lake on the shores of which stood Ioanina, the capital of Epirus — relief because we then encountered a military convoy which clung resolutely to the middle of the road.

Ioanina is a modern town except for the old district near the lake, which embraces a bazaar, a huge fortress and several minarets and mosques. We entered one or two of them to see icons similar to those Théophane intended to buy from private collectors. What did I think of them?

"Fine," I said, mendaciously. They looked too bright, too colourful and too fussy. My inclination was to tell him that whilst masterpieces speak for themselves relatively few intelligent people can recognize bad art, but thought better of it.

As I was left alone whilst he was about his business, the thought occurred that many small mosques with their domes, pendentives and squinches are unimaginative miniatures of parts of the glory of Saint Sophia. One recalls Sydney Smith's comment on the Brighton Pavilion: "It is as though St Paul's had gone down to the sea and pupped."

Théophane returned with a large, heavily protected parcel which he locked up in the boot of his car. "Seven pictures," he said. "About them I have been thinking since I last saw you. This is a matter for champagne. Let us drink where we can see the lake."

"*D'abord*," he began, "Agrapha. What do you think? Totally isolated, eh? Primitive?"

"Not at all. Difficult to get there, though. Perhaps stupidly, we went over the mountains. We learnt too late that there is a passably good road that follows the river, the Agraphiotis, but as a professional I don't follow rivers. They are deceptively easy and I was told it was flooded. When in doubt you walk high, across the knuckles of the landscape."

"But the village itself?"

"Among the best we met in the mountains. The woman of the house we stayed in adopted my wife. She washed her feet. As for the rest, hospitable. A mixed lot, Greek and Balkan refugees. A *stetl*, if you know the word."

He smiled. "Among other racial mixes, I am part Jewish," he said. "Any Vlachs there?"

"I don't know. We were both tired as hell. I remember

311

the head man, a pleasant old chap with an upturned white moustache, big enough for three. My idea of a Klepht. It was he who recommended the house of the Magdalen. Also an old priest who, we were told, did next to nothing except drink and dispense platitudes. Apart from the women who, like everywhere else in the mountains, seemed always busy, the male Agraphiotes just lolled about and gossiped."

"And you are going to write about the unwritten place, which will bring tourists to where they have never been before?"

"That's my business, just as yours is driving about collecting ideas and things you don't really want. Has Ioanina anything to offer the packagers, the pedlars of tourism, as you call them?"

"*Eh bien*, that is a matter of one's taste. One has to be curious about excessive villainy as I am. Does the name Ali Pasha have a meaning for you?"

"Yes. I've read that by an awful mish-mash of intrigue, fraud and homicide he came pretty close to stealing most of continental Greece from the Turks. In fact, I recall a picture of him," I said. "A very old man with a long white beard, leaning back in a boat smoking a hookah. He looks like a stage villain — too sinister to be true."

"So! The sketch by Louis Dupré. It is to be found in the Bibliothèque Nationale in Paris. His ancestors were compatriots of the family of my father," he added with what seemed a touch of pride. "What else do you know about him?"

As I recalled the story, Ali Pasha, the man who murdered Botsaris's father, was the descendant of an Anatolian Dervish who settled in that area, and from whom he usurped authority in Ioanina. He was supposed to have had a harem of 400 women, to have been constantly in the company of a retinue of semi-naked boys with hair down to their waists, and the court was guarded by trained assassins. He was allied to the French, but when the truce broke up he sent one of his sons-in-law to Constantinople as an envoy, and he died there, some believed by poison.

"That is true. Ali Pasha was fond of public spectacles. When he heard the news he pretended it had been contrived by his enemies. He rounded up all the immediate family, including Euphrosyne, his son-in-law's favourite mistress, and had all fifteen of them, naked and lightly bound, drowned one after another as a diversion during the intervals of a banquet."

Théophane told me how Ali Pasha's eldest son, Mukhtar had such uncontrollable lust that he frequently raped women in the public street in broad daylight, and his younger son, an exquisite called Veli, boasted that he possessed the largest library of pornography in the Near East.

Surprisingly, this bizarre court was visited not only by Byron but by other members of the intelligentsia who happened to be in the area. Théophane wondered how they reacted to being entertained amongst concubines and catamites in a palace decorated with the skewered heads of their host's enemies?

Remarkably, considering his many enemies, Ali Pasha lived on to be over eighty, but in the end, abandoned by all his former allies, he fled to the island of Nissi Ioanina in the lake below the town, where he took refuge in the upstairs room of a pavilion. Soldiers broke in and started firing through the ceiling. A chance shot caught him in the groin, and he died screaming in agony as he'd heard so many of his own victims die before him.

I could see a dozen or more egrets circling and circling, slowly, their wings bright white but unmoving in an uplift of warm air.

"Who", I asked Théophane, "is your good friend, Kalo, Kyrie Kalonaros?"

"A compatriot. It is many years that I have known him. Now, *hélas*, the dear man has operation on the throat. He has much knowledge about art. Once he was a valuer for Christie's in New York. Also, he drives the car for me when my mind is on other matters, and together we play the game of chess."

"Who usually wins?"

"*C'est moi*. My business it is to think far ahead. Do you play?"

"I scarcely know the moves, but you are perhaps aware that the game was the basis of yet another of Freud's ridiculous ideas? Since the object of the game is to checkmate, which is the symbolic killing or castration of the enemy king (father figure), and since a player's strongest piece is his queen (mother figure), good players are often motivated by parricidal urges and mother love."

Théophane thought the matter over for a moment before saying: "I loved very much my father and my mother. You were in *contre*-Freud mood when we talked together at Amphissa, *n'est-ce pas*? Have you any explanation?"

"It's a subject I know quite a lot about. My late wife, my beloved Tilly, died of cancer soon after she became a senior analyst of the Anna Freud Clinic in Hampstead."

"Could it be that you are constantly walking away from reality?"

"Not at all. I have been fond of walking since I was eight years old."

"*Eh bien*. And what is your route from Trikala?"

"Due east in the general direction of Larissa, but after about twenty kilometres we hope to climb up to some place called Vlahogiania where as far as I can make out there aren't any roads. With any luck we'll be at Elassona at the foot of Mount Olympos within four or five days. I'd better be getting back; we're setting off at dawn."

"Always on the move?" To my relief he added, "*Entendu!* I will drive you back to Metsovo where Kalo will take over. One last question: have you met many Vlachs in the Pindos?"

"A few here and there. We've seen their trucks several times. Perhaps the strangest person was a woman at Marathos, the last place before Agrapha. She was married to a local man, and they say she came from a group which camped out high above the village. Each day she took a herd of goats almost straight up the mountain where, we think, she joined them. I have an idea that in some curious way the husband managed to keep in touch with her wherever she was. Others have told us that these people still revere nature gods, the spirits of streams and forests."

"That is not a surprise for me. Man worships what he knows best. If triangles invented gods, they would imagine them to be three-sided."

"You seem to be uncommonly interested in these people. What's the reason?"

"The best of reasons," Théophane said. "Before her marriage in Smyrna, my mother was a Vlach, originally from Albania."

The Mountain

Not a good start. At dawn a thick white mist. The moist plains of Thessaly were breathing heavily. We ventured out into the empty square. All that could be heard an hour before Prime were arguments between local cats and the incessant bleep of frogs from the river Pinios. At the start of our long looked-forward-to assault on the summer home of the gods the augurs of good fortune could have served us better.

We swung out of town on the Larissa highway. We had been told that somewhere close by a derelict mosque marked the turn off to the *paleodhromos*, the classical turnpike to ancient Trikala. But it was difficult to find. We were among half-seen garages, shoddy shops and the dumps of the suburbs. Damn the frogs! We were too near their riverside romping place. Suddenly out of the murk there loomed the remains of an ivy-gripped pendentive with spandrels and narrow windows with semi-circular eyebrows. I regretted what I'd said about Ottoman architecture! It looked fine. A path ran alongside the rubble of broken pantiles and stone and beyond it a Thessalian farm where tethered cows were being milked on sun-baked dung among a gabble of guinea-fowl. Two girls and their mamma in kerchiefs must have been surprised at our exuberant greeting.

The old road? Why it was over there! As an actor peers through the curtains at his audience before the show begins, a lemon-coloured sun emerged through the thinning mist. We could see the gate and the lane and we were on our way in an ever-brightening landscape.

For insecticidal purposes the lower portions of the trunks of fruit trees are painted as white as the stockings of men at Metsovo, which brought us back to the enigmatic M. Théophane. Did I think that Kalo was his resident boyfriend, asked Katie.

I thought not. In my opinion the compulsive collector was of that class rarely recognized or talked about in Britain, a capon, an affectionate neuter with a penchant for horrendous stories. A sadistic substitute for sexuality?

"He talked with what seemed enthusiasm about the dreadful goings-on of Ali Pasha; he described how a bishop of Trikala who had stepped out of the official line was flayed alive and his body stuffed with straw before the Turks took him round in a cart on an exhibition tour." I told her how as we hurtled down to Ioanina Théophane said it was on that route that Curzon had a macabre encounter with an unfortunate traveller strapped to the side of a mule in a small box. He assumed he was a dwarf until somebody explained that his particular mode of travel was because the man had just had both his legs cut off by robbers.

To change the subject Katie bent down to examine an exquisite bunch of Madonna lilies on the banks of an irrigation ditch. Even in well-watered Thessaly the hot dry summer was well under way. Nearly all the annual species of plants had already set seed and were drying up. Nevertheless we saw Greek trefoils shimmering with blue butterflies and valerian, Love-in-a-mist, cornflowers, mulleins, St John's Wort and on sandy land the Spanish oyster plant, a thistle-like herb with golden flowers. The ancients dug it up for its edible tap-root which, according to Dioscorides "is good for such as have the arme pits and other parts of ye body foule smellie".

We began to climb. The sun poured down fiercely. The farmsteads were falling away. On open land the natives build wattle shelters like Masai *manyattas* around isolated trees to protect their sheep and goats from the heat. Estimated animal population within each compound about fifty.

Here we began to get some idea of the economics of rural pastoralism. In Trikala a butcher had told me that graziers received an annual subsidy of 3,000 drachs, a little more than £12 for each animal. What for? To reduce the scrubby vegetation to the deserts seen on most of the high tops? Ignorance is a basic problem. It is, unfortunately, possible for people to live on a rapidly eroding landscape and be almost unaware of it.

The country became hilly. We had been walking for hours and were too parched to eat what little food we had bought as emergency supplies. There were no changes in the contour lines on the last of our almost useless maps. We had imagined we should spend the greater part of the day on the plain but to the north-east we saw, faintly, a huge range of hills, and to the south the Larissa highway.

We made for a compound around the only tree in sight, a withered evergreen where a score or more of curiously mottled sheep huddled around a young lad under a thick woollen cape. We asked him about the nearest village. "Neohori," he said, and by holding up all his fingers and then those on one hand indicated it was about fifteen kilometres to the north. We trudged on with bloodshot eyes, tired and with no enthusiasm.

Sod's law again. Unless rectified promptly discontentments tend to be cumulative. With the plain far below us we clambered up a track, the wrong track, came back, tried another and at eight o'clock that night arrived at the small but sophisticated village of Neohori, where a well-stocked supermarket had been closed for about an hour, and the taverna was about a mile away up the road. We gazed longingly through the shop window.

Up came a young girl who asked if she could help. The shop closed? No problem. The owner lived nearby. She would fetch him. He seemed delighted to see us, and with the girl, a student of the guide school in Thessaloniki as interpreter we chose a supper of everything we could wish for including fresh fruit, pastries and a litre of the best white wine in the shop. Could our friend recommend anywhere beyond the village where we could put our tent down for the night? We liked soft ground.

She spoke to the shopkeeper at some length. Presumably there were alternatives. There was one phrase, *ine steeheeomonos*, which she asked him to repeat and then, turning to us, said, "Many places just beyond the bridge where a wood has been cut down for new buildings, but there is one place marked by a monument in front of an old stone wall avoided by most of the villagers. They say there used to be an ancient place of holiness there. It is *steeheeomonos*. I don't know how you say in English."

An evil place, I suggested.

She shrugged her shoulders and sighed. "Perhaps. The Germans murdered many people there, including some of my father's family, during the Occupation."

By contrast with the gauntlet of stares we had so often endured, the citizenry of Neohori were filled with goodwill. We had invitations to stop for coffee and answer their questions. We shook hands and passed the time of night with everybody who greeted us. The bent figure of an elderly man with a black eye-patch who spoke good English insisted on finding out where we were heading for. To Elassona, I told him, by way of Diasello and Vlahogiania. "There is a bus from Larissa to Elassona," he said. "You can pick it up anywhere on the main road." Because we suspect that places which rural Greeks haven't visited don't exist, we left it at that.

Beyond a number of squares were neat suburbs, each with a pump on a plinth. We filled our plastic water-container and felt the householders would not have refused us a bath in their garden.

The site we chose in the almost dark backed on to an incomplete building of red brick immediately beyond the town limits. Owls halloo-ed sadly and wraiths of mist floated up from an invisible streamlet. With gear up and in order we drank to the outcome of the day, *and* to the next one when, with any luck, we should be at least within sight of the almost unimaginable, a glimpse of our objective, the throne of Zeus.

"To us," we said, and again to the fruit of Gaia, an

excellent wine made the better by what we had sipped in the village of hospitality.

"Who's that?" Katie asked, quietly, pointing.

A scarecrow of a figure, slightly lame. Not making towards us. He moved backwards and forwards, peering under tarpaulins at builders' gear, piles of sand and a cement-mixer.

"Better have a word with him," I said.

I followed him. I don't think he had seen us. Surprise on both sides. It was Captain Hook, the man with the black eye-patch from the village. What were we doing there, he asked. I told him we were camping near the stream. If we wanted to, we could sleep in the school, he said, pointing to the red brick building. It was empty, and as caretaker he had the key. Did we want to use the toilets and the taps at the back? If so, he would turn the water on. Yes? Then would we please follow him.

Where had we come from? Not wanting to go into a long, tedious explanation, I told him Trikala. On foot? I nodded. That was a long way. Had I been a soldier? Yes. He thought so. Sergeants taught a man how to walk. In the war he had been wounded, and touched his eye-patch. I asked him where that had been. "Here," he said, "in Neohori, but I was lucky. I got away. Look!"

In front of an old stone wall stood a cenotaph inscribed with twenty or more names. All the men the Germans captured had been stood up in front of that wall and shot one after another. The bullet marks, concave depressions as if pitted out by a chisel, could still be seen in the uppermost stones. Then, as a reprisal for guerilla activities thought to have been supported by local people, the invaders had burned the village down. I could think of nothing to say. The name Neohori, the new place, occurs throughout Greece.

The caretaker showed me the water taps in the shed. I thanked him. We shook hands warmly and I went back to Katie.

Hours before dawn she woke me up at the sound of a sustained howl from somewhere near by.

"Wolf, dog or evil spirit on the prowl?" she asked.

"Dog," I said firmly. "It's been barking on and off since you went to sleep. No matter what they said in the village, I don't believe in the supernatural." I had been haunted by the thought of the old stone wall and the men who had died there.

Years ago during the Spanish Civil War an old friend of mine, Arthur Lerner, the economist and philosopher, faced death with three other members of the International Brigade. For some reason they were reprieved, and a dispatch rider arrived when they had already been lined up facing the firing-squad. "What were your last thoughts?" I asked him. He said it had happened in a farmyard, and he recalled looking down to find that he was almost standing in fresh cowpats. Feeling that it was indecent to die there he managed to inch away, nearer to one of his companions.

The next day: Monday 4 June. Because of the uncertainty about the country ahead and the thirst-provoking heat, I felt distinctly out of sorts. Our last day but one on that laborious stage is a confusion of tape-recorded impressions, starting with a shrine that became a pock-marked wall of death, and ending with egrets and the travellers through the night.

Almost the only figure in those immense landscapes were old women in black, mostly alone, hoeing away in the stubble of old tobacco plants. They were glad to be greeted; they waved their hoes and shouted back, "*Kalo taxidi.*" Working on a presumed position of Diasello due north, we struck up a sinuous track in that direction, fortified by the opinion of a shepherd and his goats, two or three of which had climbed up thorn trees, that the village was "*Makria makria*", further up, further up. At least he had heard of the place. Somebody we had asked not far from Neohori had pointed in an entirely different direction and said something we didn't quite catch but which we took to mean "difficult to find".

Eleven o'clock. Another hour had passed. It had become hot. Expecting to pass through at least one small village before Diasello, we had cut down on weight by carrying only about a pint of water in a plastic bottle. We had drunk half of it and could hear the rest splashing about in my rucksack, tantalizingly.

It took me back to the deserts of North Kenya where, with a dozen camels and four men in my care, water was a constant problem during stages of three or four days. On several occasions there wasn't enough for a wash at night nor the next morning, since I wasn't prepared to rinse my hands and face in camel urine, straight from the pump so to speak, as the boys did. With time to spare before dusk we sometimes unloaded the camels and allowed them to wander free in hummocky country with nothing visible except a complete circle of sand. There was just a chance that in an almost straight line they would make for a patch of scrub in a depression unseen by us, where they would begin to browse. At this the men would plunge their spears deep into the ground and examine the blades when they pulled them out. If just a few particles clung to the metal they concentrated on that area until they struck slightly moist sand. Then they began to dig with the exuberation of dogs which had smelt buried bones. They were looking for the line of an extremely small underground spring — enough sometimes for cooking, but with the reasonable certainty that there would be much more in that hole by the morning.

Another hour passed. Through glasses Diasello appeared as a dot on the horizon with, behind it, horizontal clouds on a mountain range. We were elated. We drank the rest of the water.

For reasons I can't explain in terms of estimated distances between horizons, landscape-reading in Greece is more deceptive than in any other country I know. Perhaps it's the light. For every mile we walked Diasello enlarged in size: it looked lower than when we first saw it, our pace quickened and our packs felt lighter too. Friends have said of me that I'm frequently surprised by the obvious. As we neared the buildings on that steep slope and saw far beyond them the white-topped peaks of the Olympos range all became clear. Another dragon of the imagination had been slain.

From the old squat buildings in layers on the way into town it looked as if the high-perched hamlet had at one time been a Turkish fort. The little streets were labyrinthine and the local folk gracious. There was none of that "Hiya feller" stuff of middle-aged Greeks who had spent their early years and their family's patrimony in the slaughter-houses of Sydney or Chicago. The place breathed self-respect. We wondered if we had climbed into another Vlach village.

We settled down and, seeing me poring over the last of our tattered maps, a well-dressed young fellow in his mid-twenties asked, simply, if he could be of any help.

Vyronos (Byron) and his brother Veni, presumably short for Venizelos, the two sons of Papastavros, apparently a rich man, had been beguiled away from studying economics in Athens to help their father during a local labour shortage. Although they didn't say so, both seemed bored to hell with life in the northernmost part of the *nomos* of Trikala. Did I really imagine they liked ordering kilolitres of *venzini* for the truck and sacks of fertilizer, when they could have been in the students' club in Panepistimiou? Would we come to their home for something to eat? Five kilometres; they would take us there and bring us back in the pick-up. No? Then perhaps another drink? We were the first tourists they had ever seen at home.

The most important question, as I put it to him, was how to get down to the floor of the valley and reach Elassona without touching the central highway from Larissa. There were not even any small roads on our map.

We were joined by his brother and together they looked

at the sheet with some surprise. "A very old map," said Veni. "I have never seen one like it. True, there is no road but there is a shepherd's track. Would you like a lift down there? No? Then look. Come down in this direction," and with his pen he drew a serpentine line. "That is a tributary of the Titarissios which joins the Pinios." In the other, the northerly direction, we were told, it flows through Elassona.

"How far will that be from here?"

"All the way? Perhaps twenty-five kilometres or a little more." And in answer to my final question: yes, we could drink from the stream. They had drunk a great deal of it when out shooting, but it was greatly improved by a touch of ouzo.

We were conducted to the edge of the escarpment where, below us, swinging down in the form of an immense letter S through a mosaic of pasturage and farmland interspersed with trees, we could see the track. This, coupled with the local advice from the brothers, set our spirits soaring.

We talked about the name Vyronos which in Greece still has a charismatic quality. Even in small villages, from Athens to Trikala, we had seen the tribute paid to him in the names of streets, cafés and restaurants. Thousands of children are baptized in his name. In town squares where inscriptions under statues have been smudged by time, some Greeks seem unable to distinguish between heroic representations of the *lordos*, or perhaps Marcos Botsaris, or even a ferocious old Klepht in battle-dress. This point is nicely made by Patrick Leigh Fermor.

Poets, he says, have strange posthumous careers. When Rupert Brooke died aged about twenty-seven in 1915, he was buried in Skyros, an island he'd never visited in his life. The Skyriots are proud of him and he is greatly honoured there. A few years ago a visitor was admiring the olive grove where the poet's grave lies and reading the inscription on the tomb, when an old shepherd spoke to him saying he'd noticed that he was admiring the grave of *O Broukis*: "We are glad to have him with us. He was a good man." On questioning, the shepherd admitted that he was not strong on letters and had never read any of the poetry, but said you could tell he was a great man, adding, "You see that olive tree over there? That was his tree."

"How do you mean?"

"He used to sit under it every day and write poetry."

Not wanting to contradict him, the visitor asked if he was sure they were talking about the same person. The shepherd was quite sure.

"What did he look like?"

"Magnificent, sir. Tall, dignified, flowing hair, burning eyes and a long white beard."

Late in the afternoon we reached what could have been a line-and-wash sketch for a picture of Arcadia by Edward Lear or Claude. Classical landscape with figures. The stream, one of the innumerable tributaries of the Pinios, the nymphs of yet another river-god, gurgled through an arcade of tall, light-dappled plane trees and willows. A dozen or more cheerful young men whom we took to be Vlachs were watering and milking goats and sheep, the latter by throwing the ewes over on to their backs and straddling them to reach their swollen teats. Some old shepherds with intricately carved crooks stood around, together with two or three women, knitting or finger-spinning on a distaff.

We didn't stay long. They had work to do; as for us, to keep up with that damned implacable task-master The Schedule, we felt we ought to tread down a few more kilometres. We shouted goodbyes and left in the company of that talkative stream.

It let us down, we felt, by swinging away from the track on the left bank which led us into flat moist country inhabited by aggressive horse-flies and mosquitoes. No chance of a peaceful night there. The ground became slightly steeper; the dirt track, joined by another, looked more used. Wheel-marks and sheep- and goat-droppings. Surrounded by hills on three sides, we came out into a grassy plateau perhaps a mile in diameter with some curious wooden contraption immediately ahead.

A long feeding-trough on trestles with at one end a metal cistern partly set into the ground and fed by a dribbling tap. "Home from home," said Katie: I was less enthusiastic. A cardinal rule for anyone who sets up camp in the bush is never to be too near to, or even within sight of, a water-hole, the focal point of tribesmen, animals and their predators.

Leaving Katie to unstrap our packs and draw more water than we had been able to squander in days, I took a turn round where the plateau began to slope. The sight of a flock of snowy-white birds, egrets, circling above where we took the stream to be, disclosed a patch of flat ground where we couldn't be seen. Katie, meanwhile had found a litre bottle of white wine in the cistern, presumably left there by somebody who would be coming back for it. Footprints were still visible in the moist sand.

We walked over to the egrets' hunting ground. After sitting with our feet in lukewarm water we supped and stretched out luxuriously, listening to the calls of owls. They weren't the species we had become accustomed to, Scops owl which murmurs *pee-oo, pee-oo*. These were Little owls (*Athena noctua*), the symbol of the city, created according to legend by the Goddess of Wisdom. Scops are remarkable for a loud ringing cry that put us in mind of the opening sequence of the bird we know so well from our northern moors, the curlew. The Greek equivalent of coals to Newcastle is that anything commonplace is like sending owls to Athens or priests to Athos where they used to swarm like bees. When Curzon became Under-Secretary for Foreign Affairs at the end of the last century he received word that the heavily bearded brethren on that peninsula were violating their vows. Unfortunately, in cipher, the word vows became cows. In the margin of the despatch Curzon simply scribbled, "Send them a papal bull."

That night we listened and gazed up at the owl-like moon until we slept. At about two in the morning I woke with a start. I heard a truck, and then another. The noise grew louder. Four or five vehicles without lights made their way toward the cistern. There they stopped. Men got out. Goats and sheep bleated. Much laughter and loud talk in the clipped vowels of the Black Departers.

Were they about to release their flocks with dogs? To our immense relief they kept them penned up and off they went. "How long will it take us to reach Elassona?" asked Katie in a tense voice. I thought about five or six hours. "Thank God" she said.

I underestimated the number of loops in that serpentine track. It took us from first light until five in the afternoon. Ahead of us for most of the way like a mirage that came and went we saw the immense ridge that marked our journey's end.

On Thursday 7 June we were hanging our washing on the balcony of a hotel remarkable only for the fact that our bedroom overlooked a pair of nesting storks, which, when they exchanged incubating duties, made a noise like dice rattling in a box.

Over supper that night we talked about how far we should venture up towards the visibly snow-capped platform of the range. Katie argued, forcibly, that from the moment we decided to make this trip we had chosen the foot of Mount Olympos as merely a tangible objective to head for. Well, surely we had arrived there, hadn't we? She pointed out that we could see the slopes from the roof of the hotel and thought they looked less inviting each time she saw them. In the Agrapha we had already done more mountain-storming than we had bargained for. Enough was enough. Didn't I remember that night under an electric pylon when the thunderstorm started to brew up?

Had the small market town of Elassona looked more attractive I might have agreed to haul the flag down then and there. Homer mentioned the ancient place, since demolished, which is more than Michelin does today. Strange, this, since for thousands of years Elassona has stood watch and ward between the rich Plain of Larissa and the mountain pass, the *Elassonitikos*, the classic invasion route of Thracians, Persians, Slavs, Huns and Turks.

Katie sighed at my intention of eventually pushing on and asked, "Well, then, what next?" I suggested that for a few days we should enjoy ourselves doing nothing in particular, and then perhaps a modest venture into those nebulous slopes to the north-east, which were under a cloud that morning. Could it be that the gods had pulled down their blinds?

I was up and about earlier than Katie and came upon several thirsty souls in a taverna beyond the market-place. The company included Spiro, a local tobacco merchant who had served his time in Richmond, Virginia; Grego, a cab-driver with a fine Mercedes bought from his earnings in Detroit; and a butcher with a South African wife. They spoke English in a variety of accents and I heard their stories out before getting down to ways of reaching the *Elassonitikos*.

Grego, their spokesman, told the story, strange to my ears but far from uncommon in Greece, about how, within a year of his getting a hard but well paid job on the Chrysler assembly line, his father sent him three photographs of a girl he had never seen, with more than a suggestion that he should marry her. Unknown to him the parents had been discussing the subject for months. He met her for the first time when she stepped off the boat. He showed me several coloured photographs. A striking-looking girl with a wry smile whom many a man might have run off with even without the property his father had told him about, together with an attestation from the best-known lawyer in Elassona.

"Gardammit, never did a better deal in my life," said Grego, and the others who had known the family for years nodded their approval. Together with his taxi business they now have a house and a small vineyard just outside town, and three daughters, one already engaged.

The others told their stories. All of them had worked abroad, helping to keep their parents until they collected their short-term pensions. The man with the flashy rings and watch who owned the tavern still had four sons in Germany, they told me.

This nation-wide propensity for emigration stems from centuries of Turkish oppression when Greeks in their millions, especially in the north, became refugees, deprived of their family holdings. Lord Curzon said there was "no precedent in modern times for this gigantic transference of populations". The problem was exacerbated after the Convention of Lausanne in 1923 where the Allies sought unsuccessfully to straighten out compulsory Graeco-Turkish exchanges. The housing shortage was such that for two or three years each box in the municipal theatre in Athens was occupied by a whole family of Greeks, their only living space.

Grego recalled stories his grandfather had told him of the road between southern Bulgaria and Macedonia which was solidly blocked by hordes of home-bound families trying to move in opposite directions, obliged to live on herb tea and roots which they dug up and boiled, together with anything else they could find. Grandpa had said that for two years his relatives close to the sea came round begging for anything they could offer the refugees, but "not those lousy Bulgars," he added.

Mention of that road brought me to what I really wanted to know about: how did one get up into the mountains from Elassona? Grego made no bones about it. We were on what he called "the wrong side of the big haul", the highest part of the *massif*. By far the easiest way was from Litohoro — that place we had seen on the bus on our way south from Thessaloniki over a month ago. There, as he put it, if you took a cab up to the half-way house, a little hamlet called Prionia, you could get to a *refuge* and then the summit in two or three hours. There really wasn't much to it.

I recalled the peaks: the highest point, Mytikas, the Throne of Zeus, with Skolio and Skala on one side and Stefani and Toumba on the other. I could repeat their name like a litany. What I hadn't realized until that morning was that due largely to perspective and the extensive plateau immediately below the utterly bare peaks, the whole vista couldn't be seen from Elassona, which is some thirty miles to the south-west. The bulk of the range extended for some forty or fifty miles to the north-east.

"Why can't we go straight over the top from here?" I asked. For answer Grego slowly raised an invisible rifle and shot me through the head. "There's a small army up there at the garrison of Olimbiada," he said. Sometimes they let civilians through in a closed truck but not often and not without special passes from the Greek Alpine Club.

"Can't we work our way round the rim of the fortifications?"

We might, he thought, if we were lucky and prepared to slip a sentry a few notes. But he admitted he didn't really know. Neither he nor his friends had ever been beyond the gates at the garrison. It was a roundabout route by a little road, but he could run us there in about an hour.

"About how far is it across country?"

He hadn't thought about it. Maybe fifteen kilometres, but very steep in places. I left it at that.

I found Katie sitting on our balcony, poring over the crossword in a month-old copy of *The Times*. "Where did you get that?" I asked.

"At the bus station," she said.

"*What* were you doing there?"

"Just talking to the Inspector, darling. Don't be so snappy. Look! Overnight we've had an addition to the family," and she passed me the field glasses.

Peering from beneath the outstretched wing of one of its parents — storks are difficult to sex — could be seen a stumpy white chick staggering about making a clicking noise in imitation of the adults. To its evident satisfaction the parent leaned over, touched its small black bill and heaved, slightly. The process is called regurgitation. Temporarily satisfied, it rolled over on its back and stopped clicking.

During the chick-rearing season storks develop prodigious appetites. Within an hour one banded specimen watched by a professional ornithologist devoured forty-four mice, two hamsters and a frog. Normally they gorge themselves on insects and amphibious dainties. Owing perhaps to the fact that the birds are regarded as emblems of fertility and worthy of protection there are still about 2,500 pairs in Greece, although as in other countries their numbers are declining.

Over drinks that evening I recounted all I had learnt from the cab-driver, emphasizing that the garrison, Olimbiada, was far higher than anything we had originally intended to essay. As I saw it, if we reduced everything we had been carrying to irreducible necessities, far from achieving the lower slopes from a respectable height we should be able to see where the gods were reputed to live during the summer. Wasn't that worth another stage or two?

There were arguments and counter-arguments against the alternatives. No, I didn't want to see what the northern flanks of the range looked like through the windows of a bus on its way to Katerini on the coast. We had already been there on the way in. Outspoken friends have said of us that on important matters Katie and I are one and she is the one, but on this issue I won hands down on a local map provided by that good fellow who gave us his radio-cab number and offered to haul us back. Could he give us the garrison number? Like hell he could, he said.

Relieved of part of our load we felt buoyant, almost cushioned on air as we strode through lark-infested stubble some two or three days later. Visually tedious until the contours began to squeeze together at something over 2,000 feet. Thereafter the dry irrigation canals became first damp and then slow-moving streamlets fed by melting snow and enlivened by banks of flowers. A botanical peculiarity about plants on steep slopes is that the higher they grow the later they flower. Their spring is delayed. Those which were beginning to look desiccated on the plains, such as a variety of gentians, saxifrages and orchids with luscious "lips", had only just achieved full sexual vigour around us.

Orchid fertilization is so complicated and varied that in their efforts to attract pollinators this huge family of some 30,000 species has been described as a floral *Kama Sutra*. Their rounded tubers resemble testicles, which is *orchis* in Greek, hence their name. Anthony Huxley, a son of the late Sir Julian relates how in medieval England orchids were known as dogs' stones or bulls' bags. Shakespeare wrote of Ophelia's "long purples" to which "the liberal shepherds give a grosser name", a phrase which must have had them rolling about in the pit.

Guileful orchids both protect and advertise their generative parts in the form of scents which usually happen to be very attractive to our senses, such as lily-of-the-valley. Several Dendrobiums offer heliotrope in the morning and lilac after dark. More remarkable from an evolutionary point of view is the way in which their lips and purses resemble the female bodies of bees, flies, small moths and other insects on which they are almost entirely dependent for fertilization.

In all this erotic chambering there is more than a touch of sadism and prostitution. A beguiled pollinator, let us

337

say a dull but extremely diligent bumble bee, is forced into ridiculous postures, often upside down to satisfy his misplaced lust. He may be physically drugged, trapped in narrow passages from which there is no escape unless he enlivens the moist ovules (ovaries) of his heavily disguised temptress. When it eventually escapes, "groggy and wet-winged" as Huxley puts it, the insect can't be aware that it has visited the wrong house, that of a sex-deficient group of plants remarkable for florid beauty and bizarre bodies which in some cases actually smell like the legitimate mates of their pollinators.

Despite the erratic nature of tracks between holdings we made good progress, climbing steadily. The sight of an old fellow leaning on a stick, watching his goats brought to mind our first glimpses of those solitaries in distant Boeotia.

What did Katie recall most vividly at the start of the trip? Without hesitation she said the *Flying Tortoise*, the wreck of the trains; two monsters smashed into small pieces. She'd never forget it, and often wondered how many people had been killed.

"Yes. But what would you pick out on the plus side?"

She thought for a moment.

"Good will. The hospitality of everyone out to enjoy themselves on the first of May but most especially those exhausted young men at the taverna that night who left their sweeping to put a wrap round my shoulders."

We mentally spooled back to other memorable times. One of Katie's recollections was her joy at the profusion of flowers in the early part of the walk; mine were of the poverty of land at the end of its tether, Arcadia reduced to an irrecoverable wilderness through lack of water and the improvidence of landowners intent only on their current income. We thought of rigours scarcely talked about at the time and were at one about that gorge, the Devil's Arse, its heat and its hurts, nicely smoothed out before night by the chance encounter with the gallant Legionnaire from Sidi bel Abbes.

About the Agrapha and its narrow cliff-hangers some hundreds of feet above the noisy torrent, the Agraphiotis, I have no mind to say more than that I might have turned back if it hadn't been easier and more prudent to press on. What I can't explain is how we were able to expend so much energy walking up to eight or nine hours most days with very little food yet rarely feeling hungry.

Thirst now, that was something different. We were often chronically dehydrated. At the sight of moist earth at the foot of a scree I had dug like a starving ant-eater. As somebody put it, you can get used to anything — which has always seemed to me a cogent argument against the minatory prospect of Hell. But where now? *Pou-pou-pou*, as hoopoes say.

No hoopoes on the stairs to Olympos, only squeaky quails, twittery larks and now and again melodious warblers which warbled in bird language wholly unknown to me.

Almost immediately above us we could make out a line of battlements partly obscured by the Gatherer of Clouds. We were within sight of our destination. It certainly looked mysterious, but I was in no mood for the supernatural. We had clambered up there to see the place believed by the ancient Greeks to be the summer home of the gods. That day the wind from the heights felt somewhat chilly.

It seems to me that myths of creation and eventual extinction vary according to the climate. In our cold north the first human beings were said to have sprung from the licking of frozen stones by a divine cow-like creature named Audumla. The Northern afterworld was a bare, misty, featureless plain where ghosts wandered hungry and shivering. Those unpleasant places were destined for serfs and commoners: the nobility with paid bards to sing about what splendid fellows they were could look forward to warm celestial mead-halls in Valhalla, and Elysian fields in Greece.

According to a myth from the kinder climate of Greece, the human race derived from a Titan named Prometheus kneading mud on a flowery riverbank, which he made into human statuettes and Athene brought to life. Without a hope in hell, the ordinary run of Greek ghosts went to a sunless, flowerless underground cavern.

Our long journey ended on the authentic note of anti-climax echoing from peak to peak. A military helicopter clattered over and encircled us twice.

The sentry at the gates of the garrison knew enough English to say plainly but politely that nobody without a military pass could enter whilst they were engaged in manoeuvres. "How long would that be? A few days? A week?" He didn't know.

Hoping for a glimpse of what that high platform looked

like from behind the gates, I asked if we could speak to the commander.

He shook his head. He had been given his instructions when he first saw us approaching about an hour earlier — and he pointed to an almost concealed pylon inside the enclosure. On the top of it could just be made out the slowly revolving arm of a radar scanner. Before he closed the gate, decisively he saluted and wished us a good journey. *"Kalo taxidi."*

Most journeys end more abruptly than they begin. We tramped down to a village, Kallithea, from which after a telephone call, Grego hauled us back to where the storks, both parents, were clattering excitedly over the emergence of their second storkling.

Among the Gods

Nearly four months later I flew from Heathrow to Thessaloniki, alone. Thoughts about the eastern face of the famous peaks on the skyline above Litohoro had become something of an obsession. As soon as we had turned our backs on Elassona I regretted we hadn't stayed on, rested for maybe another week, and then tried to add a few Olympian laurel leaves to our last long walk. But in addition to family affairs far too much work had to be attended to in London even to think of going back in the summer.

About mid-September, or maybe it could have been a little later, I put a call through to the Hellenic Alpine Club in Athens to ask what was the latest date one could be reasonably sure of getting up to the *refuge* above Litohoro without whooshing about on skis. I don't think I can ski. I've never tried. They thought mid-October or the beginning of November. They gave me the telephone number of their local manager and guide, Costas Zolotas. That helpful fellow — who speaks both German and English with curiously inverted phrases — was much of the same opinion. "*Korrekt*," he said. With him I should be there about mid-October, it had been a hot dry summer followed by much rain. In the northern Balkans clouds were already piling up.

Katie agreed to stay at home until I phoned her, first before I started the scramble and then again when I returned to the hotel. She could rejoin me in either

Corfu or Metsovo. She packed spartan gear for me — tent, sleeping-bag and woollies — and demurred when I slipped in a miniature camera and a short-wave radio the size of a pack of cards. Total weight far less than half of what we had lugged through Greece. She was apprehensive. No need to worry, I assured her. After all, I said immodestly, I had scrambled over the Mountains of the Moon in Central Africa to nearly 15,000 feet. Tim Salmon who has done a lot of walking in Greece has described Mount Olympos as a mere pimple by Himalayan standards.

Litohoro is a Chamonix or Bourg-St Maurice in miniature, a small township at the top of a hill from which serious climbers, scramblers or indolent scenery seekers can stroll up towards the youth hostel, turn sharp right to a comfortable open-air restaurant and sit down the better to have their breath taken away by one of the greatest views in Greece. Immediately ahead lies an immense V-shaped gorge of grey rock, the spectacular outflow of a torrent, the Enippeas which flows into the Aegean some five miles below the town.

Lording it over the landscape at a height of a little over 10,000 feet are the peaks subordinate to Mytikas, the very throne of the Gatherer of Clouds. In the curiously green light they stood out that morning like dark stones in a bright necklace of snow.

Zolotas turned out to be a hairy, square-shouldered fellow who looked as if he could carry one of his own mules. They were quartered, he told me, at Prionia at the very top of the gorge. This is the half-way house

343

up to the skyline. It could be reached most easily, he assured me, by local taxis on a twelve-mile loop of the forest road. Alternatively he could run me up there in his Land Rover the next day, since his wife ran the *refuge* about six kilometres above Prionia. If I held to what he called the "*Zeek sack*" of the *podidhromos*, a foot-track through the last of the trees, I could make my way up to the crest of Olympos in maybe two and a half hours. The verticals were for serious climbers.

A genial fellow, but his proposals sounded too much like a conducted tour for self-satisfaction. I told him I proposed to scramble up through the gorge on a DIY.

He looked puzzled. "*Allein*," I said. "Alone — by myself."

"*Gar nicht leicht.*" In his opinion it wouldn't be easy.

On a large-scale map he pointed to places where there were overhangs of rocks. At those points it was necessary either to take a path up to the top near the road and scramble down the other side, or to cross the stream at various points.

"*In diesem augenblick*" — just at the moment the snow was melting and the stream flooded. Now if only a week or two earlier I had come . . .

"When will you leave here?" he asked.

"Maybe in a day or two. First I want to have a look at the gorge."

"Before you depart come and see me," he said. "Then if we don't see you at the *refuge* we shall know where to look."

* * *

It looked formidable. For two or three hundred yards the left wall above the torrent is paving-stoned with blocks of ferro-concrete. These end abruptly in a confusion of screes, foot-pointed in various directions. I took to an up-going diagonal with little confidence, confirmed by the tinkle of dislodged pebbles the size of gravel. Seeing a traverse on more substantial stuff several feet above my left shoulder I soldiered on towards the apex of the first of the overhangs I had been told about.

Much more of that local lithology and I would have accepted the offer of the lift up to Prionia but the Devil, having been at his game for a long time, deals slowly, offering small rewards to ventures on the slippery stones to peradventure.

It looked fine on the down-slope — a dribble of a long track down to the torrent. What could be better after that initial survey? Surely a drink or two back in Litohoro? And so passed that day and the next.

In that time I met the trim young Mayor whose father had been with ELAS in the mountains, his chief clerk, who was interested in botany, and the charming French-speaking woman from the Information Bureau, from whom I learnt in order of importance that the weather prospects weren't too good but avalanches were rare because of the bangs from the bombs on the range on the top — meaning, presumably, behind Olimbiada — and that, to my surprise, it wasn't until 1913 that a local guide, Christos Kakkalos had helped two Swiss climbers, Baud-Bovy and Boissonas to climb to the summit of Mytikas. The operative word here is climb. The scaled an almost vertical face with overhangs. Nowadays it's done regularly by professionals but each year thousands of other summit-seekers scramble between the verticals, and I hoped to be among them. Madame said near the top of the gorge I should probably see the priest in charge of the Monastery of St Dionysius.

In the sixteenth century this saint, one of three of that name and the founder of the rule, had written somewhat sceptically about the "so-called gods" who were reputed to have lived above his retreat from "worldly affairs".

That evening I phoned Katie to say that I intended to set off the next day. Not alone, she hoped. There'd been some talk on the radio and TV about worsening weather advancing on the Balkans from the Ukraine. Thick snow in northern Yugoslavia.

"No talk of it here in the Hotel Aphrodite," I said. "In any case, I'm scrambling up with three lusty Australians tomorrow. Right now they're whooping it up in some nightspot on the coast."

"Take care, darling," she said. "Phone me as soon as you can. *Kalo taxidi*."

Worsening weather? I combed the air with my short-wave radio. Nothing but the sound of tearing calico from the BBC World Service, Thessaloniki, Belgrade, Zagreb and Ljubljana. Electronic black-out? Had it anything to do with the snow?

The manager of the Aphrodite was several shades less than helpful. No, he had heard nothing about the weather. His TV on a cable link had gone on the blink. I switched on my little machine. The same crackle. He smiled, conducted me to the door and pointed upwards to where three power cables looped towards the restaurant and the chalets at the foot of the gorge. He walked out into the back garden and told me to switch on my set again where, as I understand it, the air-waves were filled by someone describing in Greek how Athens were in danger of losing their match against Italy. The manager shrugged his shoulders. Kyr'Zolotas would know all about the weather, he assured me.

But that good fellow wasn't in his usual haunts in Litohoro, neither the café in the square nor the tavern next door. He had left in a hurry. Why? Nobody knew. Where could I find out? From the taxi-drivers, they told me.

Of the four cabs parked in the square only one was manned by its owner, listening avidly to that damned match in Athens. Reluctantly he turned it down. Kyr'Zolotas? He had driven up to Prionia two hours ago, he said. Why? Perhaps he intended to rejoin his wife at the *refuge* the next day. After all, everyone had the right to. . . . I left it at that.

A discouraging evening. Sitting on the balcony of the almost empty youth hostel in my overcoat, I sipped cup after cup of coffee, twiddling all the short-wave bands of my radio. Nothing but incomprehensible Russian and other Slavic tongues until, faintly, interspersed with static I heard the last few bars of "Lilliburlero", the nostalgic, thrice-blessed signature tune of the BBC World Service, and fragments of an announcement in English. It faded before I had learnt anything of importance but I had located the wavelength and managed to recapture the end of the news loud and clear. It would be repeated in half an hour, the announcer said.

Bad news. As Katie had foretold, a narrow but intense belt of low pressure was sweeping south-west across Central Europe. There followed reports from local correspondents in Belgrade and Bucharest. Deep snow. Main road and rail traffic had come to a standstill. But which way was the storm heading? No hints from London. I switched off the set and tramped down to the Aphrodite.

No encouragement there. The manager said he'd had a telephone call from my three friends at Katerini on the coast: they were sorry, but they'd seen TV pictures of the snow to the north and had decided to go up to Thessaloniki for a few days.

I felt gloomy, a mood shared by the whole village. They were talking about it in the tavern and the cafés, small groups around tables discussing what they'd seen on the box. They felt disgraced. A local lad had been chosen for the national team and Athens had lost by one goal. If it hadn't been for a penalty kick in the last three minutes it might at least have ended in a draw.

The weather? What weather? Oh, that *snow*! Yes, at least a fortnight before they'd expected it up there, but that sort of stuff wasn't any good for skiing. Too wet. It'd probably melt within a week. Anyhow, it might not reach them. *Real snow*, now, that wouldn't start until the end of October.

This from Christos Kakkalos, the young master of the house, namesake but as far as I could make out not otherwise related to the famous man who had guided the Swiss to the top of Mytikas nearly eighty years earlier. A not uncommon name thereabouts.

I asked him if I had time to get to the top of the ridge and back the next day. He wasn't sure, thought it might be dodgy. "Who would know?" I asked him. He named someone in the village whose son kept an eye on his small flock above Prionia and operated under a special dispensation. It was an *Ethnikos Drimos*, a national park. Christos phoned him.

Answer: ambiguous. It depended on the wind. If it stayed south-east as it was at present, I could rely on at least a couple of days of snow-free weather. But if it backed — as he thought it might — I should turn round at once.

"Why not take a taxi to Prionia?" asked Christos.

The next morning I asked myself that more than once after scrambling up the scree I'd sampled two days earlier, and slid down to a torrent I didn't much like the look of. Deepish, I reckoned. For stepping-stones the gushing water was bridged with boulders touched on narrow ledges by red paint I'd been told about by my friend the guide. Would he had been there with a helping hand.

The alternatives were to risk chucking my rucksack on to the opposite bank with a mighty swing and then jump after it from ledge to ledge unhampered. The track on the far side looked tempting, since it followed the stream without an overhang in sight. But I felt dizzy and funked it. Then maybe I could wade across? Sounded with a stick, the water proved crotch-deep and flowing fast. Not worth a thorough wetting. Upstream on my side a cliff towered over the torrent. Nothing for it but to outflank the monster on a scree similar to the one I had scrambled down.

It took me more than an hour to advance what would have been no more than perhaps a couple of hundred yards alongside the water. This roller-coastering on loose shale, precarious on the ridges on the top, had to be undergone twice. Since downright discomfort is as unpleasant to relate as it is to endure there will be only one mention of tobogganning on my bottom in a place where I couldn't trust leaning backwards on my feet.

Immediately overhead came comfort from the Gatherer of Clouds which were still scurrying resolutely from the south-west — but not long after midday when, rounding an arête near the top of the gorge, I found they were united in a classical anvil-shaped thunderhead. To hell with Zeus!

I knew the bolts of lightning would zip open swirling masses of water-vapour already tortured in their search for equilibrium. That's what happened: a few flickers like a faulty fluorescent tube and then, almost simultaneously, ferocious forks of light, a helluva crash, and a shower of hail. No place to be in a cyclonic storm. That's when I took to tobogganning — anything to get down quick.

At a height of maybe a couple of hundred feet above the torrent it's difficult to say whether I was more invigorated by the sight of an anchor-shaped peregrine plunging down on some sort of grouse-like bird in mid-air, or a young fellow approaching the stream where it was narrow enough to be jumped across from boulder to boulder in full kit.

"Sling your pack over," he shouted.

I jumped, twice. Easy enough once you've done it and landed, physically, in the outstretched arms of a friendly young fellow, a mountain goat, Nick Smith from Lichfield in Staffordshire, who did me capital service that day. We went on upstream together.

Had he heard about the threat of blizzards throughout the Balkans? No! Did he know that we had about twenty-four hours before it was likely to beat about us? No! He looked up. The sky looked bruised, bilious, but he reckoned if we hurried we could make it.

Nick was less than a third of my age, and scuttled up and down impressive slopes at least twice as fast as I could but he was patient and irrepressibly curious. He kept disappearing down cracks in cliffs to see if corners couldn't be cut off, and emerging apologetically to say that we'd better keep on where we were or climb a bit higher. He was obliged to hurry. With limited resources he'd bought a return railway ticket to Stamboul, which meant being back in Thessaloniki early the next morning to board the ongoing train. In that time he hoped to reach the *refuge* above Prionia and then get back down in time to get a lift to the bus station.

He jumped the next crossing in one impressive bound and waited whilst I laboriously waded upstream in search of shallow water. Only one crossing defeated him. The boulders were almost under water some three or four feet in depth. He sighed and looked up to the crest of the highest scree we had yet seen. The track, marked only by the ruins of railings round tricky corners, had disappeared.

"Better make ourselves some ski-sticks," he said, selecting four useful lengths of birch poles, and up we went to the knife-edge of the ridge of incoherent shale. I wondered wryly how I should have got on on my own. It took us the better part of an hour.

Half-way down the far side we saw the roofs of two monasteries a mile or more away further up the gorge. Nick, practical as ever, reckoned it a waste of time to throw away altitude by scrambling down to the stream again. As we could rely on our stout staffs why not try a traverse? he suggested. We made it, easily. At no time that day had I felt more confident. With those poles in our hands — and hindsight — we might have ignored the torrent from the start and saved a great deal of time and energy.

Another shower of hail. We ignored it. Clouds were closing in, but they were still sweeping up from the south-west. The monasteries were clinging like limpets to the walls of a cliff. The first one, St Spilio seemed deserted. I looked up. In a patch of Tiepolo-blue sky behind the great ridge, the one that housed the peaks of the gods on either side of Mytikas, I could just make out wisps of high cirrus. They were being driven in from the north-east, from the Balkans. Stratified clouds blowing in opposite directions are, meteorologically speaking, about as comforting as a thumb pointing downwards in an arena, but as I might have been mistaken I decided to say nothing.

After a great deal of bawling at the foot of the second

monastery, St Dionysios, a young but heavily bearded brother appeared on the balcony high above us. In Greek I asked him whether we should turn to the left or the right to reach Prionia. He pointed to a short-cut through their vegetable garden. When we clambered up to their level and heard the murmur of chanting we felt rather bad about the noise we'd made.

More hail. Within a quarter of an hour we reached that small hamlet where the Black pines looked fit for Christmas cards. Except for those in the restaurant everyone seemed to be getting out in a hurry. Cars, cabs and coach-drivers were herding their passengers back for the run down to Litohoro. Any chance of a drink? Yes. A meal? No, not for at least another hour. It was five o'clock and they were over-full.

How long would it take us to reach the *refuge*? A waiter anxious to retain potential customers said, "Many hours." Untrue. A schematic map outside the stables made it clear that with any luck we should find shelter within two and a half hours at the most, but as Nick kept glancing at his watch we set off again after two tins of beer and a meat roll each. My good friend had no taste for it, but I managed to sneak in a double ouzo.

If the screes in the gorge might be compared to rollercoasters interspersed with two or three Big Dippers, the serpentine tracks through the trees above Prionia were merely undulatory "in their discriminatory proportions", as they were described by an eighteenth-century botanist.* In a way which would have delighted

*John Sibthorpe, 1758-96.

Arthur Rackham the Black pines and Greek firs had been twisted and gnarled into weird shapes by the winds and snow of many winters. At their feet were the rusty-brown remains of seed-bearing plants which had survived the heat of the summer. Only a few tuberous species, such as the Autumn crocus with its drifts of purple flowers, managed to put on a fine show.

Although Nick was usually about a hundred yards ahead in his role of path-finder, I noticed that he was less of a mountain goat than he had been amongst those screes of accursed memory. He carried more weight than I did and although neither of us admitted the fact, we were both pretty tired. When I stopped for a few moments under pretext of admiring a plant or listening to a bird — a trick he saw through from the first — among those trees he sometimes stopped too.

What was that sharp indignant whistle from the ledge below us, he asked. I'd heard it myself but couldn't be sure. Through glasses I made out creatures which popped their heads out of rounded burrows in the manner of a jack-in-the-box. Although smaller they were much like Alpine marmots. We were in the company of European susliks which in late September normally gorge themselves near the snowline and begin deep hibernation. Our small colony had been rudely awakened. We soon knew why.

Mytikas and his fellows on the skyline were grumbling. In lurid light could be made out clouds — not wisps of cirrus but damned great banks of cumulo-nimbus — rolling in directly from the north-east. Outlook: ominous. The snows were upon us. A ripple of light like children's sparklers seen in the dark ran the whole length of the ridge. Subconsciously I started to count: one second, two seconds, three seconds. The storm was still probably about three miles away, but the godly — or, as I thought at the time, god-awful — grumble became a whiplash-like crack of thunder. An ear-tingler. The time: half-past six. For the first time that day Nick looked apprehensive. "How far do you think is the *refuge*?" he asked.

"Half an hour, if we scuttle," I said, optimistically.

We scuttled. Nick mounted a bank, cutting off a corner. He looked round and waved me towards him. The hail had passed over. We could see it below, wavering like veils in a breeze. The trees were thinning out. We were above the main track. We saw riders on mules and small parties. Everyone seemed to be getting out except us.

We rejoined the main track. A young Scotsman with a *piolet*, a snow-pick, in his hand approached us. How far away was the *refuge*, we asked. "Ten minutes," he said. We should see it around the next bend.

"Anybody there?"

"Yes, an elderly German couple and a Swiss mountaineer." When he left, he told us, they hadn't made their minds up whether to come down or risk spending the night there. He wasn't taking any chances: there could be a white-out before the morning, in his opinion.

He told us Costas Zolotas, the guide from Litohoro had gone off early to rescue a climber on Mytikas, or maybe Stefani. Either Zolotas had slipped — which he thought almost impossible — or he'd been hit by falling debris, and his arm had been badly broken. He'd limped down to another hut under the Ilias peak. His wife, normally in charge of *Refuge A*, had gone off to join him to make sure he was in one piece and comfortable. "A *grreat* lassie," he said. "Everybody's favourite aunt." We'd find everything in order.

We relaxed. There stood our objective, as handsome as an Alpine chalet, stout built, weather-boarded and as warm as toast. An open fire, light and a cooker from a generator.

Two scientific names were logged on my pocket recorder as I wrote the foregoing. *Cyclamen*, probably *neapolitanum*, and *Neophron*. The first the shy native species of that overblown horticulturalist's plant rarely seen native in Herefordshire. Alongside the chalet their flowers, the colour of petals of wild roses had just managed to stand above a light drift of hail.

Neophron is a fearsome-looking bald vulture, the so-called Egyptian species. Three rose like lifts from some refuse bins. I called to Nick but he was already inside asking if there were any tea available.

He stayed only to eat and drink something. He didn't much like local herb tea. We swapped addresses, promised to write, and off he went. From the balcony I watched him jog-trotting down towards the trees; a final wave and he had gone. I couldn't have had a better companion.

To my surprise and mild disappointment the elderly German couple and the man from Lausanne who had come to pay homage to Messrs Boissonas and Baud-Bovy left soon afterwards. There wasn't much I could do except ration out half a bottle of ouzo. I had the edge of the great range and the gods to myself.

Towards eleven o'clock I went out and looked up at the sky. A fine night. Had the north-easterlies blown across to Italy? I glanced towards the Bear. For what reason, I wondered, had that group of seven stars, the Septriones, been known by a variety of names, the Plough, the Wain and the Unwearied Ones, but throughout the world most commonly the Bear, *Ursa Major*? When the first white men landed on the American continent and learned to speak the language of the Indians, they pointed up north one evening and said: "Those are the stars we call the Bear." Yet a bear with a long tail, anatomically unlike any bear ever seen on earth. The Indians, delighted to hear their own opinions confirmed, said, "Yes, we also call them the Bear. Like your own God — we also call him our father."

Back in my room it felt too warm. I switched the heat down by a notch. The machine began to whirr like a bee. I flicked through my pocket diary of dates and places that began before the *Flying Tortoise* came to pieces to the west of Belgrade.

What had happened to our fellow-passenger Nacu Zdru from Kedrona in Macedonia? The last we had heard from him in London was a brief note and a front-page newspaper cutting from *The Greek American* headlined "The Silencing of John Zdru". This veteran of the Greek army with dual citizenship had been "summarily expelled from Greece" — where he owned a house — "without the benefit of even so much as a piece of paper showing the charges against him or grounds for those charges." Zdru had provided us with our Vlach vocabulary and phrase sheets which had been as passports among the last of those itinerant pastoralists.

Tired but still tense, I turned off the light and, dressed only in my underpants, went to bed.

I woke up shivering. The time: half-past four. The hum continued. I had turned up some sort of air-conditioner, a cold one. I turned it off and burrowed into the blankets. In terms of Fahrenheit or any other thermometry it had been a two-dog night. That intriguing phrase came back from a tale told by my friend John Mitchell of the Massachusetts Audubon Society.

It concerned Richard Porter of East Charleston, Vermont, aged seventy-five or thereabouts. He had never heard of an electric blanket. He didn't have central heating in his three-roomed cabin, nor a modern airtight wood stove, nor a kerosene heater, and he regularly allowed the fire in his wood stove to burn itself out each night. He wasn't averse to cold draughts, and for that reason never insulated the pine-board walls of his cabin even though the temperature commonly dipped below zero for weeks at a time. And yet in spite of his apparent lack of conveniences, Porter said, he never felt cold at night. He had devised a system of living blankets which automatically piled themselves on his bed in response to the temperature.

Porter kept a number of dogs as companions. Towns-people regularly saw him walking along back roads surrounded by his pack, a mixed crew of all shapes and sizes, some large, some small, some friendly, "and the rest too lazy to be unfriendly". He became known as the Dog King. Not surprisingly it was his subjects who kept him warm at night.

About the time when the box stove began to cool in winter, the first of Porter's alternative heating systems, a black-and-tan named Spike began to stir from his spot alongside the stove and climb on to his bed. Louise, an old bitch, joined Spike when the temperature fell still further and the other four dogs began to come in through a dog-door which he had cut into one of the panels. On really bad nights he had five intimate companions, but he could make do with only two when he felt rather chilly.

Apprehensively I got up and wiped a small port-hole in the misted window with my forefinger. It was snowing heavily. Nothing furious. The flakes floated down thickly, as can be seen in the overturned sphere of a Victorian paperweight. From outside came a shrill explosive whistle. Might have been those Balkan marmots, or some bird I couldn't put a name to.

At first light I inspected the platform where conical drifts of snow against the gauge measured three-quarters of a metre, say two and a half feet. The wind gusty, the snow fitful. During weirdly bright light somewhere between bright orange and pale purple I could see the spume blowing between occasional glimpses of the peaks. Must be mighty windy up there. Better wait an hour to see how it developed. The chances were that Costas's assistants would lead the mules up from Prionia. I had told Nick that, if it came to a pinch, two or three of us would probably stay put until midday.

Time passed, slowly. I have no gift for doing next to nothing. The generators weren't working, but with bunk made up and floors swept I set about the fire with cut blocks of fir, and soon had bits of mutton fished out of a stew and braised them nicely in a skillet with chopped onions.

By nine o'clock I set off with a staff as stout as any used by Friar John to discountenance the Devil.

The enormity of the whiteness wrinkled my eyes. Branches of a few conifers were hung about with icicles a foot or more in length, as if on a commercial Christmas tree. Between them, an encouraging sight: a raised track of solid rock, steep in places but wind-honed of all but streaks of snow. Snowscapes are notably deceptive. Small objects appear twice their natural size. As far as could be judged from its ever-narrowing perspective the track extended for about a mile, maybe more or less, before disappearing behind a hummock, probably an extensive scree of snow at the foot of a ledge. And beyond that? We should discover when we got there.

We? Yes, my companion, my staff and I. It probed with resolution where I trod gingerly. Bully for the lad from Lichfield.

How long, I wondered, had it taken him to jog down to Prionia in the almost dark? I re-enacted some of the high spots of our previous day. With thoughts on something he had told me about a winter scramble down his native hills — perhaps the Lickeys or The Roaches — I took my eyes off the track and stumbled. Better to keep to the job in hand.

From a depression a dozen or more yards to the left I again heard that shrill explosive whistle. Those marmot-like susliks? They should have been snugly underground hours ago. Walking cautiously, I left the safety of the track and made towards them. Each step probed knee-deep snow and made flatulent noises. I peered down into a long concavity in the lee of several boulders. A flock of birds like jackdaws with lemon-yellow bills was feeding amongst the exposed tops of bushes. Alpine choughs. At my appearance those masters of aerial acrobatics whirled up into the air whistling and chirruping excitedly before floating down towards the chalet.

The hummock above, which looked inconsiderable at the start, had grown immeasurably as if some mythical animal several times the size of Melville's Moby Dick had been laid low for impiety and shrouded as an afterthought at the foot of Zeus.

Because of the elusive qualities of objects seen in snowscapes I'd have taken no bets on how long it would take me to reach the Great White Whale. A backwards glance showed I was on what good master Costas called a *zeek-sack* interesting for at least one piece of lore unrecorded — as far as I know — in the writ of Proc Zoo Soc Lond,* the stepping stones of doctorates. From one of those mounting transects I looked down to the one below to see a scurry of curious nose-to-tail lemming-like

*Proceedings of the Zoological Society of London.

animals, perhaps susliks, marmots or stoats. Had they included those giant Sumatran rats to which Sherlock Holmes attributed the desertion of the *Marie Celeste* — a story "for which the world is not yet prepared" — I wouldn't have been surprised. Everything seemed to be going down when I was still trying to scramble up.

It took, perhaps, half an hour to reach the outermost flippers of the White Whale and there beyond them, stretching out into white nothingness and shown only by a slight depression, stretched the remains of the track.

It had to be faced: there was nothing of comfort above Moby Dick. More hail, lateral hail. I could scarcely see. I turned round. My own footprints were disappearing. I started to walk down, fast. The time, near eleven o'clock. That raised track up which I had clambered was becoming distinguishable only by its eminence.

Who had made it? Probably Klephts, certainly ELAS. Olympos had remained impregnable throughout the Occupation. Comforting to recognize what I had seen before: the sanctuary of the choughs, the skeletal remains of an ancient pine, perhaps the last in that snowscape without trees.

I looked behind. There was nothing except a *grisaille* of swirling hail and wet snow. Mytikas? I never saw Mytikas nor his subjects again. I had done with them.

Curious word, that: Mytikas. Until I talked to the graceful lady in the Information Bureau in Litohoro I thought it stemmed from *muthos* defined as: "A purely fictitious narrative usually involving supernatural persons, actions or events and embodying some popular ideas concerning natural or historical phenomena."*

"Not at all," she said. "It means nose-shaped, or pointed." This pleased me since many months ago, that is before we set off on this walk, I had read Geoffrey Kirk, that considerable scholar who states plainly in one of the best-known of his works: "It is sometimes hard to resist the temptation of viewing the 'Homeric world' as a real one, possessing a simple historical value of its own. The truth is, of course, that the epic is to an important extent *fictitious* — more than that, it is a fiction that contains contributions from different periods over a span of half a millennium or more. Yet the historian need not altogether despair. In its total complexity the world of the poems bears no exact resemblance to any historical setting in any historical period; yet many of its elements are based on fact and can be assessed in comparison with objective evidence disclosed by archaeology."

Heinrich Schliemann, that rich German archaeologist, imagined he had gazed on the face of Agamemnon, but the gold mask was later identified as being some small local chief. Schliemann (1822–90) paid a small army of excavators to burrow like moles into a *tell*, an enormous mound, bigger even than my Moby Dick, at Hissarlik near the coast of Turkey and discovered what he believed to be Ilium or Troy in the Troad. Nine "cities", stratified like a Neapolitan ice were buried one above the other, the seventh of which is now reckoned to be a post-Mycenaean fortress, the basis of *The Iliad*, 3,000 years of mythology and scholarly speculation.

*The Complete Oxford English Dictionary.

Who was Homer? Nobody knows. I cling to Geoffrey Kirk* who suggests in a quiet way that the greatest, the first, the prince of story-tellers, the most skilled in the quiet world of mythology, started to sing in the eighth century BC about Greece, already through her "dark age", a loose confederation which had re-emerged "as a strong and individual force in the eastern and central Mediterranean". He was probably an Ionian, probably too a-literate — meaning he couldn't read — but he had an imagination that rivalled that of Shakespeare about whom there is no known fellow.

In those deep thoughts I stumbled and at least twice failed to sound the track with my fine staff. I fell crotch-deep into a pit of snow, scrambled out, and laughed as ever Rabelais did in the face of the bishops, men whom he called those Sorbangraes and Sorbionnes, "Oddipols, Joltheads, who in their disputes do not search for truth but for contradictions only and debate."

The chalet appeared not far below, and beyond it a well-worn track. I heard the whinny of mules, the finest mules you have ever heard. They had come up from Prionia.

"Are you all right?" cried Madame Costas Zolotas from the doorway.

"No!" I said, "repeat no. I am suffering from a-Mytikasia."

Homer and the Oral Tradition, Cambridge University Press, 1976.

INDEX

Aeschylus, 2;
  Seven Against Thebes, 80
Aesop, 165
Agios Dimitrios, 244
Agios Nikolaos, 243
Agrapha, 177, 242, 244, 267, 285-6, 296, 311
Agrapha range, 244, 294, 331, 339
Agraphiotis river, 244-5, 296, 339
Akhilleas, Carlo, 155, 167, 174
Alaric the Goth, 160
Alcibiades, 41
Alexander the Great, 15
Ali Pasha, 253, 308, 311, 317
Amphissa (or Salano), 155-6, 167-8, 171-2
Anastasia, Madame (guide), 28-9, 165
Anatoli, 243
Andrews, Kevin: *The Flight of Ikaros*, 268
Andriko (Vlach train steward), 8-10, 13
Androcles, Mustapha ("Muzzi"), 218-19
Andronicos, Manolis, 174-5
Anoula, Mama, 131
Antikira, 122-3, 126, 131, 137
aphodius (dung beetle), 107
Arachova, 126
Argolis, 151

Aristophanes: *The Frogs*, 61-2
Aristotle, 15, 171
Aromanians, 9
Artemis (goddess), 188-9, 213
Asopus, river, 51, 61-2
asphodel, 48
Aspropotamus, river, 240
Athabasca, Lake (Canada), 141, 275-6, 278
Athens, 25-6, 31-2, 146;
  in Aristophanes' *Frogs*, 61
Athens, Duke of, 82
Attica, 46-7
Averof, 310

Barrett, David, 61-2
Basil II, Byzantine Emperor (the Bulgar-slayer), 150
Basilides ("Bassy"), 303-4
Baud-Bovy, Daniel, 345
bauxite, 183-5
bears, 254
bees and bee-keeping, 92-3
Benedicite (canticle), 189
Benta (Swedish student), 244, 247, 249-50, 253
Berger, John, 145
black vultures, 165-6
boars, wild, 7
Boeotia, 47-50, 51-2
Bogart, Humphrey, 263
Boissonas, Frédéric, 345
Bora (wind), 222

Borlero (mountain), 296, 298
Botsaris, Marcos, 247, 252-3, 327
Breese, Dilys, 276
Brooke, Rupert, 328
broom (*Planta genista*), 35, 52
Burton, Robert, 95
butterflies, 54-6, 170, 271-2, 287
Byron, George Gordon, 6th Baron, 253-4, 313
Byron, Robert: *Europe in the Looking Glass*, 238

Cadmus the Phoenician, 67, 70
Camberwell Beauty (butterfly), 170-1
Carlo the Cop *see* Akhilleas, Carlo
Carr, Archie, 61
Carrara (Italy), 185
Carti Vlaha-Engleza (news-sheet), 11
Castalian Spring, 160, 164
Célestin, Auguste, 95-6
centipedes, 60
Chios (island), 59
Civil, Alan, 258, 276
Clarence, Dukes of, 238-9
Coleridge, Samuel Taylor: "The Rime of the Ancient Mariner", 267n
Congo (now Zaire), 202-4
Congo, river, 279-81
Conrad, Joseph, 280
Coolidge, Harold J., 166
Corinth, Gulf of, 30, 35, 49, 81, 112, 113

Craxton, John, 150
"Curious and Curiouser" (village), 233-4
Curzon of Kedelston, George Nathaniel Curzon, Marquess, 317, 330, 333
Cyrus the Great, Persian Emperor, 62

Daphni (village), 214, 216
Daphnoula, 54
Dekelea (pass), 40, 61
Delidemi, Mount, 296
Delphi, 25, 26, 64, 146, 151, 152-4, 166
De Quincey, Thomas, 229
Desphina, 145
Despina, 37-8
Diasello, 321, 324, 325
Dioscorides, 317
Dombrenis group (islands), 114
donkeys, 236-7
Dora (Adorable), 210-14, 220
Dorst, Jan, 165
dung beetle *see aphodius*
Dupré, Louis, 312

EA (Cooperative Society), 59
EAM (resistance movement), 58
Echembrotos (flautist), 158
EEAM (Communist trade union organization), 59
Egyptian vulture (*Neophron*), 356
ELAN (resistance navy), 58-9
ELAS (resistance army), 58, 177, 183, 298

Elassona, 315, 321, 326, 332, 334
Elassonitikos, 331
Eleftherae (pass), 40
Eleuther, 158
Elgin Marbles, 26
Eliot, T. S.: *The Waste Land*, 232
Elopia, 90, 93, 96-8
emigration (from Greece), 332-3
Enippeas, 343
EP (Civil Guard), 59
EPON (Communist youth movement), 59
Epaminondas, 52
Eugenia, Aunt, 223-4
Euripides: *Ion*, 159

Fermor, Patrick Leigh:
on Valchs, 9-12, 121, 124;
on poets, 327;
Roumeli, 301
Flying Tortoise (train), 5, 6, 13, 338
Forster, E. M., 286
Francis of Assisi, St, 189
Freud, Sigmund, 163, 315
Fries, Karl, 270
frogs, 61-2

Gaea, or Ge (mythological figure), 221
Giona range, 167, 176
Golden dogs (*Canis aureus*; jackals), 220
Great Grey shrike (*Lanius excubitor*; butcher's sentinel, or watchman), 228-9

Greco, El (Domenico Theotocopoulos), 5
Grego (cab driver), 332-3, 341
Guiccioli, Countess Teresa, 254
Gus (Giorgios), 137-8

Heinzelan de Braucourt, Jean de, 203-4
Helicon, Mount, 79, 81, 85, 107
Hellenic Mountaineering and Skiing Federation, 24
Herodotus, 77, 108, 150
Hesiod, 108-9, 114, 158
Hetairia Philike (society), 254
Hillaby, Joe (author's brother), 109, 250
Hillaby, Thelma (Tilly; author's late wife), 315
Hippocrene, Fountain of, 113-14
Homer, 5, 67, 109, 158, 188, 302, 331, 362;
see also *Iliad, The; Odyssey, The*
hoopoes, 71, 156
Horace, 66
Hrisso, 244
Hunt, John, Baron, 167
Huxley, Anthony, 48, 337

Ibrahim Pasha, 253
Ignatius, Bishop, 253
Iliad, The (Homer), 148, 150
International Union for Conservation (IUCN): Athens conference, 25-6
Ioanina, 310-11

Iphigenia, Madame, 27, 29
Iphigenia, Stephanos, 29
Itea, 79, 148
Itea, Gulf of, 148

Jack (Jacques; US geologist), 16-17
jackals *see* Golden dogs
Janos (Vlach), 122-3

Kalambaka, 305
Kallithea, 341
Kakkalos, Christos (climber), 345
Kakkalos, Christos (tavern-keeper), 348
Kalonaros (Kalo; friend of Théophane), 305-6, 309, 314-15, 318
Kaloscopi, 176, 186, 189, 190-1, 199, 216
Kamatero, 34-5
Kapodistrio, "Kaiser", x, 282-3, 287, 290
Karampola, 44
Karol, 128-9
Karpenissi, 196, 198, 220-1, 239-56, 270
Kassotis, Ma, 138-9
Kastania, 299-300, 307
Katerini, 21
Katsimbalis, George ("Colossus"), 32
Kedrona (*formerly* Arvanitovlach), 255
Kerassea, 307
Kirk, Geoffrey, 363

Kirphis, Mount, 153, 166
Kirra, 140, 144, 146-7, 154, 166
Koleti, Ioan, 310
Kostandi, Andoni, 268
Koukourountsos, Mount, 297
Krissa, 148, 152, 155
Kyllini family, 236-7

Laius, King, 162-3
Lamia, 22, 167, 176, 182-5, 221
Lancaster, Sir Osbert, 31, 59
Lang, Andrew, 65
Larissa, 285, 315
Larissa, Plain of, 332
Larsen, Kurt, 142-3
Lausanne, Convention of (1923), 333
League of Neighbours (Amphictionies), 154, 158
Lear, Edward, 36
Leigh Fermor, Patrick *see* Fermor, Patrick Leigh
Lerner, Arthur, 323
Levi, Peter, 50-1, 54, 78, 148, 157
Levkas, 240
Linné, Carl von (Linnaeus), 55-6, 170
Liossion, 31, 34
Litohoro, 19, 21, 334, 342-3, 345, 353
Lycabettus (Athens), 30
Lysander (Spartan admiral), 62
Lyte, Henry, 266n

McDougall, Doc, 142
McFarlane, Andy, 193, 198, 201, 209

Macmillan, Harold, 26
Magda, 128-9
Makronisos, 183, 196
Maliakos Gulf, 221
Malmsey wine, 238-9
Mandelstam, Osip, 94
Mangakis, George, 144
Marathos (hamlet), x, 244, 279, 281, 286
marble quarries, 185
Marceau, Marcel, 225
Maria Theresa, Empress of Austria, 6
Marin, Captain Jean-Paul, 280, 281
Marmara, 226-7, 229
Mavrolithari, 176, 194, 209-10, 216, 308
Megaros brothers, 42
Megdova bridge, 244, 255, 264
Megdova, river see Tavropos river
Melissohori, 86-7, 90
meltemi (wind), 28
"Men of the North" (BBC radio series), 276
Meteora, 305
Metsovo, 302, 305, 307, 315
Meyer, Reb, 160-1, 165
Missolonghi, 253-4
Mitchell, John, 358
Mitsotakis, Constantine, 58
Montaigne, Michel de, 4
mosquitoes, 140-3
Mouzaki, 299
Mukhtar (son of Ali Pasha), 313

mulberry trees, 81
mullein (plant), 266-7
Mytikas (mountain peak), 334, 345, 354, 362;
    see also Olympos range

Neohoraki, 63
Neohori, 320-2
Nicos (blacksmith), 57-8
Nietzsche, Friedrich, 79, 177
nightingales, 119-20
Nikolitsi, 230, 232, 239
Notopolos, Nico, 283-4;
    wife (Nicolaina), 285, 289

Oceanus (god), 221
Odysseus, 65
Odyssey, The (Homer), 64, 151
Oedipus, 22, 162
Offenbach, Jacques: *Orpheus in the Underworld*, 52-3
Olimbiada, 334
olives and olive trees, 150
Olympos range (and Mount Olympos), 15-18, 21, 331, 343-4, 356-8;
    see also Mytikas,
OPLA (secret police), 59
orchids, 337-8
Orphean warblers, 156
Orthodox Church: ceremonies, 103-4
Ossa (mountain), 21

Page, T. E., 94
Palatine Anthology, The, 206
Paleohori, 227

INDEX

Panagia Kliston (Gorge of the Virgin), 41
Pandion, King of Attica, 72
Pantermalis, Dimitrios, 15-16
Papadopoulos, George, 246-7, 296
Papadopoulos, Loula, 252
Papandreou, Andreas, 58
Paralia, 131, 133
Parcs Nationaux du Congo Belge, 203-4
Parkio, 265
Parnassus, Mount, 153
Parnis, Mount, 34
Parnis range, 37, 40
Paul, St, 15
Paul II, King of Greece, 26
Pausanias, 2, 30;
  on Seven Gates of Thebes, 78-9;
  on river Asopus, 61;
  on Kirra, 148;
  on Delphi, 152;
  on Pythian games, 158;
  on Stymphalides, 299;
  Guide to Greece, 50-1
Penelope (wife of Odysseus), 65-6
Perouse, Lieutenant Ramond, 135-6, 183-4
Persian Wars, 146, 148
Petriades, Peter, 25, 26-7
Phaedriades cliffs, 147, 152, 164, 167
Philip II, King of Macedon, 21
philotomo ("face"), 29

Phokis, 146, 150, 153
Phyle, 37, 40
Pili, 56
Pindar, 67
Pindos range, 155, 167, 292
Pinios river, 301, 317, 328
Pira, 176, 193-4, 198, 207, 282
Pitsi, 239, 242
Plaka (mountain), 296, 298
Plataea, Plataeans, 49, 51, 61
Platanos, 198, 199, 239
Plato: Critias, 270
Pleistos, river, 152
Pliny the Elder, 70
Plutarch, 51
Porter, Richard, 358
Preston, Peter, 262
priests, 59, 87
Prionia, 334, 343-4, 348, 349, 353, 364
Prodromos, 114
Putnam, Anne Eisner, 204
pygmies (the Little People; Congo), 202-4
Pythia see Delphi,
Pythian Games, 157

Quintilian, 110

Ray, John, 55
Reid, Forrest, 207
Resistance movements (war–time), 58-9
Ruskin, John, 4
Ruwenzori (Mountains of the Moon; Africa), 281

Sacred Way, the, 140, 146
St Dionysius, Monastery of, 346, 353
Saint-Exupéry, Antoine de, 244
St Omer, Nicholas de, 82
St Spilio monastery, 352
Salmon, Tim, 343
sanctuaries, 156-7
Scarfe, Laurence, 3-5
Schliemann, Heinrich, 363
Scythians, 76-7
Segesta (Sicily), 109
Shelley, Percy Bysshe, 244
Sibthorpe, John, 353n
silk and silkworms, 82
Skala (mountain peak), 334
Skolio (mountain peak), 334
Skourta, 50, 53
Smith, Nick, 350, 353, 356, 359
Smith, Sydney, 311
Socrates, 42
Solon, 154
sparrows, 100-1
Sparta, 52, 146
Spencer, Herbert, 3
Sperkios, river, 221, 239-40, 243
Spirides family, 223
Spiro, Thomas, 116-17
Stamatis brothers, 149, 152
Stefani (mountain peak), 334
Stevenson, Robert Louis, 200
Stoneman, Richard, 238
storks, 335-6
Sturt, Charles, 263
Swift, Jonathan, 110

Tavropos, Lake, 299
Tavropos, river, 244, 255, 264-5, 299
Te-Chee Poo, Dr, 25
Thebes, 22, 47-8;
    Seven Gates, 52, 64, 68, 79;
    rivalry with Plataea, 61;
    author visits, 64-80, 167, 175;
    in Odyssey, 64;
    silk manufacture, 82
Theo (husband of Dora), 211, 213
Theodosius I, Byzantine Emperor, 159
Theodosius II, Byzantine Emperor, 16
Théophane:
    author meets, 73-4, 82, 173-4, 176, 209;
    entertains author in Metsovo, 302-14;
    driving, 307-8;
    Vlach mother, 315;
    sexual nature, 317
Theophrastus of Lesbos, 149, 159
Thermopylae, 22
Thessalians, 152
Thessalonika, 15-16, 19
Thessaly, Plain of, 300, 301
Thomas, Dylan, 122
Thracians, 77
Thucydides, 109
Timfristos range, 221, 241, 244, 259
Titarissios, river, 327
Tolstoy, Count Leo, 279

INDEX

Torcello, 1-5
tortoises, 300
Toumba (mountain peak), 334
Tower, Christopher: *Oultre Jourdain*, 188n
transhumation, 124, 293
Trieste, 6
Trikala, 177-8, 242, 285, 299, 301-6, 315-16
Tringia, 307
Twain, Mark, 71

Uranium City (Saskatchewan, Canada), 141, 143, 274

Vardoussia range, 167, 212, 220, 242
Vathi, 79
Velhouiotis (*pseud., i.e.* Ares), 304
Veli (son of Ali Pasha), 313
Veni, 325
Venice, 1-5
Venizelos, Eleftherias, 271
Viniani, 267
Virgil: *Georgics*, 91-2, 101; on olives, 150
Vlachs (Wallachians): nature of, x, 9-11, 124;
language, 9, 11;
author meets, 120, 233;
transhumation, 124;
herding, 285, 289;
in Metsovo, 308;
Théophane and, 315
Vlahogiania, 242, 321
Voltaire, François Marie Arouet de, 35
Vyronos (son of Papastavros), 327-8

Wainwright, Alfred, 36
Walton, Izaak, 119
Wells, Robert, 91-2
Wesley, John, 70
White, Gilbert, 156
winds, 222, 224-5
wolves, 254, 274-5, 294
World Wildlife Fund, 25

Xironomi, 104-5

Zdru, Nacu (John), xi, 11-13, 252, 357-8
Zolotas, Costas, 347, 353, 355, 359, 361
Zolotas, Madame Costas, 343, 347, 355, 364

LARGE PRINT

ISIS publish a wide range of books in large print, from fiction to biography. A full list of titles is available free of charge from the address below. Alternatively, contact your local library for details of their collection of ISIS books.

Details of ISIS unabridged audio books are also available.

Any suggestions for books you would like to see in large print or audio are always welcome.

**ISIS
7 Centremead
Oxney Mead
Oxford OX2 0ES
(0865) 250333**

BIOGRAPHY AND AUTOBIOGRAPHY

Lord Abercromby	**Childhood Memories**
Margery Allingham	**The Oaken Heart**
Hilary Bailey	**Vera Brittain**
Winifred Beechey	**The Reluctant Samaritan**
P. Y. Betts	**People Who Say Goodbye**
Christabel Bielenberg	**The Road Ahead**
Kitty Black	**Upper Circle**
Denis Constanduros	**My Grandfather**
Dalai Lama	**Freedom in Exile**
W. H. Davies	**Young Emma**
Phil Drabble	**A Voice in the Wilderness**
Joyce Fussey	**Calf Love**
Valerie Garner	**Katherine: The Duchess of Kent**
Gillian Gill	**Agatha Christie**
Jon & Rumer Godden	**Two Under the Indian Sun**
William Golding	**The Hot Gates**
Michael Green	**The Boy Who Shot Down an Airship**
Michael Green	**Nobody Hurt in Small Earthquake**
Unity Hall & Ingrid Seward	
	Royalty Revealed
Brian Hoey	**The New Royal Court**
Ilse, Countess von Bredow	
	Eels With Dill Sauce
Clive James	**Falling Towards England**
Clive James	**May Week Was in June**

BIOGRAPHY AND AUTOBIOGRAPHY

Paul James	**Margaret**
Paul James	**Princess Alexandra**
Julia Keay	**The Spy Who Never Was**
Dorothy Brewer Kerr	**The Girls Behind the Guns**
John Kerr	**Queen Victoria's Scottish Diaries**
Margaret Lane	**The Tale of Beatrix Potter**
T. E. Lawrence	**Revolt in the Desert**
Bernard Levin	**The Way We Live Now**
Margaret Lewis	**Ngaio Marsh**
Vera Lynn	**Unsung Heroines**
Jeanine McMullen	**A Small Country Living Goes On**
Gavin Maxwell	**Ring of Bright Water**
Ronnie Knox Mawer	**Tales From a Palm Court**
Peter Medawar	**Memoir of a Thinking Radish**
Jessica Mitford	**Hons and Rebels**
Christopher Nolan	**Under the Eye of the Clock** (A)
Christopher Ralling	**The Kon Tiki Man**
Wng Cdr Paul Richey	**Fighter Pilot**
Martyn Shallcross	**The Private World of Daphne Du Maurier**
Frank and Joan Shaw	**We Remember the Blitz**
Frank and Joan Shaw	**We Remember the Home Guard**
Joyce Storey	**Our Joyce**
Robert Westall	**The Children of the Blitz**
Ben Wicks	**The Day They Took the Children** (A)

(A) Large Print books also available in Audio.

GENERAL NON-FICTION

Estelle Catlett	**Track Down Your Ancestors**
Eric Delderfield	**Eric Delderfield's Bumper Book of True Animal Stories**
Phil Drabble	**One Man and His Dog**
Caroline Elliot	**The BBC Book of Royal Memories 1947-1990**
Jonathan Goodman	**The Lady Killers**
Joan Grant	**The Owl on the Teapot**
Anita Guyton	**Healthy Houseplants A-Z**
Helene Hanff	**Letters From New York**
Dr Richard Lacey	**Safe Shopping, Safe Cooking, Safe Eating**
Sue Lawley	**Desert Island Discussions**
Doris Lessing	**Particularly Cats and More Cats**
Martin Lloyd-Elliott	**City Ablaze**
Vera Lynn	**We'll Meet Again**
Richard Mabey	**Home Country**
Frank Muir & Denis Norden	
	You Have My Word
Shiva Naipual	**An Unfinished Journey**
Colin Parsons	**Encounters With the Unknown**
John Pilger	**A Secret Country**
R W F Poole	**A Backwoodsman's Year**
Valerie Porter	**Faithful Companions**
Sonia Roberts	**The Right Way to Keep Pet Birds**
Yvonne Roberts	**Animal Heroes**
Anne Scott-James	**Gardening Letters to My Daughter**
Anne Scott-James and Osbert Lancaster	
	The Pleasure Garden
Les Stocker	**The Hedgehog and Friends**

WORLD WAR II

Margery Allingham	**The Oaken Heart**
Paul Brickhill	**The Dam Busters**
Josephine Butler	**Cyanide In My Shoe**
Reinhold Eggers	**Escape From Colditz**
Joyce Grenfell	**The Time of My Life**
John Harris	**Dunkirk**
Vera Lynn	**We'll Meet Again** (A)
Vera Lynn	**Unsung Heroines**
Frank Pearce	**Sea War**
Maude Pember Reeves	**Round About a Pound a Week**
Wing Cdr Paul Richey	**Fighter Pilot**
Frank and Joan Shaw	**We Remember the Blitz**
Frank and Joan Shaw	**We Remember The Homeguard**
William Sparks	**The Last of the Cockleshell Heroes**
Anne Valery	**Talking About the War**
Robert Westall	**Children of the Blitz**
Ben Wicks	**The Day They Took the Children (A)**

POETRY

Felicity Kendall	**The Family Poetry Book**
	Long Remembered: Narrative Poems

COOKERY

Jennifer Davies	**The Victorian Kitchen**

REFERENCE AND DICTIONARIES

The Lion Concise Bible Encyclopedia
The Longman English Dictionary
The Longman Medical Dictionary

(A) Large Print books also available in Audio.

TRAVEL, ADVENTURE AND EXPLORATION

Jacques Cousteau	**The Silent World**
Patrick Leigh Fermor	**Three Letters From the Andes**
Robin Hanbury-Tenison	
	Fragile Eden
Mike Harding	**Footloose in the Himalaya**
John Hillaby	**John Hillaby's London**
Patrick Marnham	**So Far From God**
Robert Morley	**Around the World in 81 Years**
Dervla Murphy	**On a Shoestring to Coorg**
Dervla Murphy	**The Waiting Land**
Eric Newby	**Love and War in the Apennines (A)**
Salman Rushdie	**Jaguar Smile**
Sir Ernest Shackleton	**South (A)**
Tom Vernon	**Fat Man in Argentina**
A.Wainwright	**Wainwright in the Limestone Dales**
Mark Wallington	**Boogie Up the River**
Mark Wallington	**Five Hundred Mile Walkies**
Dylan Winter	**A Hack in the Borders**

(A) Large Print books also available in Audio.

HEALTH AND SELF HELP

Wendy and Sally Greengross
Living, Loving and Ageing

Margaret Hills
Curing Arthritis

Longman Medical Dictionary

Sarah Lewis
Eating Well on a Budget

Dr Geoffrey Littlejohn
Rheumatism

Kenneth Lysons
Earning Money in Retirement

Dr Brice Pitt
Making the Most of Middle Age

Neville Shone
Coping Successfully With Pain

Dr Tom Smith
Heart Attacks

Elaine Stritch
Am I Blue? How to Live With Diabetes

George Target
Your Arthritic Hip and You

Nancy Tuft
Looking Good, Feeling Good

Denys Wainwright
Arthritis and Rheumatism

Claire Weekes
The Latest Help for Your Nerves

Claire Weekes
More Help for Your Nerves

Rosemary Wells
Your Grandchild and You

Dr Robert Youngson
Everything You Need to Know About Your Eyes

Dr Robert Youngson
How to Cope with Tinnitus and Hearing Loss

SHORT STORIES

A. E. Coppard	**The Higgler and Other Stories**
Thomas Godfrey	**Country House Murders, Volume 1**
Thomas Godfrey	**Country House Murders, Volume 2**
Thomas Godfrey	**Country House Murders, Volume 3**
Graham Greene	**The Last Word and Other Stories**
Nathaniel Hawthorne	**Tanglewood Tales**
Henry James	**Daisy Miller and Other Stories**
M. R. James	**Ghost Stories of An Antiquary** (A)
M. R. James	**A Warning to the Curious** (A)
Saki	**Beasts and Superbeasts**
Alan Sillitoe	**The Far Side of the Street**
W. Somerset Maugham	**Ashenden** (A)
Peter Ustinov	**The Disinformer**
Robert Westall	**Antique Dust**
Marguirete Yourcenar	**Oriental Tales**

HUMOUR

Molly Keane	**Treasure Hunt**
Barry Pain	**The Eliza Stories**
Tom Sharpe	**The Great Pursuit**

(A) Large Print books also available in Audio.

1	21	41	61	81	101	121	141	161	181
2	22	42	62	82	102	122	142	162	182
3	23	43	63	83	103	123	143	163	183
4	24	(44)	64	84	104	124	144	164	184
5	25	45	65	(85)	105	125	145	165	185
6	26	46	66	86	106	126	146	166	186
(7)	27	47	67	87	107	127	147	167	187
8	28	48	(68)	88	108	(128)	148	168	188
9	29	49	69	89	109	129	149	169	189
10	30	50	70	90	110	130	150	170	190
11	31	51	71	91	111	(131)	151	(171)	191
12	32	52	72	92	112	132	152	172	192
13	33	53	73	93	113	133	(153)	173	193
(14)	34	54	74	94	114	134	154	174	194
15	35	55	75	95	115	135	155	175	195
16	36	56	76	96	116	136	(156)	176	196
(17)	37	57	77	97	117	137	157	177	197
(18)	38	58	78	98	118	138	158	178	198
19	39	59	79	99	(119)	139	159	179	199
20	40	60	80	100	120	140	160	180	200

201	201	241	261	281	301	321	341	361	381	91
202	202	242	262	282	302	322	342	362	382	92
203	223	243	263	283	303	323	343	363	383	93
204	224	244	264	284	304	324	344	364	384	94
205	225	245	265	285	305	325	345	365	385	95
206	226	246	266	286	306	326	346	366	386	
207	227	247	267	287	307	327	347	367	387	96
208	228	248	268	288	308	328	348	368	388	97
209	229	249	269	289	309	329	349	369	389	98
210	230	250	270	290	310	330	350	370	390	99
	231	251	271	291	311	331	351	371	391	0
	(232)	252	272	292	312	332	352	372	392	
	233	253	273	293	313	333	353	373	393	
	234	254	274	294	314	334	354	374	394	
301	235	255	275	295	315	335	355	375	395	
302	236	256	276	296	316	336	356	376	396	
303	237	257	277	297	317	337	357	377	397	
304	238	258	278	298	318	338	358	378	398	
305	239	259	279	299	319	339	359	379	399	
306	(220)	240	260	280	300	320	340	360	380	400

401	406	411	416	421	426	431	436	441	446
402	407	412	417	422	427	432	437	442	447
403	408	413	418	423	428	433	438	443	448
404	409	414	419	424	429	434	439	444	449
405	410	415	420	425	430	435	440	445	450